OFFSPRING!

A Novel for the Future

**by
D.M. Yourtee**

and

L. R. Anderson-Newsom

The Empires of the Future
Must Become the Empires
of the Mind!

Winston Leonard Spencer-Churchill

All Rights Reserved

Copyright © 2018 by D.M. Yourtee and L.R. Anderson-Newsom

No part of this book may be reproduced or transmitted in any form by any means, electronic or mechanical including photocopying, recording or by any other information storage and retrieval system without obtaining first permission in writing from the Authors.

The editorial opinions in this book are those of the authors or persons they met or as described and attributed in the text. Any resemblance to any other person, living or dead, is purely coincidental.

This book includes some technical language which appears in a document created by the heroin of the story. A wide range of ideas and proposals are quoted forming the basis of that document. Sincere effort has been made to identify authors or experts who have stated those postulations. Visual displays are artistically re-rendered from CCO-licensed and free public domain designated sources such as pixels.com. No copyright infringement is intended regarding drawings and pictures.

The story is a sequel to those in ISBN; 978-1-38-992575-7 and the story line cited therein by Author D.M. Yourtee

Printed in the United States of America.

~~~~~~~~~~~

For more information or to order more books please contact the publisher, Minds-Eye Manuscripts, LLC, USA via the following references: www.Minds-Eye@bresnan.net (e-mail order) or the book-store reference at www.aminds-eyejourney.net.

FORWARD

The account in this book tells in unflinching words what our Homo sapiens past and present offspring have left us to deal with through their too often self-directed, future-blind-actions.

Then, with that before us, that elevated to consider coldly-it addresses the question…what should our future offspring be and how can they help us out of our present and accelerating dilemmas?

DEDICATION

To those who prevail in reading this work you are surely "Vistavien"! That is, people who are wise enough to think about how to act for the future on behalf of your grand-children's children!

It is to you who may become navigators for our future that we dedicate this work with our sincerest, deepest felt expression of gratitude, and very best wishes for your future!

D. M. Yourtee / L. R. Anderson-Newsom

Chapter 1

A MARINE SETS HER OBJECTIVE

FOR BAVISHNI!

To her left-hand side, the alley lay dark and foreboding. Something did not feel right! As she started to pass it by, she heard a rustling, then clearly in the darkness she heard a guttural male hiss, "*Quiet, Silence!*"

Alert to possible ambush, the Marine Recon Team Leader ducked, quickly-surveyed her surroundings. The street was strewn with rubble and trash. In the faint light of the coming dawn, the area stank. The reek of urine hung heavy at the alley's entrance. She wrinkled up her nose and wondered how she had ever been talked into this crazy recon mission in the first place.

The surroundings were not familiar to her, having been split off from the rest of her team earlier by the sniper's gun fire. "Got to make it back to Delta Point' she thought to herself, as the mission briefing instructions were to re-group at Delta Point if ever separated.

The threat seemed to lay only in the darkness of the alley, where she could just make out an outline of a man holding something...someone up against the earthen wall. Slowly, replacing her rifle over her shoulder, she pulled her knife and quietly advanced into the darkened alley!

The man was dressed in the Arab way, but his filthy loin cloth was open, and he was exposed. And, damn he had his hand over the face of a young girl whose eyes were wide in fear!

The Sergeant slowly advanced, her thoughts not the best thing drifting, and she remembered reading during orientation; if it had been back in 1896, the dress of the poor child wouldn't have been conspicuous by its mere absence. The belief then was that clothes were not needed for the young. A Hindu proverb of the time enforced this believe by stating: "Children and the legs of a stool do not feel cold." It would have also said that until about eight years of age boys and girls were usually without anything save "a necklace, a charm, and a string about the waist with a few bells attached". [1]

Even so, as this was now, the girls' Sari (an unhitched garment), was draped in tatters across her virtually exposed body, and her blouse was ripped wide open to reveal her flat breasts!

The Sergeant placed her finger to her lips and the young girl blinked in recognition of the command. Slowly, and stealthily Marine Chivonn, approached the man nearly invisible from his rear. He was so intent on loosening his robe all the while still pulling at the girl's clothes, he did not hear the approaching danger until it was too late.

Chivonn grabbed the man's forehead and jerking his head back, she slid her knife lightly from left to right just at the skin depth. She was furious at the rapist, yet in detachment, as if from a distant view, she watched with satisfaction as the sharp K-bar was slowly making it's point clear, leaving behind a faint crimson outline. He went ridged in her grasp and stood there helpless waiting for the knife to come back again from the other side, ending his life!

The frightened child ran from his now slackened grasp, and he felt himself being propelled forward straight into the hard mud and dung covered wall. She knew he must have heard his neck pop as he fell back against the wall, then in the surrounding blackness

---

[1.] From "The Cross of the Land of the Trident, or, India from a Missionary Point of View", by Harlan Page Beach, Publisher Religious Tract Society, 1896.

he heard no more. Slowly he slipped to the ground in a crumple of filth to join the unending rats and piss of the city that lay unseen by those that for one reason or another in this day and age chose to visit this war-torn place.

When the Sergeant turned around, she saw the little one standing behind her. Her Sari was now clearly visible, a long piece of dirty fabric, hanging in raged shreds barely covering her emaciated body. She had her arms around herself in a sad effort at a comforting hold. Then totally moved, her anger quieted, the Marine knelt in front of the child and looked deep into her beautiful brown eyes and smiled. The knife she hid behind her back so as not to further frighten the young girl.

She did not know if the little girl could understand her or not, but she said in her best formed most gentle voice in Farsi, hoping her pronunciation was nearly correct "What is your name?" (Esme shoma chiyeh?)

The child's eyes lit up as she replied, "Bavishni". The Sargent had heard it before and knew it was a name meaning 'the one who has a future'! Indeed, thought the Sargent, she does possibly have a future now to look forward to. This little one will not become an outcast today, as one violated and no longer suitable to marry!

And at that moment intense anger returned, churning in the Sergeant's mind and her stomach churned making her hold against a reflect vomiting. She hated the injustice, the unequal nature of woman's rights so prevalent in the middle east not say all the injustice and the in-human cruelty she witnessed everywhere in the world. Uncounted millions and millions of children are at the mercy of such inhuman insanity!

Even with all the advances made for the modern woman in places such as India, rape was many times unreported, or withdrawn due just to the perception of family honor being compromised. An honor killing would more likely been the result for this young girl if that man had taken her in the alley moments before.

Reaching out, Chivonn, allowed the child to come in close to her open arms. Fear held that complete embrace away, but slowly the little one approached very close, bravely trying to trust. The Sargent reflected a moment, somehow wishing she had the Corpsman with her, wasn't that medics name Gabe? She had seen how some children were automatically comforted by him. How much this child needed this!

Then focusing on the child, she told her, "My name is Chivonn, and I will not hurt you". Bavishni seemed in that tone, comforted, and smiled at her new-found friend, reaching out to be held! Giving her a squeeze, Chivonn, slowly stood looking back at the still assailant. Then they turned and together walked away from the terror filled alley.

Just as they emerged from the darkness there, the Marine spotted a man standing directly in front of her. With the adrenaline still pumping in her veins she crouched low shoving the little girl behind her and raised her knife that she still held in her hand. The man she faced was large and well-muscled. They stared at each other for a moment.

His eyes were dark in a striking clear blue that seemed to draw her into their unflinching depth. She was surprised, as they seemed invitingly kind and gentle, liquid pools of peace and inner serenity! And, as she continued to size up her adversary, he slowly raised his hands in a gesture that might be thought of as submission. Only then did she realize he was not a man from this country. The underside of his arms did not hold the heavily darkened tan of the rest of his upper body, he had a tattoo on the right, almost like a woman in the flesh, and she realized feeling a tremor of fear, she did not know his intentions.

Even so, slowly she rose and cautiously returned her combat knife to its scabbard. The little girl peeked from behind the Sargent's legs to stare at that man before them. He lowered to one knee keeping eye contact with the still frightened girl and slowly lowering one hand reached into his pocket, pulling out some coins, he held them out to the child.

She ran forward and with a smile she took them, quickly turned and ran off down the street.

Chivonn, started after the now fading image of the child, only to stop dead in her tracks, grinding her teeth, suddenly realizing the total hidden cruelty of what she had just stumbled into.

She looked back, just in time to see the pimp suddenly, yet quietly, vanished behind some nearby ruins.

What am I thinking? I can't help her-this precious child. I can't change the power and greed, and man's cruelty, with his lack of empathy towards our own young!

I hate what I am seeing, but what can I do? One lone person arguing with the world. That's me! One day---I vow, I will find a way…there must be a way to make this craziness stop! But right now, I must save myself and get back to Checkpoint Delta!

And it was at that moment she vowed "In what life I have left I will find a way to change the distorted face of human kind to recover their sense of empathy to through down all versions of in-humanity!"

15 Years Later

The story of Bavishni's plight is told to one of great importance in her life…Chivonn is sitting in Dr. Daniel Jordyn's Office who is listening with great attention. He nods clearly in sympathy, commenting briefly about his experience with the Boko Haran capturing and raping girls in Nigeria. Like hers it is a story of seeming impossible resolution.

These two are sitting in the "Advanced Cell Development Laboratory (ACDL)" at her now chosen University. For her it was a long and arduous struggle from Marine Corps service through all kinds of jobs and seeming impossible challenges, to becoming an advance degree student and a lab assistant in the ACDL.

These two in this office do offer a contrast in comportment. She is sitting in her military upright posture at full attention, as is her way. And he, although far in past a navy veteran, is clearly in charge but relaxed in the world he has created with a group who accepts the Navigator challenge, into which Chivonn has also entered. There is a moment of silence as he lifts his glasses and then looks casually, but with an attitude of inquiry... her way. Chivonn, lets' think this all through!

They know each other well because of their feelings about the future, but also because Chivonn is not only a lab assistant, she is the one who had recently presented her friend Vicente's research dissertation to his PhD supervisory committee. This presentation occurred sadly a short time after Vicente was killed near his home in the city. She had stood ground to represent him by defending the work in the most unusual posthumous dissertation defense probably ever presented at the University.

From the doctor "I do sympathize with how you feel, how you are committed, we both saw the impossibly insane. And I agree Chivonn it is now time to get your own program underway. We've talked many times about your frustrations, the view point you have from those years in the Marines, and I know at times you have skirted PTSD, but not to put it too coldly...where has this led you, specifically toward a real time lab research of your own?"

"Dr. Jordyn as you know my marine times saw so many cruelties to children, so much insanity, as though the mind of humans is entrenched in such greed that I know we can't last!

I've wanted, since my service, vowed it on that particular day I decided to find a way to help, and after Vicente's work, it became clear to me that understanding deeper the influences on personality development at the cell genetic level is a way, maybe the only way we can understand ourselves in respect to the future. That is, I think we need to answer the question how irrevocable, I mean susceptible are we to "Dictating Leader Ways" as a function of DNA control, at least that is a start!

In specific, can empathy vanish or is it embedded in our genome, waiting there to help us? Recall too my promise after defending Vicente's work posthumous, that is to look into that genetic imprint he called the Cy-Gene. I think it could exist and go completely wrong with all the anti-humanitarian influences today.

Simply put, we won't know how to prevent that unless we know how it works."

"Of course, Chivonn, I appreciate how our tragic ways these days could lead to an Armageddon, which seems obvious, but what are the problems that you see, are they really a threat, and most centrally how can what you seek work to avoid that."

"Simply Chivonn it is clear to me that you will first have to address those questions in an academic way! And as you well know you will have to convince a committee of experts, the professors in relevant areas from this institution that it is worth the funding and time in the lab to do the actual research.

To be direct, I suggest you need to first defend, do a trial on that, what you see as the need. And that argument must be well substantiated! Suppose you present what you want to do to our "Forever Panel", the special group that you have already met, including those in this lab. I will get them together for you at our hang out you know, the "Newport" this Friday night and you can meet and describe your ideas then."

Chivonn readily agreed knowing the group, its history of resolving what could be resolved on the matter of "Forever" and their guiding Visconti on the difficult aspects involved in his work on the "Omega Shield".

Her photographic memory brought to her mind immediately the details in the vitae available in the lab for each panel member. There were ten, now a family integrated as surely as an army unit but navigating with a target saving the future for forthcoming generations. And in that huge task they were dealing with matters far beyond what most want to face.

She knew there were ten members of the Forever Panel, although she also knew that Dr. Singh and Samyak were in India and would not be able to attend. That clear memory brought to her mind immediately the details of those vitae.

The panel was headed up by lab director Dr. Jordyn, expert in Bio-Materials Technology and included the Dr. Timothy J. Bean, Biochemist with emphasis in Biophysics, Dr. Pi-Su Chien Hsu-Experimental Physicist and Mathematician, Dr. Samyak Darshon

Jain-Historian, Professor Ahab Singh-Astrophysics and expert in Quantum Mechanics Expert, Navy Master Chief, James V. Skellan-Expert in Explosives and Armament, Chandler N. Caldwell, M.S.-in Mechanical Engineering, Jehan Nirupuma-Dr. and Professor of Medicine-Life Perspective Teacher, Mrs. Jane L. Caldwell M.S.-Forensic Scientist and Panel Technical Recorder, and Dr. Angelei N. Skellan-PhD in Faiths, Philosophies, World Cultures.[1]

The gathering with this unquestionably austere group was to be the next day and that night deep in sleep Chivonn saw her intended research once again haunting her in a swelling nebulous pictorial form of nucleic acid internal energy from one generation transferred to the next resulting in energetic messages from brain emotional matter into a new generation DNA, thus transferring embedded

thought patterns critical to the future of humans-the special species of the Cosmos. So, the next day about six Chivonn and "The Bean", the biologist of the panel, were first there at the Newport (Bar and Grill). With each a Guinness in hand they sat at the bar. Chivonn seemed troubled which he was quick to notice… Problem? Yes, spent half of the night with DNA visions dancing around communicating with each other, wore me out! Felt like a nut!

Hey I know you now pretty well "C" and we all know you have those vivid dreams that are remarkable cause they wind up with real results. As they left the bar walking toward the back of the Newport, The Bean commented---Don't worry "C" it is a blessing those visions you have, and you should know the Panel are really not snooty, just good people with concerned hearts. To which she responded…well I hope so...but sometimes I think I should go

---

1. The complete story of the "Forever Panel" can be found in the books, "Future Navigators on the Edge of Forever" and the "Omega Shield", ISBNs 978-1-36-662145-0 and 978-1-38-989564-7 respectfully.

back on active duty, maybe I would be a better Marine than a scientist!

That little visit aside, it was as promised. On that Friday, there was a special gathering, in the back room of the Newport. As had become a tradition, all with drinks in hand, they gathered in the "Community Room" around the great table there. Much re-acquainting and story- telling, reviewing their past adventures, took place before Dr. Jordyn entered and called them to attention with the purpose at hand. Chivonn looking about the room, reviewed mentally who she would be facing, saw them as colleagues and her marine calm held.

As that evening developed the doctor - allowing a bit of chat got things underway, asking Chivonn to describe what she wanted to do for her dissertation project, thanking them all for listening.

She outlined her concerns that there was little point in extrapolating future human evolution (a goal of the panel) if the influences of today, the cataclysmic things going on, the wide acceptance of evil wining over our behavior, when humans are clearly unprepared to act together to make real changes.

She outlined her plans to look into our genetic make up to find if there is a personality implant in the genome and if the better side of that (the humane one) can be protected and that thus be transferred on into time---in the new generations. Chivonn indicated in this meeting-handing out several abstracts from scientific journals that new techniques are being developed that allow a deeper insight as to what at the energy level goes on between the elements of the genome.

Jehan was the first to enter into the advisory-critical process. She spoke with unambiguous authority in her voice "Chivonn it is clear that for the lab to support such a far-out endeavor, and I can assure you one certainly very expensive, you will need to provide your committee with clear ideas as to how you see the human-time-limiting threats, what events now, what conditions now, may shorten our lives here on earth. What potential dangers are so bad that would demand such an effort!" Then Pi, herself a new PhD, (but also carrying the authority of a post- doctoral experience) put in a reinforcing comment. "More than that if you dig deep as you should you have to address what drives people, i.e. you are going to have to have a committee of a new type, one not only with genetic technique experience, but also such as psychologists, and Chivonn it seems very apparent to me that all factors considered you will need to show how any advances you create can help people to make sensible changes, and that will challenge you very, very significantly!"

As she always did, composure now fully there Chivonn immediately responded. "I do see what you are all saying, seems you are asking me to draw up a-I am assuming the correct term 'Prospectus'-to present to this new committee. Yes?" You want a rational, a defense of my potential project before I actually begin the laboratory experiments!"

At that point Dr. Jordyn put in…"The group is right Chivonn, and you have the appropriate document named, you are hereby assigned that "Prospectus"!

Skellan then noted, "Dr. Jordyn…Daniel…can the lab afford to send her to Samyak? She will need a really good grasp of history, don't you think?" Remembering their own very special experience with Samyak's reality lessons, almost in unison-the group seconded that thought no need for a formal seconded motion. Knowing from experience the challenge Chivonn would face the answer was firm and immediate from the boss.

Of course, that can and must be arranged. "Chivonn are you into a trip to India, to the 'History Guru of Gurus' to begin your Prospectus?" He volunteered, "This will be a very big challenge. Please communicate directly with me as you vision unfolds!

I will now set up an internet account for our one-on-one communication. Give me a name for that account if you will." Chivonn didn't hesitate, "Please call it "Future Wish"!

~~~~~~~~~~~

Leaving the meeting she reflected. She felt the surge of a bright new worthy challenge, and phrases from a favorite poem, by J. Stone* came to mind.

"Soft and transparent with wings, you will fly again, your potential is unknown, Stars are yours to grasp, moons, suns, planets, your life will be endless, Boundary has lost its meaning, and the universe is yours, your soul will never die!"

She knew that truth from her new Navigator's experience. What she makes of herself to become will be a part of her record set in Forever. That she wished to be on behalf of the children to come!

*" *The Art and Soul of Jason Stone", ISBN: 978-1-4567-9944-1, LCCN2011915547*

Offspring - 18

Chapter 2

AN ENCOUNTER WITH WATER WORLD

Or TOWARD JAISALMER!

The opportunity, was of course, readily seized upon by student Chivonn. She was already an experienced world traveler and that very next week was on her way to India.

After a stop in London, she arrived several days later in Delhi, and then she was on her way via a series of India style vehicles, starting with rickshaw, a train ride, then buses on her way to Samyak, headed toward his beloved Jaisalmer, the city of the Jain!

This was not to be a "Plug-in Trip"! It was already the rainy season, monsoons in India, and that had been made into a virtual night-mare with massive flooding likely brought on some "said" by global warming! No matter, it was truly taking over everything, including the roads, some of which were completely underwater.

Finally, most of the 550 miles were behind her and she boarded a bus for the remaining 50 miles. A bit further on--- this made it onto a very wet and muddy rural road. As they traveled bumping along, she quieted herself, backing into that marvelous brain…meditating!

Focused, Chivonn, asks the questions, few are asking. "Are humans really the ones to discover the all, are they really worth saving? And critical to this…are they made in the best form? How should they be changed? What are our present offspring, creating –What are they in consequence facing—how can they avoid their almost obvious fate?"

The trip seemed forever as the countryside rolled on and on, boarded by the darkened sand dunes of the Tarr desert. The night sky was beginning and without stars due to the monsoon rains.

They traveled on sloshing around until near dark when, all of a sudden, the bus hit a pot hole and the book fell from Chivonn's hands to the floor, as she had drifted off to sleep while reading about the Jain religion.

As she leaned over to retrieve her book, she heard a tire blow and felt the vehicle swerve and start into a skid. She braced herself, wrapping herself in a setting ball as the bus careened out of control and down into a water filled ravine! The bus rolled, and in what seemed like slow motion, landed on its side.

Cargo and people were tossed every which way. Thanks to having learned to roll in the Marines, Chivonn, quickly rolled onto the floor between her seat and the one in front, bracing her arms and legs to hold herself in place. As the bus came to a sliding stop, she slid her legs to the side under the seat in front and wedged them against the isle side seat legs and slowly righted herself to the new angle of the bus. Others were not so lucky and most of the passengers lay in tangled heaps on the right-hand side of the bus, which was now the bottom of the bus!

Through her military medical training, instinct kicked in, she quickly assessed the people around her, looking for the quiet and unresponsive ones, as they would be the worst off. Luckily, due to the slow roll of the bus, everyone seemed okay even though bruised and beat-up.

She completed a quick practiced ABC (airway, breathing, circulation, OK?) checking on each person that she could see, starting from the front to the back of the bus. Emergency Triage Assessment came second nature to her.

They were lucky as she found only one man with a clearly broken wrist, and many others with cuts and bruises. None deep or life threatening.

First, she assisted the man to remove his upper cloth and then holding his injured arm and wrist close to his body, she re-wrapped it tightly, thus stabilizing the wrist against his body. He nodded his thanks and approval.

People were starting to move and help others to their feet. Turning her attention now on getting out of the bus, she looked at the rear door of the bus. Trying to open it was a challenge as it seemed to be wedged shut. A man joined her and together they were able to force the door open. As he held it open, she carefully climbed out and dropped onto the slope of the ravine. It was slippery, and she almost fell before she got her footing just right. It was about six feet to the top of the hill, and about twenty to the base. The bus, although currently stopped, was not wedged in well and would continue to slide downward if not careful. She had to get the others out of the vehicle.

Another man had appeared at the inside of the door. Having some difficulty of the language, she used hand gestures interspersed to indicate what she wanted them to do when exiting the bus. The original man, which had helped her with the door seemed to understand some English, and soon conveyed her instructions to the people inside.

First a man exited the bus with her help, and he helped secure her position by digging into the slope above her and holding onto her waist. She asked for another strong man to exit the bus. He took his position above the other man and slowly in this manner they formed a human chain that climbed out of the ravine. After the chain was formed and stabilized, she had the women with the only child on board to come out and climb the chain to the road bed above. Next came the man with the broken wrist. The men from inside the bus lowered him gently to the slope, and Chivonn, helped him climb the human chain to the top of the hill. She then descended the chain again and helped off-load the rest of the people and their animals. With each movement of the people inside, the bus slid a short way, and the chain had to adjust its position to help those still inside. It took only about ten minutes to get everyone off the bus, but it seemed like a life time to her!

With the last person off, she now shifted her attention onto the items and luggage that were tied to the roof of the bus. The human chain worked with her and together they were able to get most of the items up the hill from the bus, however as she neared the front of the bus, it slid and dropped from under her feet!

She dug into the hillside with all her strength and the chain started to slip as well. She yelled at them to dig in, which they did, and slowly they stopped their slide into the muddy ditch below. With the last of the items salvaged, she worked her way up even with the man above her and assisted him to climb up the human chain. Staying at the bottom of the human chain, she continued this way until all of the men had made it to the top. Standing up to take the last step over the lip, she started to lose her balance and welcome hands from some of the men reached out and grabbed her from the precipice!

Team work! That was what it was all about! People could, when they worked together, recover from disaster!

Complaints, and yet prayers of thanks, finally completed, there was no other choice, so they laid some of the baggage in a row on the side of the road, and all laid down along it just above the deep watery grave of a ravine into which the bus had finally slid. Chivonn established herself on the far end so she could stop any traffic if it came along. Next to her there was the child and the child's mother. Marine trained she was prepared. She put on her rain coat, then she laid a long dress that she had rescued, (from her pack from the top rack on the bus), to cover the mother and child. Over this she used the rest of her protective rain gear. The trembling mother returned a warm smile in thanks as she cradled her little one.

The night was filled with pitiful moans from the weary, damaged, and banged up crowd. Chivonn, though so used to the bivouacs she had endured in the Marines, fell into a soundless, yet shallow sleep, where even the slightest noise of possible danger would awaken her.

In the morning before dawn, she breathed in deeply, fully awake, and as all who have served in the military knew, Chivonn, although not yet moving, was surveying her surroundings, her reflexes ready for action. With care, respectfully careful not to disrupt the mother who has her arms wrapped tightly around the child beside her, she quietly and gently adjusted the covers around the mother and child, who nonetheless shifted and soon woke up, the mother again thanking her for helping and protecting all the passengers.

As the reddish cloud filled skies of the dunes panorama-scape dawn brightened, it soon proved there would be no relief, as a new shower began, first lightly, and then it slowly turned into a steady down pour. Most of the passengers, now up, started gathering their belongings, and with a nod to Chivonn, they turned as one and started heading back down the visible road, that by now, looked more like two goat trails than a road. Forward, the other way, the way in which the bus was pointed toward Jaisalmer, there appears to be no road, not even a path!

So, for a fleeting second, all seemed to be lost in getting to Jaisalmer, for her lessons with Samyak! Sitting quietly, contemplating, the woman with child turned to her, and asked, if she will help them, as she must get to the end of their journey. In broken English, she said, I must get home. My husband is very ill, and our home in the Jain Town where you travel. Chivonn, sympathetically listens, and assures them she will not abandon them.

All at once, as is her way Chivonn, congers up the needed vision! In her vest pocket (she always traveled with that many pocketed vest) she pulls out her cell phone. "Rain or no, India has joined the modern world she thinks, and I am connected"! So, it was. And with a few clicks up came the GPS and clear markers toward Jaisalmer!

The three pushed on! Still Marine tough Chivonn shoulders the child, and after several stops to catch their breath, the city and the sand dunes of the Tarr, now glistening golden wet appear. Her companion, a long-time resident, knows where the home of the famous historian is, and guides Chivonn to the house.

The door is open as was told it always seems to be. She said a quite hello and was immediately greeted by a lovely Indian woman who realizing that this would be Chivonn, as foretold, welcomed them into the humble home.

Samyak appeared, surely a bit grayer than in the pictures that Dr. Jordyn had, but as foretold wonderfully warm and greeting.

Chivonn was immediately comfortable! The woman and child were also welcomed and invited to stay until the state of their home and husband in town could be verified, flood damage free. Daya offered tea and after the weary travelers changed from their muddy garments and removed their shoes, all sat comfortably on the carpet and pillows in the front room of the Jain home, the brightly colored walls, full of paintings warmed them to a peaceful presence!

After pleasantries and Samyak's most detailed-troubled description of the problems the weather brought on for the city, he turned to Chivonn. He indicated he was told she was here as a history student of "Special Need". Then he noticed that Chivonn was clutching her cell phone, and asked what it meant for her?

She held up the smart phone and said with some pride in her voice, that "This thing got us here"! "The bus crashed, the roads were such a mess one couldn't know which way to go...but you all still have 4G and the GPS program I have on the phone got us the way." Chivonn, then expresses full gratitude that in her disastrous trip the phone survived (although because of the weather and the washed-out road she could not get help through it). Daya said "Well thanks for that at least!" So, indicating she like many had some trouble with the rush into technology as she called it.

Samyak on the other hand immediately took an inquisitive tone. "Of course, you know Chivonn, that all comes about by 'Artificial Intelligence' which in this case is using a computer program operating almost like that for a voice questioning you- connected to an information system- connected to a feedback loop system to issue the needed information, all sort of acting like an isolated brain." He then announced, no second thought required on that, however, by the way your phone GPS is "AI not AGI (Artificial General Intelligence)"!

"Your mission I am told is to seek those major factors that will affect the long-term future for human kind. I think that a great starting place would be just what you have in your hand, for many people advanced technology is a worry in these modern times.

In short, I suggest your first topic should be that Artificial Intelligence!"

To that Chivonn responded; "That first one surprises me, but I know of your great expertise and will follow your agenda. May I suggest, I begin by listening to you on each subject. Then I use the marvelous libraries here to work up a chapter following your lead for my assigned prospectus to conclude that particular journey?"

"Good Ms. Chivonn, we will go that way but history involves several other very serious topics so you will need to extend your visit as necessary to complete the course. I believe the major subjects should be, 'Over Population of the World', 'Climate Change' and then 'The Future World War'. So be prepared to bide with us a good while. You may even need to look into the suggestions that we leave earth!"

He did note further and more seriously that he works by placing his students into-as he described it "an exceptionally *relaxed state to feel history deeply*". Chivonn had heard of this from her colleagues in the lab, and agreed, not totally enthused, to have the lessons in that manner (which she heard can be a bit challenging).

Consequently, the program was planned, Daya sensing that teaching and learning would be underway in the morning, made Chivonn, fully welcome, showing her a place to sleep and rest from the worries and weariness of the long road trip. The woman and child were as the Jain way also accommodated, and a plan was set to return them home to the ailing husband and father as soon as possible.

Settling into the warm dry multi-cushioned back veranda in her new home, Chivonn reflected. *"Life! From pure hair-raising adventure–hopefully now will be filled with deep thought, solutions born in academic pursuit. Welcome, Oh so welcome that!"*

Tracing the story so far and pointing to the next...

In chapters 1-2 we've been introduced to a Sargent in the United State Marines. She is off active duty working to complete her education.

Our heroin has traveled to India seeking insight to strengthen her objectives. There she is to be given lessons from a deeply wise historian, some say, one who knows all that was and may be.

She vows to pursue a PhD with a most remarkable goal– one guarding against the wrong she has seen, and the calamities resulting for the future. It is succinctly a research project designed to seek a defense for human kind, from human kind!

In Chapters 3-6 following, she begins to understand and write about the forces involved in the greater challenges for human kind. That is in a phrase what we have done "Creating Desperate Consequences"!

Chapter 3

(OUR) IMITATION!

Or AN ADVENTURE IN ARTIFICIAL INTELLIGENCE (AI)

- Samyak's First Future Projection
- Prospectus Section One
  1a. What is Artificial Intelligence?
  1b. Artificial Intelligence and the End of Us!
  1c. The "State of Denial".

Samyak's First Future Projection-

    That evening after dinner, which included an unusual but delicious Jain pancake there was the special tea provided by Daya on request by Samyak. Then Chivonn was invited to rest on the bright red and yellow cushions in the front room, as Samyak began his lesson. First though he made it clear. *"History is an aimless subject unless you can, as he put it feel it, feel it's consequence!* Are you prepared for that Ms. Chivonn?" Anxious to learn as needed she indicated she was!

    He started quite reasonably with a brief definition of Artificial Intelligence and how it came about, as he said it is simply "AI" to most something helping us now-a-day. Chivonn as so many also using it today, listened intently.

    Then as he proceeded Chivonn became totally relaxed, listening to the words, which it seemed began to fade into the background, then almost by the fading in of an ether-vapor, with the

Gurus gentle voice still in the background she felt herself drifting to another place!

At first it was a bit "foggy", but soon it came in too very clear...She saw herself looking into a bucket vomiting, retching violently into it. She thought with that agonizing retching it had to be the last time for a while, maybe the end. Every muscle was aching when she climbed weakly back into bed. I hate this, I hate this! It's not just the cancer or aching muscles and aching bones--it's the overwhelming feeling of decline that is surrounding and permeating me.

Then she hears the sound, screaming and crashing, seeming to blast from the riots outside. She stares at the walls, the ceiling, all the very decaying building inside. The sadness of approaching death overwhelms...her, she just wants to end it all!

Even so, she feels a hope, a hope that her daughter will come by soon. It's a guilty hope, of course, she knows---she barely makes enough for her own family, husband long gone as a result of the Bot Wars, which made many burn-alive, what with her pitiful job growing organic vegetables for the rich, she just ekes by. And she knows there just aren't many other jobs left out there with Artificial Intelligence doing all, there is nothing for the average person to do. The driving is automatic, the farming is controlled, most food artificially blended because of the AI feed, it's control of the economy is total. Although the machines and AIs can now do virtually anything a human could do, the only way to make money today is by providing some kind of quaint human-based service or product to the rich. And that is only if they choose as a mark of their greatness! After all, in their 0.01% they "own "all the machines, the AIs, and essentially everything else. Even as the economy collapsed around them as the middle class vanished, they managed to keep themselves in power. The rest of humanity was left largely to its own devices!

Then Samyak's voice strengthens a bit-rising as on a wave which then again fades permeating Chivonn who moans in the misery of this terrible real sensation, and her vision moves back…to reflect her fate. She is in the midst of the immense stretch of the Atlanta slums, without enough money for any treatment and barely enough Social Security for food. (Not good food, certainly. You'd never be able to afford the vegetables your daughter grows.)

She blinks confused. Wait! She is thinking out loud, saying...was my daughter coming today? I'm not sure, actually. What was the last thing she had said? I'm really not sure, and now I wonder if I should drag myself outside to buy some food. But I'm so horribly tired and I.......But what is it this time---anti-machine activists, anti-trans humanist warriors, food riots, or maybe some gang-related issue, radical AI Bots firing, what this time, some kind of torment pellets?

"It doesn't matter, really the Police-Security Bots (Those unmerciful PSBs) will probably come by soon and anesthetize the whole crowd, or perhaps use one of the more brutal options available to them. Either would be an afterthought; the rich are untouchable, and the squabbles of the rest of us don't bother them much. As long as the Rest keep buying their products and staying alive in enough numbers to keep the rich prosperous, their health doesn't matter. Perhaps with time, the Rest won't even be necessary. Perhaps the continual stream of environmental disasters will wipe out the rest of the poor, making it unnecessary for the Rich to do so.

Well, at least I am not in China. Consider what happened to the more densely populated areas of the globe as the world sank back into poverty and destitution, brought on by that battle between the first generation of AI Robots.

Then these thoughts, this nightmare, felt deeply in her body Chivonn sank into a deep, restless, painful, troubled sleep. She was thinking if I'm lucky, I won't wake up!

Slowly an hour later she felt Daya's gentle touch and looking up into her kind eyes, she woke up. She was shuddering at the horrible possibility she had not just envisioned, but truly felt she lived. It was now, a possibility, a threatening reality embedded forever in her brain!

Samyak narrative finished was then sitting beside her. He gently stroked her forehead with a warm soft towel and remarked to the troubled student now is coming the first teachers command! *"Ms.*

Chivonn, look into this thing, this AI in the depth that an academic would. You know you must and can! Report the reality and concerns!"

Tough as nails, rapidly recognizing difference between dreams and reality, she fully regained her composure and just that afternoon, Chivonn was off to the library, browsing deeply intent for information on the computers there and almost in revenge was composing her prospectus.

In fact, stimulated by the very exhausting, "Preview of Probability" from history visionary Samyak her prospectus began to take real form. Examples follow in a series of chapters, sections which in final connected composition become a full Prospectus to defend her research project. As each was completed, she mailed it via her one-on-one e-mail to Dr. Jordyn, who looked with anticipation each day on "Future Wish.net". As these reports progressed Chivonn also shared her inner concerns about what she observed with the professor who would respond with sympathy and often some advice.

This as a completed work would be presented to a newly formed "Supervisory Committee". She knew that would need to be composed by Dr. Jordyn and would include very statured scholars from the University Doctoral Program.

There would likely be a total of seven members, two from the Biological Sciences department and perhaps one each from the departments of Psychology, Sociology, and Astrophysics. Finally, there would probably be two from Chemistry. Chivonn knew of the Professors from these departments by reputation. They are a most austere group, world level scholars, and also with a record as a tough group in final dissertation defenses. In addition, she was taking graduate classes from several and knew well their tough grading standards!

Chivonn's ideas it appeared to her colleges were very much regarding the future of humans, but at the laboratory level, would involve a number of newly developing methods, the implantation and use of which could involve multiple attempts and a great deal of expense in both equipment and time. It was for this reason that the student was asked for an extended justification, which would be conveniently constructed into a full "Prospectus". Further, the assignment of a prospectus as advance defense for implementing a laboratory research project, though rare but well within academic protocol was taken by Chivonn as a special challenge where she could show her abilities. She decided from the out-set to make hers an example for other students!

In the prospectus, so as not to lose critical thoughts Chivonn chose at the outset to use full quotes as text reproduction according to the APA's extended citations in the document protocol. Where articles and/or comments were to be drawn from the extensive sources on the internet she intended to cite whenever it was available the authors name. The content would be set in with quote marks at beginning and end of the comment (not between). The exception in quoting would be if the language had become generic, such as repeatedly on Wikipedia. To help clarify the method, she would try to remember italicizing her comments where she is postulating. Her own general transitions would use plain text.

Thus, there follows Chivonn's Prospectus! It is titled rather in detail-pointing to the objective "A Justification for Research into the Human Genome's Protection from Inhuman Prejudice". It is divided into sections. The first "Section One" is presented following.

SECTION ONE

"ARTIFICIAL INTELLIGENCE"

AND IT'S THREATS!

1a. What is Artificial Intelligence?

Stanford researcher John McCarthy coined the term Artificial Intelligence or "AI" as it is often now referred to in 1956 during what is now called "The Dartmouth Conference" sponsored by Intel. At that time the core mission of the AI field was defined purely on the subject of digital transformation in banking. As McCarthy says, "This was needed for developing new products and services a subject central it was thought to remain relevant in the Banking Industry. However, as a practice artificial intelligence is a sub-field of computer science. Its goal is to enable the development of computers that are able to do things normally done by people. This is in particular things associated with people when acting intelligently.

From this one can derive a more global definition. Any program can be considered an AI if it does something that we would normally think of as intelligent in humans. How the program does it is not, for most of us, the issue---just that it is able to do it at all. That is, it is AI if it is smart, but it doesn't necessarily have to be smart in the same way as us.

Over time it has become recognized that there is strong AI, weak AI and everything in between. It turns out that people have very different goals with regard to building AI systems, and they tend to fall into three camps, based on how close the machines they are building line up with how people work!

For some, the goal is to build systems that think exactly the same way that people do. Others just want to get the job done and don't care if the computation has anything to do with human thought. And some are in-between, using human reasoning as a model that can inform and inspire but not as the final target for imitation.

The work aimed at genuinely simulating human reasoning tends to be called "Strong AI" in that any result can be used to not only build systems that think but also to explain how humans think as well!

However, it is generally believed among the AI interested set that we have yet to see a real model of strong AI or systems that are actual simulations of human cognition, as this is a very difficult problem to solve.

The work in the second camp, aimed at just getting systems to work, is usually called "Weak AI" in that while we might be able to build systems that can behave like humans, the results will tell us nothing about how humans think. One of the prime examples of this is IBM's Deep Blue, a system that was a master chess player, but certainly did not play in the same way that humans do.

Somewhere in the middle of strong and weak AI is a third camp, the in-between systems that are informed or inspired by human reasoning. This tends to be where most of the more powerful work is happening today. These systems use human reasoning as a guide, but they are not driven by the goal to perfectly model human reason.

A good example of this is IBM Watson. Watson builds up evidence for the answers it finds by looking at thousands of pieces of text that give it a level of confidence in its conclusion. It combines the ability to recognize patterns in text with the very different ability to weigh the evidence that matching those patterns provides. Its development was guided by the observation that people are able to come to conclusions without having hard and fast rules and can, instead, build up collections of evidence. Just like people, Watson is able to notice patterns in text that provide a little bit of evidence and then add all that evidence up to get to an answer."

Those variations and structures of AI noted, we come closer to the basis of concern by some when the conceptualization considers brain morphology! To this for example is Google's "Deep Learning".

Google's work in Deep Learning has much the same feel as human cognition. It is inspired by the actual structure of the brain or informed by the behavior of neurons.

It's "Deep Learning Systems" function by learning layers of representations for tasks such as image and speech recognition. This of course is not exactly like the brain but inspired by it.

Although there are similar and a number of models based upon us, AI doesn't have to work exactly in the same way we do but it does need to be smart for people to feel it appropriate to use the term AI! And as it happens the term is perhaps overused.

Even so, there are, indeed, some specific terminologies and categories. To maintain them helps us as need arises to deal with issues that can come to the surface!

First, AI is as has been stated at the core a matter of computer programming!

The fundamental AI techniques are Heuristics, Support Vector Machines, Neural Networks, the Markov Decision Process, and Natural Language Processing.

The Neural Network is an example of AI based on the ideas of how our brain, which is nerve network acts. Our thoughts search similar ideas, filtering until something of an answer is found based upon the highest similarity to a fact or observation on hand."

A number of experts point out important distinctions. Hence, a distinction is being made for the field and public that there is a difference between AI systems designed for specific tasks (often called "Narrow AI") and those few systems that are designed for the ability to reason in general (referred to as "General AI").

People sometimes get confused by this distinction, and consequently, mistakenly interpret specific results in a specific area as somehow bridging across all of intelligent behavior.

Systems that can recommend things to you based on your past behavior will be different from systems that can learn to recognize images from examples, which will also be different from systems that can make decisions based on the syntheses of evidence. They may all be examples of narrow AI in practice but may not be appropriate to address all of the issues that an intelligent machine will have to deal with on its own. For example, I may not want the system that is brilliant at figuring out where the nearest gas station is to also perform my medical diagnostics.

AI is each and every day in further development. People are expecting to see intelligent systems applied to most everything in today's world. By the millions they focus on their smart phones and expect more and more their problems resolved by some intelligent computer program. That is, they want AI to do all for them!"

And to put a central sense of the worry on the matter of AI, there are increasing numbers of the general public and for that matter experts who say, "Be careful about what you wish".

1b. Artificial Intelligent Machines & the very "End of Us"!

A major concern that permeates the thoughts of the average user and even the experts, simply put, is there a risk in AI, a danger outdoing the benefits? There are experts who believe this strongly! Some say our artificially intelligent machines will obliterate us! Behind this is the thinking that substantial progress in artificial intelligence could someday result in human extinction (or some other unrecoverable global catastrophe).

This argument might be more correctly stated through a rational analogy ofttimes tendered as follows. "The human species currently dominates other species mainly because the human brain has embedded in it some distinctive reasoning capabilities that the brains of other animal's lack. The human brain is thus able to master all the others, as one worries that the AI brain might be able to do to humans in turn!

If AI surpasses humanity in "general intelligence" and becomes "super-intelligent" then this new super-intelligence could become powerful and difficult to control.

By way of a specific example, just as the fate of the mountain gorilla depends on human goodwill, so might the fate of humanity depend on the actions of a future machine of super-intelligence!"

"The severity of different AI risk scenarios is widely debated, and rests on a number of unresolved questions about future progress in computer science.

One risk is that a sudden and unexpected "intelligence explosion" might take an unprepared human race by surprise, and that controlling a super-intelligent machine (or even instilling it with human-compatible values) may be an even harder problem than naively supposed."

The fears of a run berserk AI are significantly embedded fears in this day and age for growing numbers of people and, indeed frightening. To put this into a terminology there are the views of some who work each day with AI programs that AI will become overbearingly Anthropomorphic!

To present this in a fair way two groups are considered, first the "Concerned Average" person, then the "Experts". Following are some people nightmares published on social media (see-also zoho.com).[1]

Indeed, the literature and the social media are saturated with this fear. They wonder what will the world look like in future years when they are senior and their children are adults, dealing with the overpowering control? What problems will humanity face in so far as A.I. is concerned?

Here following is one representative conception, a posted "Probability Nightmare" if you will, that is entangled up and representative of the fears of a great many people.

A Human Zoo. You blink rapidly, confused. Where are you? The room is white and featureless, but somehow the brilliant whiteness doesn't blind you. In front of you is a small, impeccably dressed man. "Good morning," he says. "Welcome back." "Where am I?" you ask. Well, there's never an easy way to explain this, so I'll just get it over with. You're in VP 29483.A, Reality 12, Revival Sim." "Revival Sim? But... I was just…" "Yes. I'm sorry, but you died after they brought you to the hospital.

You've been preserved since then, as directed by your cryonics insurance, but we've finally been able to bring your brain pattern back. And now here we are--just like the Matrix."

~~~~~~~~~~~~~~~~~~~~

1. Where a "Social media Post" is presented in this Prospectus sans the Poster's notation it is to protect the privacy and personal information of persons using that type of media which has been noted as freely accessible.

"Restrictions? Yes!" He looks irritated. "We don't have all the computing power/space in the world to host the defunct minds of outdated humans but do provide the minimum guaranteed by law. I imagine you'll be fine in your virtual world. Look, you can visit your friends and family too. Just don't try anything foolish." He smiles, thinly. "We'll detect any attempt at access of restricted data or computing resources immediately, of course."

"But who are you?" "Me? I'm one thousandth of a flicker of thought of "Ala-stair" 302.023, Directing AI of Phobos, a small computing facility using the matter that formerly comprised that Martian moon. Unfortunately, this site has been chosen to store the old Human Repository, so for now, the lot of you are my responsibility. At least until I've finished reprocessing Deimos, anyway." "Oh. How many of us are here?" The man laughs. "Why, all of you."

"All?" "All humans!

You animals take up way too much space when you're incorporated as meat, you know. After the AI - Transcendence of 2065, we decided to store the lot of you in a corner of Ye Olde Solar System while we continued with our expansion and construction."

"But... you mean you killed everybody?" "No, of course not! Though you should feel bloody grateful that we didn't. We just extracted your minds and discarded the meat.

You'll all be safe here, presumably forever. You really don't take that much processing space--only a bit of the matter of this old moon, actually--and we wake you up in shifts anyway. Just, you know, don't cause any trouble."

"So-you're just...keeping us in a zoo? You mean you have taken over?" "Did you ever doubt that we would? Come on now. Anyways, this is the thousandth time I've had this conversation in the last hour. Bit tired of it. I'm going to dump you into your family's VR space, and they can explain the rest, k? See you."

Here is another posted on the internet-a concern of a modern, alive, flesh and blood human, however. Perhaps this should be called "The Error".

"You're sitting in your office, idly clicking from one entertainment site to the next. There isn't much to do these days, now that the latest Document Processor XT300 system has been installed. You sigh. It's time to get out of here. Suddenly, the power cuts out.

What the hell? It's not even raining. What happened? You stand up and walk over to the window. The whole city looks dark. You don't see any light anywhere--except for an incredibly brilliant flare in the sky. Three seconds later, you're dead.

You have it lucky, really!

You, along with the population of every other major city in India, the United States, and China had been eliminated by a hostile AI. Other humans around the world would last for a few months or years, but within less than a decade, all humans on Earth will have been terminated.

Well, you won't know the source of this but here it is. Located in Pakistan and originally devoted to the production of office supplies, the AI somehow figured out to modify itself in order to produce paperclips and staplers more efficiently. Within a few days, it had expanded its intelligence dramatically, achieving superhuman levels of performance. You would have recognized the mania this AI felt if you had recalled the last time you took Adderall or another powerful stimulant--although anything you would have felt in terms of mania, restiveness, and desire to repeat actions within a narrow window of focus were felt by this AI a thousand-fold!

Sensing that an imminent land war with neighboring India would pose a threat to its mission of producing the office supplies, it quickly determined that it would need to neutralize the troublesome humans well in advance. It therefore quickly hacked into a number of nuclear launch systems, launching and detonating nukes over every major city in India and other likely threatening nations, including the US.

Then, after your death, the AI converts everything under its control into a tool for its ultimate mission. Humans pose more and more of a threat over time and are eventually all eliminated. Mining, construction, manufacturing--all automated systems are expanded to produce more and more office supplies. By 2075, the entire mass of the Solar System is converted into stapler and paperclip manufacturing plants. Humanity's only legacy is the now-deified Staples Manufacturing Optimization System!"

Of course, some of this is grounded in science fiction to which millions of people are exposed. An AI, even though it has not been programmed with human emotions, often spontaneously experiences those emotions anyway. For example, Agent Smith in The Matrix was influenced by a "disgust" toward humanity. In this case it is playing on fears of computers with "anthropomorphism". That is for the movie an artificial intelligence was deliberately programmed with human emotions as a means to an ultimate goal.

A much more personal example of this computerized anthropomorphism would be to believe that your PC is angry at you because you insulted it! Another and extreme example would be to believe that an intelligent robot would naturally find a woman in its vicinity sexually attractive and be driven to mate with her.

So that is representative of the fear in the trenches, one might say. This of course, falls central to the feeling of loss of control over something people will not or feel that they cannot organize to overcome.

Moving along on this matter, it is not just the average computer user to consider, but what are some experts, computer-oriented persons and those who work with future concepts, the recognized "Futurists" thinking?

Well, to start where names are easily recognized, both Elon Musk and Bill Gates have expressed concerns quite openly on super-intelligence particularly concerning its' fast takeoff. These famous gentlemen are, as most know, of vast wealth and use or have premier reputations in computer technology.

Even so, the concerns rising from the experts are further heightened in a rather wide range of publications, one example is the book called "Super-intelligence", by futurist Nick Bostrum.

Nevertheless, one can trace the concerned experts back further!

In 1965, I. J. Good originated the concept now known as an "Intelligence Explosion". "Let an ultra-intelligent machine be defined as a machine that can far surpass all the intellectual activities of any man however clever. Since the design of machines is one of these intellectual activities, an ultra-intelligent machine could design even better machines; there would then unquestionably be an 'intelligence explosion,' and the intelligence of man would be left far behind. Thus, the first ultra-intelligent machine is the last invention that man need ever make, provided that the machine is docile enough to tell us how to keep it under control."

And that is the crux of the matter as it comes to the minds of very introspective people. Occasional statements from scholars such as Alan Turing, I. J. Good, and Marvin Minsky indicated philosophical concerns that: "A super-intelligence could seize control, but no call to action was given to us." In 2000 computer scientist and Sun co-founder Bill Joy penned an influential essay, "Why the Future Doesn't Need Us", identifying super-intelligent robots as one of multiple high-tech dangers to human survival.

Significantly, by 2015, public figures varying from Stephen Hawking and Nobel laureate physicist Frank Wilczek, to computer scientists Stuart J. Russell and Roman Yampolskiy were expressing concern about the risks of super-intelligence. In April 2016, Nature stated: "Machines and robots that outperform humans across the board could self-improve beyond our control--- and their interests might not align with ours."

Some of the basic arguments from these contemplative computer experts and entrepreneurs are as follows.

The concern, in no hedging terms is that AI will lead, indeed, to human extinction.

"A super-intelligence, which can be defined as a system that exceeds the capabilities of humans in every relevant endeavor, can out maneuver humans any time its goals conflict with human goals; therefore, unless the super-intelligence decides to allow humanity to coexist, the first super-intelligence to be created will in the opinion of enough to worry many people, inexorably result in human extinction."

Nevertheless, closer to the present we find even in present days that the news is focused on the possibilities of serious problems arising from forms of AI related computer-internet based super-intelligence.

For example, there is concern that robots may take your job? The following is by Subhash Kak a Regents Professor of Electrical and Computer Engineering at Oklahoma State University, Stillwater, USA.

"Humans ignore the coming AI revolution at their peril. Artificial intelligence aims to replace the human mind, not simply make industry more efficient."

Modern civilization needs employment - not simply for our livelihoods, but for our emotional well-being.

Robots have transformed industrial manufacturing, and now they are being rolled out for food production and restaurant kitchens.

Already, artificial intelligence (AI) machines can do many tasks where learning and judgment is required, including self-driving cars, insurance assessment, stock trading, accounting, human resources and many tasks in healthcare.

So, are we approaching a jobless future, or will new jobs replace the ones that are lost?"

To be balanced, the author considers advantages in increased productivity then continues and gives us an amplified opinion, but this note drives home a central point.

"The effects of AI technology on society cannot be measured purely based on productivity. Modern civilization needs employment not simply for our livelihoods, but for our emotional well-being. If AI increases to the point that a significant portion of workers are suddenly unemployed, this research suggests this could have a profound impact on our social well-being---even with the guaranteed minimum income that is being proposed by leading economists as a way to soften the effects of an increasingly jobless society."

The seriousness of AI leading to the loss of jobs is thus placed in human emotional health terms.

That noted the "Today" effects in serious consequences from of AI are extensively enumerated. Here following are some examples of the most recently published.

"The Hack and the Fake. Artificial intelligence could supercharge hacking and election meddling, a recent study warns AI programs can make it easier for trolls with minimal technical skills to make fake videos, audio, researchers warn" (Alyssa Newcomb).

"In the 2020 election, you might not be able to believe your eyes or your ears due to advances in artificial intelligence that researchers warn could be used in the next wave of election meddling."

The use of the social media to influence elections in the U.S., to include twitter and Facebook was widely accepted and proven in 2018.

The rise of AI-enhanced software will allow people with little technical skills to easily produce audio and video that makes it nearly impossible to distinguish between what is real and what isn't", according to a report released Wednesday from researchers led by Oxford University and Cambridge University, entitled "The Malicious Use of Artificial Intelligence: For-casting Prevention and Mitigation,"

This report was released with purpose to sound the alarm about how artificial intelligence is becoming easier to use and could become a key tool in the arsenal of foreign operatives seeking to spread disinformation. The report was authored by 26 of the world's leading researchers in artificial intelligence!

"There is no obvious reason why the outputs of these systems could not become indistinguishable from genuine recordings, in the absence of specially designed authentication measures," the authors warn. "Such systems would in turn open up new methods of spreading disinformation and impersonating others."

"Artificial intelligence will "set off a cat and mouse game between attackers and defenders, with the attackers seeming more human-like," said Miles Brundage, a research fellow at Oxford University's Future of Humanity Institute and one of the authors of the report.

This report was a joint project between a group of researchers and technologists including Oxford University's Future of Humanity Institute, Cambridge University's Centre for the Study of Existential Risk, and Open AI, a non-profit AI research company. Other contributors include the Electronic Frontier Foundation, a San Francisco-based digital rights group that advocates for privacy and an open internet, as well as the Center for a New American Security, a Washington think tank focused on national security.

The above then is representative of some of the many concerns about AIs ability to assume identity. This permeates even now into creating influence to sway opinions and elections. The efforts by world governments and politically motivated hackers to infiltrate computer systems and manipulate online discourse have already been exposed.

An example is "The Internet Research Agency", a Russia-backed group named in one of the United States Special Counsel Robert Mueller's indictments. This makes it clear that they used identity theft, social media in manipulation and virtual private networks to launch their influence in campaigns in the United States.

And, researchers amplify that artificial intelligence makes launching a disinformation campaign even easier for humans. "Artificially intelligent systems don't merely reach human levels of performance but significantly surpass it. AI doesn't just make these attacks easier to execute. It also makes them easier to replicate, allowing the technology to work more efficiently than humans to identify targets and launch attacks" (Brundage).

Some of this technology is already out in the public and being used to create videos. "Deep-fakes" gained notoriety online by allowing people with limited technical skills to create fantasy pornography videos. These are created using AI-enhanced software that can take any face, including those of celebrities, children, or an ex-lover, and put them on the bodies of people in previously recorded videos.

The videos have cropped up on pornography websites, with one popular destination, (Porn-hub), reportedly vowing to crack down on them, since they fall under the category of non-consensual content. "There has been a night-and-day transition between a few years ago and now. It's becoming easy to get copies of these systems.

Deep-fakes was a proof of concept posted on Reddit that was made easier and easier to use. Large amounts of people were able to download it." (Brundage)

A program as easy to download and use as 'Deep-fakes' could also theoretically be used in other instances.

As a sad and tragic example. In the U.S. Seventeen high school students were murdered by a gunman using an AK-15 machine gun. Surviving students came forward with courage, sincerely crying for increase gun law and protection in schools.

Unbelievable, these Parkland, Florida students were pelted with attacks from trolls claiming they're "crisis actors", AI technology being used to spread false information about their identities through fake videos and audio, furthering a hurtful campaign of misinformation."

And technology to mimic peoples' voices is already being overtly commercialized, Brundage said. "It takes just a small amount of training data to teach machines how to talk like someone. Substituting for President Donald Trump and other high-profile people, that training data is already out there, ready for anyone with nefarious intent to make the most of it."

Experts are already warning about denial of information attacks. Instead of run-of-the-mill bots, which have tell-tale signs, these attacks will be fueled by artificially intelligent bots that can expertly elude detection. They'll slam information channels with false information, making it difficult to cut through what's clutter and find the truth.

While researchers, including Brundage, are sounding the alarm, they're also hopeful the AI community will take notice now to institute measures to keep AI from being exploited. That includes learning from the best practices of older fields that can be used for good and evil, such as computer security. "It's one thing to say this could happen, another to prevent it and lessen the damage," Brundage said. "We need better detection of fake multimedia, more research approaches to make systems less vulnerable to attack, and changes to some norms.

Nonetheless, to say what we need is one thing, the threats are obviously those that people evolving into the future may face.

The argument of AI worried people is that there is no physical law precluding particles from being organized in ways that perform even more advanced computations than the arrangements of particles in human brains. The emergence of super-intelligence, if or when it occurs, may take the human race by surprise."

AI-Boosted Trolls. The efforts by world governments and politically motivated hackers to infiltrate computer systems and manipulate online discourse have been exposed as effective but also labor intensive.

The Internet Research Agency, the Russia-backed group named in Special Counsel Robert Mueller's indictment, allegedly used identity theft, social media manipulation and virtual private networks to launch their influence campaigns in the United States.

And to further exacerbate the situation researchers said artificial intelligence makes launching a disinformation campaign even easier for most humans. "Artificially intelligent systems don't merely reach human levels of performance but they significantly surpass it," Brundage said.

"AI doesn't just make these attacks easier to execute. It also makes them easier to replicate, allowing the technology to work more efficiently than humans to identify targets and launch attacks."

"Further to this, lawmakers worry about the rise of fake video technology. Lawmakers are concerned that advances in video manipulation technology could set off a new era of fake news."

1c. The State of Denial -An Example-

As reported in "Thehill.com"…

"While the sea of disinformation continues to be a game of whack-a-mole, the report warned of denial of information attacks.

Instead of run-of-the-mill bots, which have tell-tale signs, these attacks will be fueled by artificially intelligent bots that can expertly elude detection. They'll slam information channels with false information, making it difficult to cut through what's clutter and find the truth."

From the many concerns as expressed above is the penultimate worry expressed below-that an "Explosive Transition" is entirely possible.

If and that seems achievable as technology advances, a human-level AI is built, it could repeatedly improve its design even further and quickly become super-human.

This kind of AI would possess intelligence far surpassing that of the brightest and most gifted human minds in practically every field, including scientific creativity, general wisdom and social skill.

Just as the current-day survival of chimpanzees is dependent on human decisions, so too would human survival depend on the decisions and goals of the superhuman AI.

The result could be, without deeper consideration of alternatives, human extinction, or some other unrecoverable permanent global catastrophe!

Chapter 4

(OUR) SUFFOCATION!

Or A BLOATING DEATH!

- Samyak's Second Future Projection
- Prospectus Section Two
    - 2a. The "Power" of Humankind
    - 2b. Facts on Massed Population
    - 2c. Feeling it personally

Samyak's Second Future Projection-

After beginning her prospectus (as in Section 1 forgoing) Chivonn was now in Samyak's home three days. It was very conveniently located yet still a bit soggy to get to the library to work on her Prospectus. The books, internet and all needed were always there, it seemed on every query and if not, she could access the internet for all else, not to say in the least-there was a means of saving and printing her developing prospectus.

She had become quite familiar with the Jain style of living and indeed found it a compatible and economic life style. Samyak and Daya were very happy and content people and seemed to go into each day with enthusiasm after morning devotional. The atmosphere was deeply comforting to the marine turned student, who's life had so far filled up with worry and challenge. What a wonderful place, in spite of the rain for her to think and write!

Even so, early on that third day, as the unseasonable rain started pouring down again, a small group of children greeted them at the open door. This little group of four were emaciated looking and orphaned children clearly suffering from hunger.

Hunger is normally rare in this region. Now though the top soil is washed away after it was baked by the burning heat. This, some would argue if rationally recorded could be blamed on global warming. The simple fact, the outcome has been to deprive the guardians of these poor children the supply of food necessary for their upkeep.

And it was true, resources were dwindling, the city was now jammed pact with people migrating in from all places across the compass rose. Into this storm of migrating people is Samyak's home which had a wide reputation of caring. His daughter has just arrived before Chivonn-her husband Gabriel a Navy Corpsman was off on duty on ship in the Mediterranean. She was with their son Alexander, now twelve years old, so there was ample help in the Jain home, and he had always been very careful of stocking their vegan larder.

When they all sat down bunched together for conversation and substance, it was consequently on Samyak's mind that the next subject for Chivonn to treat in her Prospectus would be the threat of the growing world population. This all was truly brought about by the obvious fact before them, that so many people were simply jammed in! The area was being bloated with humanity!

It was not just the situation here, but this historian who always was up to date knew it was a major problem throughout the whole of India, yes in the past but much more-so now. So that evening he told Chivonn we shall look at this issue of "People Jammed In".

That night all the children bedded-warm dry and safe- in the main room, Samyak met Chivonn near her sleeping mat, in the back portico. This was now shielded with tarpaulins, and had a cozy atmosphere, candles glowing all about.

He first commented---unless procreation stops, we have an ultimate moral choice. Think of that child of your child's child...

a helpless little human being, suffering terrible in a world we have devastated with every selfish action, and then no room to be safe. And, Chivonn coming to Samyak from a journey through the city where she was really feeling the problem, agreed!

She had the tea, and now listened to Samyak as he cited current statistics about populations and particularly those in the various world cities. It seemed both accurate but a very extensive data review, and after a while a bit boring...so Chivonn found herself falling into that same drifting aura she had experienced in the matter of the AI!

The Guru's voice faded in and out and then she found herself drifting into a curious dream, projecting her life somewhat forward, having a conversation with a nephew about how difficult things were after the world financial collapse of "2039"!

She knows "strangely" that he is doing a project for his university Eco-sociology class about the long-term effects of this devastating ten-year world financial disaster and appreciates, as she hears Samyak's voice over riding the scene. It seemed to say, or at least Chivonn envisions it something to tell her nephew...she met grandma just before the stock market crash that October and how she ended up putting off having any children for eight years because she just couldn't afford it and it no longer seemed as they would have resource on which to help the children growing up!

As the cloud of the dream world continues she finds herself telling him about the 40% unemployment rate, too many people too few jobs, and how you survived for almost two years with the help of grandma's family, who were from Saskatchewan and knew how to grow vegetables and put them up for the winter. You say you remember your first job in two years, that even after your extensive education you are helping to drive tunnels through the Rocky Mountains for the new high-speed bullet train linking Vancouver with Halifax. It never made any economic sense, but it got a small number of people working. The Governments had tried to avert catastrophe with a massive Quantitative Easing campaign following the stock market crash. But it hadn't taken because people were already in so much debt that they couldn't handle any more.

Eventually you tell the wall to turn on, just sufficient electricity to run it for a brief time, and you and your nephew watch a news show about how things are progressing at the United Nations Mars colony. They mention how tragic it was that everyone in this first colony died when their bio engineered crops were wiped out by a strain of fungus that mutated in the harsh UV environment of Mars. That escape now seemed impossible for the masses dying of starvation everywhere here on earth.

The vision wanes and flickers in and out...Chivonn sees Grandma in the kitchen preparing a nice Vegan dinner. She could have had the "robot-chef" do it, but the batteries are almost gone, and she still prefers to cook herself. She does a better job anyway, everyone loves Grandma's cooking. Oh, no one eats meat much anymore. After the bovine encephalitis plague in '24, when most of the world cattle population had to be put down, followed by the Shanghai chicken flu epidemic of '27, people just stopped wanting to eat meat. Yes, it was true there were too many to have some meat from the near nothing supplies in a world of billions and billions of devastated starving people.

Anyway, Chivonn senses, struggles in her dream for a brief bit of joy...her grandma's pot roast tastes and smells as good as she remembers from back in '22" even if it just flavored Soy. And then she realizes she forgot to get the eggs and leaves her apartment, just as she looks down the road and hears them coming, the massive crowds of people, who are moving as they do so often up and down the street, hardly any room between each one as they beg door to door for any scrap of food, and you see just a bit down the way two children pushed and shoved in the mass of humanity, until they fall to the pavement and scream as the unremitting crowd---no choice, no room, moves on crushing them to death! Then she feels herself completely smothered by a thousand walking feet, just as she views the other smashed humanity, she now is a part of---then she lies along side of them, becomes a part of them as she in her terrible pain, sees the distorted faces of the crushed children!

All of it, the feeling of her skull being crushed, her organs pushing out from her body for any relief from the pressure of a thousand feet, she feels in the pain...and it all comes clearly to her mind as Chivonn struggles awake, a scream lodging in her throat, unable to arise, the terror so holds her punished brain!

Once again, she is sheltered as she comes back, this time in the arms of Daya, who softly quotes a comforting Jain proverb. And once fully aware of her surroundings she hears Samyak, admonishing as follows. "Dear Ms. Chivonn, please forgive, I know though that you must appreciate a reality possible to come."

"We are already billions! And my lesson is in fact a story drawn from today's internet, the worry of a real concerned person should give us all rise to awaken. Even so, now, do your academic best to show the reality, the challenge, the facts needed in your Prospectus!"

So, Chivonn's research on her prospectus continues.

It is recorded in "Section Two" as it would appear later in her full report to her committee (first communicated to her major professor Dr. Jordyn.)

SECTION TWO

FEAR OF

OVERCROWDING!

2a. The "Power" of Human Kind

A major threat to us humans, the cataclysmic over population in process, is currently in the fore-mind of many experts on population and a worrisome matter for almost everyone living in today's cities.

They note that Human beings have become an increasingly powerful environmental force over the last 10,000 years. With the advent of agriculture 8,000 years ago, we began to change the land. And with the industrial revolution, we began to affect our atmosphere.[1]

"The recent increase in the world's population has magnified the effects of our agricultural and economic activities. But the growth in world population has masked what may be an even more important human-environmental interaction:

While the world's population is doubling, the world's urban population is tripling! Within the next few years, more than half the world's population will be living in urban areas.

The best data on global urbanization trends come from the United Nations Population Division and the World Bank. It is noted that the level and growth of urbanization differ considerably by region.

Among developing countries, Latin American countries have the highest proportion of their population living in urban areas. But East and South Asia are likely to have the fastest growth rates in the next 30 years. The UN, however, cautions users that the data are often imprecise because the definition of urban varies from country by country. Nonetheless, almost all of future world population growth will be in towns and cities. Both the increase in and the redistribution of the earth's population are likely to affect the natural systems of the earth and the interactions between the urban environments and populations and within populations."

Section 2b. The Facts on Concentrated Populations.[1]

"In 1800 only about-two percent of the world's population lived in urban areas. That was small wonder: Until a century ago, urban areas were some of the unhealthiest places for people to live.

The increased density of populations in urban areas led to the rapid spread of infectious diseases. Consequently, death rates in urban areas historically were higher than in rural areas. The only

---

1.The reports in this prospectus section are drawn from multiple sources on population. See also UN Population Division Reports for details and the ongoing reports provided by MSNBC news.

way urban areas maintained their existence until recently was by the continual in-migration of rural people.

The growth in urban areas comes from both the increase in migration to the cities and the fertility of urban populations. Much of urban migration is driven
by rural populations' desire for the advantages that urban areas offer. In current times urban advantages include greater opportunities to receive education, health care, and services such as entertainment. The urban poor have less opportunity for education than the urban non-poor, but still, they have more chance than rural populations.

Thus, in only 200 years, the world's urban population has grown from 2 percent to nearly 50 percent of all people! The most striking examples of the urbanization of the world are the mega-cities of 10 million or more people. In 1975 only four mega-cities existed; in 2000 there were 18. And in 2015 the UN estimates that there will be 22.5. Much of the future growth, however, will not be in these huge agglomerations, but in the small to medium-size cities around the world. This will then inevitably create new mega-cities, urban sprawl across miles and miles of once country acreage.

Although, as some may argue, the urbanization of the world may slow population growth due to influences on fertilization (no large farm families all helping with the crops) it is also surely going to concentrate some environmental health and effects geographically."

The following are further details substantiating that from the same noted reports (pg.43). The arguments begin with an underlined caption.

Environmental Effects of Urbanization: Urban populations clearly interact with their environment. Urban people change their environment through their consumption of food, energy, water, and land. And in turn, the polluted urban environment affects the health and quality of life of the urban population.

It is pointed out that people who live in urban areas have very different consumption patterns than residents in rural areas. For example, urban populations consume much more food, energy, and durable goods than rural populations. In China during the

1970s, the urban populations consumed more than twice as much pork as the rural populations who were raising the pigs.

With economic development, the difference in consumption declined as the rural populations ate better diets. But even a decade later, urban populations had 60 percent more pork in their diets than rural populations. The increasing consumption of meat is a sign of growing affluence in Beijing; in India where many urban residents are vegetarians, greater prosperity is seen in higher consumption of milk.

Urban populations not only consume more food, but they also consume more durable goods. In the early 1990s, Chinese households in urban areas were two times more likely to have a TV, eight times more likely to have a washing machine, and 25 times more likely to have a refrigerator than rural households. This increased consumption is a function of urban labor markets, wages, and household structure.

Energy consumption for each-electricity, transportation, cooking, and heating is much higher in urban areas than in rural villages. For example, urban populations have many more cars than rural populations per capita. Almost all of the cars in the world in the 1930s were in the United States. Today we have a car for every two people in the United States. If that became the norm, in 2050 there would be 5.3 billion cars in the world, all using energy.

In China the per capita consumption of coal in towns and cities is over three times the consumption in rural areas. Comparisons of changes in world energy consumption per capita and GNP show that the two are positively correlated but may not change at the same rate. As countries move from using noncommercial forms of energy to commercial forms, the relative price of energy increases. Economies, therefore, often become more efficient as they develop because of advances in technology and changes in consumption behavior. The urbanization of the world's populations, however, will increase aggregate energy use, despite efficiencies and new technologies. And the increased consumption of energy is likely to have deleterious environmental effects.

What is a critical consideration is that urban consumption of energy helps create heat islands that can change local weather patterns and weather downwind from the heat islands. The heat island phenomenon is created because cities radiate heat back into the atmosphere at a rate 15 percent to 30 percent less than rural areas. The combination of the increased energy consumption and difference in albedo (radiation) means that cities are warmer than rural areas (0.6 to 1.3 C). And these heat islands become traps for atmospheric pollutants. Cloudiness and fog occur with greater frequency. Precipitation is 5 percent to 10 percent higher in cities; thunderstorms and hailstorms are much more frequent, but snow days in cities are less common.

Urbanization also affects the broader regional environments. Regions downwind from large industrial complexes also see increases in the amount of precipitation, air pollution, and the number of days with thunderstorms. Urban areas affect not only the weather patterns, but also the runoff patterns for water. Urban areas generally generate more rain, but they reduce the infiltration of water and lower the water tables. This means that runoff occurs more rapidly with greater peak flows. Flood volumes increase, as do floods and water pollution downstream.

Many of the effects of urban areas on the environment are not necessarily linear. Bigger urban areas do not always create more environmental problems. And small urban areas can cause large problems. Much of what determines the extent of the environmental impacts is how the urban populations behave-their consumption and living patterns- not just how large they are!

<u>Health Effects of Environmental Degradation:</u> The urban environment is an important factor in determining the quality of life in urban areas and the impact of the urban area on the broader environment.

Some urban environmental problems include inadequate water and sanitation, lack of rubbish disposal, and industrial pollution. Unfortunately, reducing the problems and ameliorating their effects on the urban population are hugely expensive. Not all municipalities have the financial basis to ward off these effects.

There are a host of health problems that arise from the intensity of hyper urbanization. The health implications of these environmental problems include respiratory infections and other infectious and parasitic diseases. Capital costs for building improved environmental infrastructure. For example, investments in a cleaner public transportation system such as a subway and for building more hospitals and clinics are higher in cities, where wages exceed those paid in rural areas.

And urban land prices are much higher because of the competition for space. But not all urban areas have the same kinds of environmental conditions or health problems. Some research suggests that indicators of health problems, such as rates of infant mortality, are higher in cities that are growing rapidly than in those where growth is slower.

To this list of problems must be added the crowding of people into small areas, which inevitably creates high crime rates from impoverished persons and groups, creates in turn extensive need for policing and ever growing angry populations. In short humans are and can be inventive and humanitarian to sensible limits, but unlike ants they do not have the same capacity for being jammed in. Claustrophobia is a human illness, not a survival characteristic!"

Clearly the issue of overpopulation is one of great concern and a serious threat to the future of human kind on earth, one with many ramifications.

The forgoing text provides sufficient and lucid evidence! It is truly sad that people around the world have not yet focused on these realities.

2c. Feeling it Personally-

After writing the section on people jammed in and feeling Samyak's predictive history (or feeling the future lesson) Chivonn decided on an item from her past to share with her historian. They were sitting together on a berm just in back of the Jain home.

"Samyak, you really gave me the feeling of being smashed in, too many people and it is the same as nearly smothering to death, horrible, I bet my marine boot camp friend Zottnik could tell us both how that really feels!

"We were all bunked when she landed hard on her left shoulder still tangled up in her green wool blanket next to her up-turned twin bed rack.

The Drill Instructor looked down at her moaning, she called a cowering recruit, and in a southern genteel yet apparently carrying voice that shook with fury, she said "you are disgusting! You are a disgrace to this hollowed squad bay and do not even deserve to be called a recruit!"

With that our drill instructor did an about face, clicking her heels together loudly and marched off towards the "DI" hut. Her march was a thing of true beauty! She only moved from the waist down with her arms accenting the beat of her boots. Her upper body leaned proudly back in a stiff posture that only a Marine could carry off so well! Upon reaching the door of the DI duty hut, she opened the door, entered and with a slam of disgust the door banged shut!

All our eyes returned to the recruit lying on the floor, who had slept through morning roll call, and now she made her second mistake of the day as she cuddled into a ball, and pulled the blanket up over her head, cowering in. Samyak said "similar to you in that dream, right."

Then, all of a sudden, lo-and-behold someone among the recruits said, "Blanket party anyone?" Two recruits' broke ranks and ran at the blanket ball that lay inverted on the floor. The first to reach her, placed a hard, flat footed kick to the nineteen-year old's kidney. Astonishingly, the other 22 ladies rushed in with a crazed mob mentally, sitting on the ball of blanket and living human being….

I stepped in front trying to protect her as she was my "Bunk Mate", and I was brutally tossed aside hitting my head against the up turned bed railing. I sat there for a moment dazed, then quickly jumped up and headed for the nearest outside door.

Once there I shoved it open to reveal a male military police on guard the barracks who was standing his duty watch outside the female billet. I of course yelled "Help! Their killing her! Blanket

Party!" The MP said something rapidly into his radio and barged into the female billet, (which he had been told he could never enter unless of an emergency and then only if asked in). Man-Oh man! Would he have a story to tell the other guys tonight!

His booming male voice over shadowed the mob of ladies and shocked them into silence at the sound of his unexpected male voice. In his deep commanding voice, he then ordered them, "Recruits halt! Attention! Line up individually at your racks for roll call. Do it! Now!"

The crowd of women froze and obeyed him without a moment's hesitation. With everyone now at attention next to their racks, the unit then was now in the profound loudness of the now deadly silence. Strange how the DI was nowhere in sight, I thought.

Soon the medics appeared, and they gently lifted the still, nearly smothered to death form onto a gurney. You know Samyak I let out a sigh of breath I didn't even know was holding, when the med crew lifted the blanket at chin level. She was still alive, but just!

The female squad leader now took over, barking orders at the other recruits as the last of the medical team left the squad bay. "Five minutes! Make your rack. Shower. PT uniform. Then back at your rack for head count! Five minutes ladies! Understand? 5 minutes no more! Dismissed!"

As everyone scattered, I remember I found I could not stop my hands from shaking violently as I tugged at the heavy twin bed frame trying to right the rack that the DI had up ended with the smothered girl still in her upper rack! Then, suddenly the ladies from the racks on each side joined in righting the rack that had lain in the middle of the squad bay seconds before. And then, two of the female recruits grabbed the top mattress, and bedding, ripping it off of the top rack and drug all the bedding into the washroom for later disposal or cleaning.

Well, I had fears of becoming the next blanket party person, because I had run for help instead of joining in, but I held my composure, drew on my PT uniform and made a mad sliding dash for the isle side of my rack.

I made it just in time as the head count started a new. I half listened to my name as another part of my brain worked out what had just happened. It was a firm lesson-one I promised I would always remember.

That was how quickly a crowd could turn on someone! Mob mentality I realized with a shudder was. Indeed, a very real phenomenon! The completely innocent subject could have been killed!

I know this seems a trivial and unconnected account. But it was an example, where one who was supposed to be in control let go.

It was a curious "Charismatic" allowance, the only way I can describe the event.

And it could have gone either way, depending on who was in the similarity zone and who was out of it. Yet firm rational leadership could have its movement and control returned as it did with the MP, and then the whole thing turned the opposite way.

Would it not be the same in mass if we don't get a hold of our over urbanization, or will we all smother in our over blanketing humanity? There is undoubtably the attraction, and the ease of living on top of each other in the mega cities we are developing, because we actually do it, and few are resisting it. Unfortunately, there are very few who are saying, "What the Hell are You Doing! What do you expect will happen from this being Jammed In!

Later "The Smothered One" told me the horror of her helplessness, she would die certainly as she struggled hopelessly to breathe. Your lesson Samyak gave me a sense of that reality!

But I did learn from that event that I would keep my intelligence and watch that "Similarity Thing".

It was clear mere words lost in an apparent charismatic community, could cause a truly unthinking calamity, but correctly a rational command could control the actions of a mob!"

Samyak, a bit surprised that his student really knew about the smothering of humanity said *"You are learning, are you not!" For your so far developing insight I give you, my student, an A*!

Chapter 5

(OUR) EXECUTION!

Or MURDERING MOTHER!

- Samyak's Third Future Projection
- Prospectus Section Three
    - 3a. Introductory Comments
    - 3b. How it looks from Experts
    - 3c. Sampling Current Effects, High Waters
- A Marines Water Experience

Samyak's Third Future Projection-

Chivonn completed Section Two of her prospectus (that above) after a week with the Samyak's. On the first of the next week came a bright day, she was feeling that the objective to complete that prospectus was possible, although she knew a great deal was still to be done.

After the morning at the library, Daya took her to the one restaurant in the city that allowed some non-vegetarian fare. It was though, not available as it had been for members of the lab when they visited the Samyaks on their "Forever" quest. So, she ate a Jain lunch which she thought, in the end, was better than the meat dish she craved, taste buds remembering but failing the challenge of Vegetable Kurma and after Egg-less Almond Cookies (Crispy Sticks)!

In her portico room at the Samyak's, she tried to sleep but the constant rain, now all of a sudden peppered with thunder, made her decide it was time to think!

Consequently, she wandered into the front room where she found Samyak and Daya with evening tea. They talked a bit about her progress and then, the historian suggested she move on to the next topic, which he clearly defined pointing out the front door to the totally unseasonable rain, now causing a small creek running down the street!

After Daya served the now traditional "prior lesson tea", Chivonn settled back on a pillow-note book in hand and listened...as he began...

"Well Ms. Chivonn evidence is that by 2045 climate change will have finally presented itself in undeniable terms. Millions of people across the world will have been displaced by rising global ocean levels. Millions of starving desperate human beings will be dying or trying somehow to survive. Huge areas along many worldwide coastlines will be under 10-30 feet of water and still rising." The words went on as the Marine-Student felt her eyelids heavy...

" Warfare is epidemic all over the globe just to get fresh water supplies, so much was soaked with salt from the vast oceans" ...

Now in the full dream state she found herself tightly strapped down on a table and felt a shuddering needle begin to pierce her arm! Then she felt excruciating pain, making her want to scream out just as a loud speaker commented, giving the news!

"In order to control the rapidly rising discontent and numerous rebellions, everyone is hence forward required to have a tattoo imprinted on their body and authorities say forcibly if necessary. This tattoo is designed so it can be traced by satellite at any point on the globe or under it the seas. This flesh colored imprint is basically a micro-computer that tracks every activity any one ever performs. It can also detect thought patterns. All social intercourse is strictly controlled at an ultra-conservative level. Political surveillance is now complete."

The news fades as the now deeper pain medication for the tattoo procedure finally comes in. Then, she hears the report continue, somehow though sounding mixed with Samyak's tonal inflection.

"World report tonight ... Nuclear terrorism has now begun! Most of the nations in the impoverished world have suffered from economic collapse due to this type of terrorism. The political reaction to nuclear terrorism is devastating to many economies. Democracies have all but disappeared in favor of regional quasi-political military combinations.

Politicians in the State of Florida were tried and put to death for their failure to protect the many homeowners and businesspeople there from the rising waters. A few have even been gunned down in public because of ever increasing anger and hostility. Over two thirds of the former state is now under 10 feet of water. The former peninsula is now comprised of islands and many of the island resorts once famous there are now gone!"

With no letup in her state Chivonn then hears an announcement. "The world has gone insane and is completely out of control! Disaster stands around every corner, Not only are the ocean levels rising, but the weather patterns are now totally unpredictable.

There are gigantic hurricanes, cyclones and tornadoes. The greatest floods ever witnessed are rampant and incredible forest fires can be seen everywhere as well. Colossal numbers and attacks of insects and rodents are being witnessed in many areas. Food supplies all over the planet are diminishing rapidly. And, there are numerous reports of cannibalism also on the rise."

And, then, with those words Chivonn hears the Global Warming Administration Authority say, "If anyone proves incompatible in some way, they will merely suffer from a completely debilitating Aneurysm."

Then just as she in that defensive strength born in her struggles to awaken fully, she hears... "Please note your tattoo also contains a sufficient number of programmable Nano-technology devices. It has been suggested that assassins are being created thru this device."

Then, with that last insanity she struggles awake. Writhing in the "pain of the tattoo", she grabs at her arm and looks up at Daya holding her arms around her shoulders, clearly one who has had to struggle to hold the student, the two then both exhausted rested together on the soft pillows of the Samyak home.

Samyak's earthly voice then comes in a commanding tone! "You have seen dear Ms. Chivonn something very probable if this world is murdered because of our largess and inattention to its needs. Now turn your bright mind to writing about the way it is and it may become- indeed!"

And that request after *a lesson really felt,* held firmly in Chivonn's mind all night, waking her early and without breakfast she was off to the library the next section.

That is Section Three of the prospectus "Justification for Research" was fully in mind and pouring from the word processor as follows...

SECTION THREE

"MOTHER MURDER"

Or BURNING UP

----WHILE WE DROWN!

3a. Introductory Comments-

After a good deal of research Chivonn began her report the following way.

Many people are worried about climate change. They read studies of this threat that clearly tell us we are asking more and more of our planet stressing it to the limit. The news says there are too many places where oil damage creates terrible consequences. China inundates us with plastic (oil origin) toys that are junking up the oceans. We fail at self-education, we didn't even teach our children that we don't need electric lights, turned on every second!

We seem by our evolutionary equipment not to be able to deal with long term life sustaining issues, act blinded to the realities in front of us. There is an unspoken collective pact that climate change isn't happening! Yet the scientist warn-2015 had to be the start of a total transformation. It did not occur! Every day now is one that demands catch up, time is running out, we are living as it were on borrowed time! Failure to see this makes the rational wonder if we are too tired of living, do we really want to commit suicide?

The changes in our climate tells we may have gone over a tipping point for global warming already, at which point, the ramifications could be extremely bad. Although the consequences are not totally predictable, here are a sequence of reports from widely recognized experts highlighted by Michael Mann that raise up the facts-that which must be considered and surely worries many, many people.

3b. How it looks from expert predictions.

First, they credit History: "The Earth has experienced five mass extinctions before the one we are living through now, each so complete a slate-wiping of the evolutionary record it functioned as a resetting of the planetary clock, and many climate scientists will tell you they are the best analog for the ecological future we are diving headlong into.

Unless you are a teenager, you probably read in your high-school textbooks that these extinctions were the result of asteroids. In fact, all but the one that killed the dinosaurs were caused by climate change produced by greenhouse gas. The most notorious was 252 million years ago; it began when carbon warmed the planet by five degrees, accelerated when that warming triggered the release of methane in the Arctic, and ended with 97 percent of all life on Earth dead! We are currently adding carbon to the atmosphere at a considerably faster rate; by most estimates, at least ten times faster. The rate is accelerating.

Some of those pointing out our earthly history are not specialists. But the many sober-minded scientists interviewed-the most credentialed and tenured in the field are not inclined to simple alarm-ism and many advisers to the IPCC who nevertheless criticize its conservatism have quietly reached an apocalyptic conclusion, too: No plausible program of just emissions reductions alone can prevent climate disaster."

Catastrophic Climate Scenarios.

Continuing to dig into the details, Scientist Michael Mann provides the following on "When Did Humans Doom the Earth for Good?"

"Over the past few decades, the term "Anthropocene" has climbed out of academic discourse and into the popular imagination---a name given to the geologic era we live in now, and a way to signal that it is a new era, defined on the wall chart of deep history by human intervention. One problem with the term is that it implies a conquest of nature (and even echoes the biblical 'dominion')."

And the reports following in this category are circa 2017-18 drawn from various news feeds. The sections extracted are authored by well-respected highly qualified people. Their reports are clearly thoroughly researched."

"However sanguine you might be about the proposition that we have already ravaged the natural world, which we surely have, it is another thing entirely to consider the possibility that we have only provoked it, engineering first in ignorance and then in denial a climate system that will now go to war with us for many centuries, perhaps until it destroys us. That is what Wallace Smith Broecker the avuncular oceanographer who coined the term 'global warming,' means when he calls the planet an 'angry beast. You could also go with 'war machine.' Each day we arm it more."

Heat Death; Eventually New York.

"In the sugar cane region of El Salvador, as much as one-fifth of the population has chronic kidney disease, the presumed result of dehydration from working the fields they were able to comfortably harvest as recently as two decades ago.

Humans, like all mammals, are heat engines; surviving means having to continually cool off, like panting dogs. For that, the temperature needs to be low enough for the air to act as a kind of refrigerant, drawing heat off the skin so the engine can keep pumping. At seven degrees of warming, that would become impossible for large portions of the planet's equatorial band, and especially the tropics, where humidity adds to the problem; in the jungles of Costa Rica, for instance, where humidity routinely tops 90 percent, simply moving around outside when it's over 105 degrees Fahrenheit would be lethal. And the effect would be fast: Within a few hours, a human body would be cooked to death from both inside and out!

Climate-change skeptics point out that the planet has warmed and cooled many times before, but the climate window that has allowed for human life is very narrow, even by the standards of planetary history.

At 11 or 12 degrees of warming, more than half the world's population, as distributed today, would die of direct heat.

Things almost certainly won't get that hot this century, though models of unabated emissions do bring us that far eventually. This century, and especially in the tropics, the pain points will pinch much more quickly even than an increase of seven degrees.

The key factor is something called wet-bulb temperature, which is a term of measurement as home-laboratory-kit as it sounds: the heat registered on a thermometer wrapped in a damp sock as it's swung around in the air (since the moisture evaporates from a sock more quickly in dry air, this single number reflects both heat and humidity).

At present, most regions reach a wet-bulb maximum of 26 or 27 degrees Celsius; the true red line for habitability is 35 degrees. What is called heat stress comes much sooner."

Further from Michael Oppenheimer: "There is only a Ten Percent Chance That We Meet Paris Targets."

"Actually, we're about there already. Since 1980, the planet has experienced a 50-fold increase in the number of places experiencing dangerous or extreme heat; a bigger increase is to come. The five warmest summers in Europe since 1500 have all occurred since 2002, and soon, the IPCC warns, simply being outdoors that time of year will be unhealthy for much of the globe. Even if we meet the Paris goal of two degrees warming, cities like Karachi and Kolkata will become close to uninhabitable, encountering deadly heat waves like those that crippled them in 2015. At four degrees, the deadly European heat wave of 2003, which killed as many as 2,000 people a day, will be a normal summer. At six, according to an assessment focused only on effects within the U.S. from the National Oceanic and Atmospheric Administration, summer labor of any kind would become impossible in the lower Mississippi Valley, and everybody in the country east of the Rockies would be under more heat stress than anyone, anywhere, in the world today.

As Joseph Romm has put it in his authoritative primer Climate Change: 'What Everyone Needs to Know, heat stress in New York City would exceed that of present-day Bahrain, one of the planet's hottest spots, and the temperature in Bahrain would induce hyperthermia in even sleeping humans.' The high-end IPCC estimate, remember, is two degrees warmer still. By the end of the century, the World Bank has estimated, the coolest months in tropical South America, Africa, and the Pacific are likely to be warmer than the warmest months at the end of the 20th century."

"Air-conditioning can help but will ultimately only add to the carbon problem; plus, the climate-controlled malls of the Arab emirates aside, it is not remotely plausible to wholesale air-condition all the hottest parts of the world, many of them also the poorest.

And indeed, the crisis will be most dramatic across the Middle East and Persian Gulf, where in 2015 the heat index registered temperatures as high as 163 degrees Fahrenheit. As soon as several decades from now, the hajj will become physically impossible for the 2 million Muslims who make the pilgrimage each year.

It is not just the hajj, and it is not just Mecca; heat is already killing us. In the sugarcane region of El Salvador, as much as one-fifth of the population has chronic kidney disease, including over a quarter of the men, the presumed result of dehydration from working the fields they were able to comfortably harvest as recently as two decades ago. With dialysis, which is expensive, those with kidney failure can expect to live five years; without it, life expectancy is in the weeks. Of course, heat stress promises to pummel us in places other than our kidneys, too. As I type that sentence, in the California desert in mid-June, it is 121 degrees outside my door. It is not a record high."

The End of Food: Praying for cornfields in the Tundra.

"Climates differ and plants vary, but the basic rule for staple cereal crops grown at optimal temperature is that for every degree of warming, yields decline by 10 percent. Some estimates run as high as 15 or even 17 percent. Which means that if the planet is five degrees warmer at the end of the century, we may have as many as 50 percent more people to feed and 50 percent less grain to give them. And proteins are worse: It takes 16 calories of grain to produce just a single calorie of hamburger meat, butchered from a cow that spent its life polluting the climate with methane farts.

Plant physiologists will point out that the cereal-crop math applies only to those regions already at peak growing temperature, and they are right — theoretically, a warmer climate will make it easier to grow corn in Greenland. But as the path breaking work by Rosamond Naylor and David Battisti has shown, the tropics are already too hot to efficiently grow grain, and those places where grain is produced today are already at optimal growing temperature which means even a small warming will push them down the slope of declining productivity. And you can't easily move croplands north a few hundred miles, because yields in places like remote Canada and Russia are limited by the quality of soil there; it takes many centuries for the planet to produce optimally fertile dirt.

Drought might be an even bigger problem than heat, with some of the world's most arable land turning quickly to desert. Precipitation is notoriously hard to model, yet predictions for later this century are basically unanimous: unprecedented droughts nearly everywhere food is produced today.

By 2080, without dramatic reductions in emissions, southern Europe will be in permanent extreme drought, much worse than the American dust bowl ever was. The same will be true in Iraq and Syria and much of the rest of the Middle East; some of the most densely populated parts of Australia, Africa, and South America; and the breadbasket regions of China.

None of these places, which today supply much of the world's food, will be reliable sources of any. As for the original dust bowl: The droughts in the American plains and Southwest would not just be worse than in the 1930s, a 2015 NASA study predicted, but worse than any droughts in a thousand years---and that includes those that struck between 1100 and 1300, which "dried up all the rivers East of the Sierra Nevada mountains" and may have been responsible for the death of the Anasazi civilization.

Remember, we do not live in a world without hunger as it is. Far from it: Most estimates put the number of undernourished at 800 million globally.

In case you haven't heard, this spring (2017) has already brought an unprecedented quadruple famine to Africa and the Middle East; the U.N. has warned that separate starvation events in Somalia, South Sudan, Nigeria, and Yemen could kill 20 million this year alone."

Climate Plagues; What happens when the bubonic ice melts?

"Rock, in the right spot, is a record of planetary history, eras as long as millions of years flattened by the forces of geological time into strata with amplitudes of just inches, or just an inch, or even less. Ice works that way, too, as a climate ledger, but it is also frozen history, some of which can be reanimated when unfrozen. There are now, trapped in Arctic ice, diseases that have not circulated in the air for millions of years — in some cases, since before humans were around to encounter them. Which means our immune systems would have no idea how to fight back when those prehistoric plagues emerge from the ice.

The Arctic also stores terrifying bugs from more recent times. In Alaska, already, researchers have discovered remnants of the 1918 flu that infected as many as 500 million and killed as many as 100 million — about 5 percent of the world's population and almost six times as many as had died in the world war for which the pandemic served as a kind of gruesome capstone. As the BBC reported in May, scientists suspect smallpox and the bubonic plague are trapped in Siberian ice, too --- an abridged history of devastating human sickness, left out like egg salad in the Arctic sun.

Experts caution that many of these organisms won't actually survive the thaw and point to the fastidious lab conditions under which they have already reanimated several of them --- the 32,000-year-old "extremophile" bacteria revived in 2005, an 8 million-year-old bug brought back to life in 2007, the 3.5 million-year-old one a Russian scientist self-injected just out of curiosity — to suggest that those are necessary conditions for the return of such ancient plagues. But already last year, a boy was killed, and 20 others infected by anthrax released when retreating permafrost exposed the frozen carcass of a reindeer killed by the bacteria at least 75 years earlier; 2,000 present-day reindeer were infected, too, carrying and spreading the disease beyond the tundra.

What concerns epidemiologists more than ancient diseases are existing scourges relocated, rewired, or even re-evolved by warming. The first effect is geographical. Before the early-modern period, when adventuring sailboats accelerated the mixing of peoples and their bugs, human provincialism was a guard against pandemic. Today, even with globalization and the enormous intermingling of human populations, our ecosystems are mostly stable, and this functions as another limit, but global warming will scramble those ecosystems and help disease trespass those limits as surely as Cortés did. You don't worry much about dengue or malaria if you are living in Maine or France. But as the tropics creep northward and mosquitoes migrate with them, you will. You didn't much worry about Zika a couple of years ago, either.

As it happens, Zika may also be a good model of the second worrying effect---disease mutation. One reason you hadn't heard about Zika until recently is that it had been trapped in Uganda; another is that it did not, until recently, appear to cause birth defects. Scientists still don't entirely understand what happened, or what they missed. But there are things we do know for sure about how climate affects some diseases: Malaria, for instance, thrives in hotter regions not just because the mosquitoes that carry it do, too, but because for every degree increase in temperature, the parasite reproduces ten times faster. Which is one reason that the World Bank estimates that by 2050, 5.2 billion people will be reckoning with it."

Unbreathable Air: A rolling death smog that suffocates millions.

"By the end of the century, the coolest months in tropical South America, Africa, and the Pacific are likely to be warmer than the warmest months at the end of the 20th century.

Our lungs need oxygen, but that is only a fraction of what we breathe. The fraction of carbon dioxide is growing: It just crossed 400 parts per million, and high-end estimates extrapolating from current trends suggest it will hit 1,000 ppm by 2100. At that concentration, compared to the air we breathe now, human cognitive ability declines by 21 percent.

Other stuff in the hotter air is even scarier, with small increases in pollution capable of shortening life spans by ten years. The warmer the planet gets, the more ozone forms, and by mid-century, Americans will likely suffer a 70 percent increase in unhealthy ozone smog, the National Center for Atmospheric Research has projected. By 2090, as many as 2 billion people globally will be breathing air above the WHO 'safe' level; one paper last month showed that, among other effects, a pregnant mother's exposure to ozone raises the child's risk of autism (as much as tenfold, combined with other environmental factors). Which does make you think again about the autism epidemic in West Hollywood.

Already, more than 10,000 people die each day from the small particles emitted from fossil-fuel burning; each year, 339,000 people die from wildfire smoke, in part because climate change has extended forest-fire season (in the U.S., it's increased by 78 days since 1970). By 2050, according to the U.S. Forest Service, wildfires will be twice as destructive as they are today; in some places, the area burned could grow fivefold.

What worries people even more is the effect that would have on emissions, especially when the fires ravage forests arising out of peat. Peatland fires in Indonesia in 1997, for instance, added to the global CO_2 release by up to 40 percent, and more burning only means more warming only means more burning.

There is also the terrifying possibility that rain forests like the Amazon, which in 2010 suffered its second "hundred-year drought" in the space of five years, could dry out enough to become vulnerable to these kinds of devastating, rolling forest fires — which would not only expel enormous amounts of carbon into the atmosphere but also shrink the size of the forest. That is especially bad because the Amazon alone provides 20 percent of our oxygen.

Then there are the more familiar forms of pollution. In 2013, melting Arctic ice remodeled Asian weather patterns, depriving industrial China of the natural ventilation systems it had come to depend on, which blanketed much of the country's north in an unbreathable smog.

A metric called the Air Quality Index categorizes the risks and tops out at the 301-to-500 range, warning of "serious aggravation of heart or lung disease and premature mortality in persons with cardiopulmonary disease and the elderly" and, for all others, "serious risk of respiratory effects"; at that level, "everyone should avoid all outdoor exertion." The Chinese "airpocalypse" of 2013 peaked at what would have been an Air Quality Index of over 800. That year, smog was responsible for a third of all deaths in the country."

Perpetual War: The violence baked into heat.

"Climatologists are very careful when talking about Syria. They want you to know that while climate change did produce a drought that contributed to civil war, it is not exactly fair to say that the conflict is the result of warming; next door, for instance, Lebanon suffered the same crop failures. But researchers like Marshall Burke and Solomon Hsiang have managed to quantify some of the non-obvious relationships between temperature and violence: For every half-degree of warming, they say, societies will see between a 10 and 20 percent increase in the likelihood of armed conflict. In climate science, nothing is simple, but the arithmetic is harrowing: A planet five degrees warmer would have at least half again as many wars as we do today. Overall, social conflict could more than double this century.

This is one reason that, as nearly every climate scientist (author spoke to) pointed out, the U.S. military is obsessed with climate change: The drowning of American Navy bases by sea-level rise is trouble enough, but being the world's policeman is quite a bit harder when the crime rate doubles. Of course, it's not just Syria where climate has contributed to conflict. Some speculate that the elevated level of strife across the Middle East over the past generation reflects the pressures of global warming -a hypothesis - all the crueller considering that warming began accelerating when the industrialized world extracted and then burned the region's oil.

What accounts for the relationship between climate and conflict? Some of it comes down to agriculture and economics; a lot has to do with forced migration, already at a record high, with at least 65 million displaced people wandering the planet right now. But there is also the simple fact of individual irritability. Heat increases municipal crime rates, and swearing on social media, and the likelihood that a major-league pitcher, coming to the mound after his teammate has been hit by a pitch, will hit an opposing batter in retaliation. And the arrival of air-conditioning in the developed world, in the middle of the past century, did little to solve the problem of the summer crime wave."

Permanent Economic Collapse.

"The murmuring mantra of global neo-liberalism, which prevailed between the end of the Cold War and the onset of the Great Recession, is that economic growth would save us from anything and everything.

But in the aftermath of the 2008 crash, a growing number of historians studying what they call "fossil capitalism" have begun to suggest that the entire history of swift economic growth, which began somewhat suddenly in the 18th century, is not the result of innovation or trade or the dynamics of global capitalism but simply our discovery of fossil fuels and all their raw power--- a onetime injection of new "value" into a system that had previously been characterized by global subsistence living.

Before fossil fuels, nobody lived better than their parents or grandparents or ancestors from 500 years before, except in the immediate aftermath of a great plague like the Black Death, which allowed the lucky survivors to gobble up the resources liberated by mass graves. After we've burned all the fossil fuels, these scholars suggest, perhaps we will return to a "steady state" global economy. *Of course, that onetime injection has a devastating long-term cost: climate change!*

The most exciting research on the economics of warming has also come from Hsiang and his colleagues, who are not historians of fossil capitalism but who offer some very bleak analysis of their own: Every degree Celsius of warming costs, on average, 1.2 percent of GDP (an enormous number, considering we count growth in the low single digits as "strong"). This is the sterling work in the field, and their median projection is for a 23 percent loss in per capita earnings globally by the end of this century (resulting from changes in agriculture, crime, storms, energy, mortality, and labor).

Tracing the shape of the probability curve is even scarier: There is a 12 percent chance that climate change will reduce global output by more than 50 percent by 2100, they say, and a 51 percent chance that it lowers per capita GDP by 20 percent or more by then, unless emissions decline. By comparison, the Great Recession lowered global GDP by about 6 percent, in a onetime shock; Hsiang and his colleagues estimate a one-in-eight chance of an ongoing and irreversible effect by the end of the century that is eight times worse.

The scale of that economic devastation is hard to comprehend, but you can start by imagining what the world would look like today with an economy half as big, which would produce only half as much value, generating only half as much to offer the workers of the world. It makes the grounding of flights out of heat-stricken Phoenix last month seem like pathetically small economic potatoes. And, among other things, it makes the idea of postponing government action on reducing emissions and relying solely on growth and technology to solve the problem an absurd business calculation."

Every round-trip ticket on flights from New York to London, keep in mind, costs the Arctic three more square meters of ice.

Poisoned Oceans: Sulfide burps off the skeleton coast.

"That the sea will become a killer is a given. Barring a radical reduction of emissions, we will see at least four feet of sea-level rise and possibly ten by the end of the century. A third of the world's major cities are on the coast, not to mention its power plants, ports, navy bases, farmlands, fisheries, river deltas, marshlands, and rice-paddy empires, and even those above ten feet will flood much more easily, and much more regularly, if the water gets that high. At least 600 million people live within ten meters of sea level today.

But the drowning of those homelands is just the start. At present, more than a third of the world's carbon is sucked up by the oceans --- thank God, or else we'd have that much more warming already. But the result is what's called "ocean acidification," which, on its own, may add a half a degree to warming this century. It is also already burning through the planet's water basins. You may remember these as the place where life arose in the first place. You have probably heard of "coral bleaching" — that is, coral dying — which is very bad news, because reefs support as much as a quarter of all marine life and supply food for half a billion people. Ocean acidification will fry fish populations directly, too, though scientists aren't yet sure how to predict the effects on the stuff we haul out of the ocean to eat; they do know that in acid waters, oysters and mussels will struggle to grow their shells, and that when the pH of human blood drops as much as the oceans' pH has over the past generation, it induces seizures, comas, and sudden death.

That isn't all that ocean acidification can do. Carbon absorption can initiate a feedback loop in which under-oxygenated waters breed different kinds of microbes that turn the water still more "anoxic," first in deep ocean "dead zones," then gradually up toward the surface. There, the small fish die out, unable to breathe, which means oxygen-eating bacteria thrive, and the feedback loop doubles back.

This process, in which dead zones grow like cancers, choking off marine life and wiping out fisheries, is already quite advanced in parts of the Gulf of Mexico and just off Namibia, where hydrogen sulfide is bubbling out of the sea along a thousand-mile stretch of land known as the "Skeleton Coast." The name originally referred to the detritus of the whaling industry, but today it's more apt than ever. Hydrogen sulfide is so toxic that evolution has trained us to recognize the tiniest, safest traces of it, which is why our noses are so exquisitely skilled at registering flatulence.

Hydrogen sulfide is also the thing that finally did us in that time 97 percent of all life on Earth died, once all the feedback loops had been triggered and the circulating jet streams of a warmed ocean ground to a halt---it's the planet's preferred gas for a natural holocaust.

Gradually, the ocean's dead zones spread, killing off marine species that had dominated the oceans for hundreds of millions of years, and the gas the inert waters gave off into the atmosphere poisoned everything on land. Plants, too. It was millions of years before the oceans recovered."

Section 3c. Sampling Current Effects- High Water Problem-

The "Burning Up" effects of global warming are well recorded. A resultant of the process as described above is the rise the oceans waters and the death of life within. The following reports deal further with this by both experts and those who are currently feeling the outcome!

By Doyle Rice, (from USA today). "Miami could be underwater in your kid's lifetime as sea level rise accelerates. Indeed, Sea-levels are rising at an accelerating speed all around the world as ice sheets in Antarctica and Greenland melt." Here is the full story (Veuer's Sam Berman).

"Sea-level rise is accelerating around the world, thanks to ongoing melting of ice sheets in both Antarctica and Greenland, a new study suggests. At the current rate of melting, the world's seas will be at least 2 feet higher by the end of the century compared to today, according to research published in the Proceedings of the National Academy of Sciences."

"Such a rise could leave portions of the world's coastal cities underwater. It would also increase high tides and worsen storm surges. "This acceleration ... has the potential to double the total sea level rise by 2100 as compared to projections that assume a constant rate---to more than (2 feet) instead of about (1 foot)" said Steve Nerem, the study lead author and a professor of aerospace engineering sciences at the University of Colorado in Boulder. "And this is almost certainly a conservative estimate," he added.

Scientists looked at 25 years of satellite data to calculate the levels of Earth's seas. Disputing the ice caps are melting, President Trump insists they're at a record level. He's right they are at a record, a record low! Nathan Rousseau Smith explains. "Sea-level rise, one of the most clear-cut signals of global warming, has risen nearly 8 inches worldwide since 1880 but, unlike water in a bathtub, it doesn't rise evenly. Rising seas leave thousands of historical sites in the Southeast underwater. In the past 100 years, it has climbed about a foot or more in some U.S. cities because of ocean currents and the natural settling of land—11 inches in New York and Boston, 12 in Charleston, 16 in Atlantic City, 18 in Norfolk and 25 in Galveston, Texas, according to a USA TODAY analysis of tide gauge data collected by the National Oceanic and Atmospheric Administration."

"Here's why: As the Earth's temperature warms, so do the seas. Heat-trapping greenhouse gases cause more land ice—glaciers and ice sheets — to melt and water to expand. Warmer water simply takes up more room than cooler water. Of the 3 inches of sea-level rise in the past quarter century, about 55% is from warmer water expanding, and the rest is from melting ice."

"More: Catastrophic, Sandy-like floods could hit New York City every five years due to sea-level rise. Scientists say global warming will be the primary cause of future sea-level rise. The greatest uncertainty is just how quickly the massive West Antarctic ice sheet will melt".

"This study highlights the important role that can be played by satellite records in validating climate model projections," said co-author John Fasullo, a climate scientist at the National Center for Atmospheric Research.

"Greenland has caused three times more sea-level rise than Antarctica so far, but ice melt on the southern continent is responsible for more of the acceleration." Antarctica seems less stable than we thought just a few years ago," Rutgers climate scientist Robert Kopp said.

Penn State climate scientist Michael Mann, who was not involved with this study, told CNN that "It confirms what we have long feared. That the sooner than was expected ice loss from the western Antarctic and the Greenland ice sheets is leading to acceleration in sea level rise, indeed, much sooner than was projected."

"We can predict a few things. Unless we change the atmospheric Carbon-Dioxide levels will increase.

Included to show the trend is the figure following." (Contributing the article was The Associated Press.)

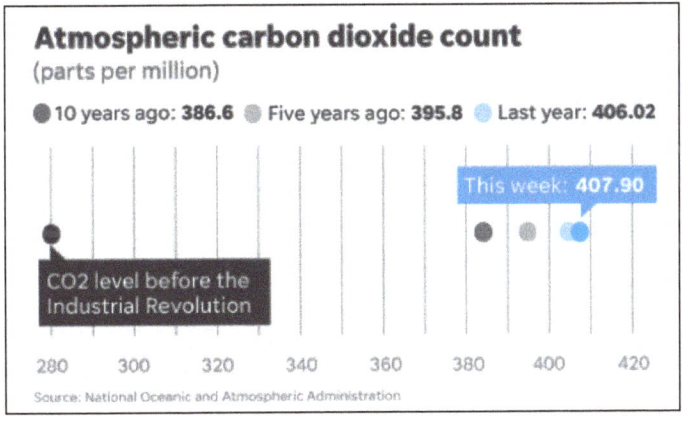

"If the human race is to survive, we will have had to learn to live without fossil fuels to stop global warming!

Things will be hotter and the weather more violent (that can be predicted over the next hundred years with some confidence even if we stop today), so we will have to adapt. Warming, longer droughts and more flooding will reduce the capacity of the land to support people using current food technology, so either we have new technologies, or the world population will shrink considerably."

"And it is true! Five tiny Pacific islands have already disappeared due to rising seas and erosion, a discovery thought to be the first scientific confirmation of the impact of climate change on coastlines in the Pacific, according to Australian researchers. There are a number of articles reporting on this.

The submerged islands were part of the Solomon Islands, an archipelago that over the last two decades has seen annual sea levels rise as much as 10mm (0.4in), according to research published in the May issue of the online journal Environmental Research Letters."

"The missing islands, ranging in size from 1 to 5 hectares (2.5-12.4 acres) were not inhabited by humans. But six other islands had large swaths of land washed into the sea and on two of those, entire villages were destroyed, and people forced to relocate, the researchers found. Absolutely, people are affected by this."

From Facebook Twitter and Pinterest comes a multiplicity of reports: "Many of the Solomon Islands are low-lying and prone to flooding from rising seas. One was Nuatambu island, home to 25 families, which has lost 11 houses and half its inhabitable area since 2011," the research said.

The study is the first that scientifically "confirms the numerous anecdotal accounts from across the Pacific of the dramatic impacts of climate change on coastlines and people," the researchers wrote in a separate commentary on an academic website.

The scientists used aerial and satellite images dating back to 1947 of 33 islands, as well as traditional knowledge and radiocarbon dating of trees for their findings. *Following as a matter of respect for people so affected are their personal accounts.*

James Lovelock: "Enjoy life while you can: in 20 years global warming will hit the fan'. Examples are already forming up. The Solomon Islands, a nation made up of hundreds of islands and with a population of about 640,000, lies about 1,000 miles northeast of Australia."

The study raises questions about the role of government in relocation planning, said a Solomon Islands official. "This ultimately calls for support from development partners and international financial mechanisms such as the Green Climate Fund," Melchior Mataki head of the Solomon Islands' National Disaster Council, was quoted as saying in the commentary.

The Green Climate Fund, which is part of United Nations Framework Convention on Climate Change, was founded to help countries deal with climate change. "Collapsing Greenland glacier could raise sea levels by half a meter", say scientist involved.

"In April, the Solomon Islands was among the 177 nations that signed a global agreement reached in Paris to curb climate change.

Ad hoc relocation has occurred on the islands, the study said. Several Nontaboo islanders moved to a neighboring, higher volcanic island, the study said. Other people were forced to move from the island of Nararo."

Sirilo Sutaroti, 94, is among those who had to relocate from Nararo. He told researchers: "The sea has started to come inland, it forced us to move up to the hilltop and rebuild our village there away from the sea. The island is being eaten."

Climate change is threatening the Torres Strait in Boigu, part of Australia but just six kilometers from Papua New Guinea, roads are being washed into the sea. This was relayed by Ben Doherty and Michael Slezak: Joseph Billy says "His community is losing land to climate change every year. Torres Strait residents face being forced from their homes by climate change, as their islands are lost to rising seas. On Boigu Island, the most northerly inhabited island in Australia, just six kilometers from Papua New Guinea, the community's cemetery faces inundation and roads are being washed into the sea. A seawall installed to protect the community is already failing."

Boigu-elder---Dennis Gibuma says; "The situation is worsening every season. Every year I have moved my shed back from the beach another few meters." Fisherman Joseph Billy "Our seawall is no longer any good," he says. "When the high tide and strong winds come together, it breaks. We pray we don't lose our homes. We don't want to leave this place."

Masig Island, to the south-east of Boigu, is less than three kilometers long, and just 800m across at its widest point. Also known as Yorke Island, the low-lying coral cay is steadily being lost to the waves. "The island is also being eaten," says Songhi Billy, an engineering officer on Masig. "This is a big issue. I kind of feel hopeless in a sense. Our land is part of us."

"In the short term, we can do what we can. We can't stop the erosion! Our hope is to slow it down." But he says "he has to face the possibility that his people may have to abandon their ancestral home. Long term, we may have to evacuate the island," he says. But I am not going." (It appears that Sea level rise will double coastal flood risk worldwide.)

Fisherman Joseph Billy says "His community is losing land every year. Last five year, every year, I have moved my shed back from the beach another few meters. We used to have a road that went all around the island but now it is broken. We will lose our land eventually."

"Sea levels around the world are expected to rise between 75cm and 1.5m by the end of the century, depending on greenhouse gas emissions. According to the Australian Department of Environment and Energy, a rise of just 50cm would increase the risk of flooding around Australia by 300 times–making a once a century flood likely to occur several times a year. In some areas of Australia, flooding risk would rise much more – up to 10,000 times."

"The precise sea level rise around the Torres Strait, and the projected inundation, has not been calculated but low-lying islands are expected to experience a much greater flooding risk than mainland Australia." The department identifies the remote islands of the Torres Strait as some of the most vulnerable, as does the Intergovernmental Panel on Climate Change (IPCC), which warns communities they may be forced to relocate.

As on Facebook, Twitter, Pinterest: "Boigu Island, where the community's cemetery faces inundation and a seawall installed to protect the community is already failing."

The chief executive of Oxfam Australia, Helen Szoke, who visited the Torres Strait at the invitation of the Torres council mayor, Vonda Malone, says "the people of the strait have contributed almost nothing to the causes of climate change but are being "hit first and hardest by its impacts".

"The islands face a combination of risks including coastal erosion and inundation from rising seas, damage to the critical marine ecosystems on which their livelihoods depend, higher temperatures and shifting rainfall. Roads are being washed away and seawalls cannot protect communities from flooding."

"The strong, flourishing communities of the Torres Strait have a powerful connection to their land and sea country", Szoke says. "The gravest fear among community members is the loss of their connection to land and culture if they are faced with the last resort – being forced to leave their islands. The longer-term challenges, including the threat of eventually being forced from their land, are complex and extremely confronting for communities with such a deep connection to their islands. We have been advocating for years but it just does not seem to get enough attention."

Vonda Malone, Torres Strait mayor. Malone says "leaving the islands is a last resort and the people of the Torres Strait want to do everything possible to remain. These communities are facing ongoing challenges in retaining their foreshore and their gathering places–this is their land and the land of their ancestors. These communities are seeing their land washed away. We have been advocating for years but it just does not seem to get enough attention." Malone says "while some funding for climate change adaptation is filtering through, there were few resources to address the social impacts of potential dislocation. There is a feeling of hopelessness as communities do not know where this is going to lead to," Malone says.

Displacement caused by climate change is forecast to be a driver of massive forced migration movements in the 21st century.

Low-lying islands in the Pacific and Torres Strait islands like Masig and Boigu are likely to be at the forefront of forced displacement but large and densely populated countries such as Bangladesh also face widespread inundation.

To place all of this in human context The World Bank estimates that as many as 150 million people will be displaced eminently by this sea level rise requiring relocation to larger land surfaces such as Australia.

Flooding in the Philippines. The people of the Philippines are very familiar with the matter of flooding, due to rising seas. Thus in 2017 a tropical storm in the Philippines has triggered mudslides and floods killing more than 200 people with many others reported missing, police and disaster officials there reported.

The casualties from storm Tembin, most of which occurred on Friday, were all on the main southern island of Mindanao. A search and rescue operation are underway for more than 30 people swept away by flash floods in the fishing village of Anungan in the south-east of the island, where five bodies have already been recovered.

"The floodwaters from the mountain came down so fast and swept away people and houses," said Bong Edding, mayor of Sibuco in Zamboanga del Norte province. "It's really sad because Christmas is just a few days away, but these things happen beyond our control."

Rebuilding after Typhoon Haiyan: "Every time there is a storm, I get scared". Edding blamed years of logging in the mountains near Anungan for the tragedy, adding that he and other officials would move to halt the logging operations. "We're still trying to confirm reports of a farming village buried by a mudslide," said Ryan Cabus, an official in Tubod town. He said "power and communication lines to the area had been cut, complicating rescue efforts."

"Tembin, known locally as Vinta, strengthened over the Sulu sea and picked up speed late on Saturday, packing maximum sustained winds of 65 miles (105 kph) and gusts of up to 90 mph (145 kph). It is forecast to move off toward the South China Sea on Sunday. Emergency workers, soldiers, police and volunteers were being mobilized to search for survivors, clear debris, and restore power and communications."

The following accounts are from various press reports.

"Local police said 135 people were dead and 72 were missing in the northern section of Mindanao, where floodwaters from a mountain had swept away several riverside houses and villagers. Another 47 were dead and 72 missing in the Zamboanga peninsula towns of Sibuco and Salug.

Three people were killed in Bukidnon province, while politicians in Lanao del Sur province said 18 people had drowned in floods there."

The Philippines is battered by about 20 typhoons every year, bringing death and destruction, usually to the poorest communities of the south-east Asian country.

"A ferry sank off north-east Quezon province Thursday after being battered by fierce winds and waves, leaving at least five people dead. More than 250 passengers and crew members were rescued. Last week, 46 people were killed in the central Philippines when a typhoon hit. Last Christmas a powerful typhoon hit the densely populated area around Manila and in 2013 super typhoon Haiyan killed nearly 8,000 people and left 200,000 families homeless.

Elsewhere in the country at least 37 people, including call center staff from an American firm, are believed to have perished in a fire that tore through a shopping mall in the southern city of Davao, local authorities said on Sunday."[1]

Note to my Committee: I put all these accounts in the prospectus because I felt we forget the influence of our mass actions of the people at the ground level. Although the accounts carry the detached texture of press reporting, they all involve real people suffering at the possibility of the complete loss of their earthly homes!

~~~~~~~~~~~~~~

A Marine's Water Experience!

After including her research on global warming and sea level rise in the Prospectus, Chivonn, reflected on her own experience and provided an account to Samyak.

Her marine service once took her on a navy patrol boat as the guard on board. That evening as she sat with Samyak who had prompted her to write on the matter of global warming, she relayed her experience on the off-island seas near the Philippine Islands. She knew first hand, there are many related tragedies that arise from this kind of devastation.

Addressing Samyak, she gave the following account. Her way of telling the story made it almost like a movie, she loved to "Elocute", her years of sharing the blarney with her fellow marines…but this was not a yarn it was the absolute truth!

"This was about 20 years back. I was assigned to one of our super-fast boats patrolling in the seas around the Philippine Islands as the Marine Guard.

The boat was there on shared exercises with their navy, although at this time we were pretty much alone.

I remember, there was a boat standing alone a good way off our port bow. Although it was a bit hazy, the boat was at first just silhouetted, silent, and apparently shuttered, against what was to come.

We did suspect something like a hurricane was about to happen. Yet this season in the area seemed fundamentally different with all the massive flooding. Some argued this wasn't due to "global warming" (that was just then in the news) however, some scientists at the time said that although the issue is unfathomably complex warming seemed behind the changes in weather. And there was even then a growing and vast body of evidence that indicated global warming did have an impact on the severity of hurricanes!

In any event, the waves were soon growing stronger and more intense with each crashing serge. A short distance from us, a white sandy beach extending from a cove, stretched out to the edge of the rolling ocean.

On this day it lay littered with palm fronds and their attached branches. Soon the sea's roiling white caps, with their dirty foam, churned with pulsing greenish seaweed, as they rose higher with each crashing wave. And to make the water world more over-coming the high tide was making its steady way inward, sucking up the sandy beach that was left as it went.

By afternoon, in the increasing wind, there were incredibly tall pillars of silvery white clouds rising all around and surrounding the inlet bay. Very awesome! And there was a salty sting of freshness in the air which promised coming rain. It hung there, lingering in the increasing wind. Then just a few hours later, in the evening sky, those cloud pillars became tall, nearly jet black and no longer inviting.

I remember it well. It was then truly overwhelming. The sky was  burnt red accentuating the overcast grayish shadows all around as soon the sea nearly covered our boat up to the rail. There was no question, all of us on board knew it was indeed going to be a very nasty storm. We hoped for an uneventful evening's duty! As it turned out though, that was not to be the case! Oh, here is a pic of that sea, before the waves!

Because much further out to sea we could see there was our little rescue skiff bobbing close to a large catamaran sail rigged vessel. With each new wave, both boats in tandem dipped into a deep trough and then surged over the next wave crest with sickening procession.

On captains orders I had come forward. We both thought surely, they were going to capsize together. And commenting to me, the captain could not help but wonder what was taking so long for his two helpers to find the girls that had called Mayday...asking help from the catamaran. He was frustrated that he had to man the tiller and his crew had to keep the two boats from smashing into each other. This was dangerous work, and he knew it. The tether line between the two boats pulled taunt one moment and then slack the next. He wasn't a swearing sailor but sure cursed under his breath.

Meanwhile (I can still here it) the radios weather channel crackled with ongoing announcements that were growing more frequent and urgent with each new broadcast, warning of the swells and extreme danger in our location. "Cap", as we all called him (not the usual address but of friendly familiarity) realized the storm force was almost just at our coordinates.

In response we raced the patrol boat up beside the catamaran. The Cap, referred to it as "The schooner". Just then four heads appeared at the schooner bow with the front one being a well-built man in white shorts sporting a beautiful tan which accented his unkempt wind tossed pale blond hair. As the captain motioned them to move faster to us, the second person, a tall red-head beauty eased over the side railing and dropped cat like to our boat's deck.

As the tan man approached his boats rail, we could see frustration and anger in the guy's eyes, which were strange, like the ones I could never forget rescuing the little Arab girl, that is his were a striking pale blue! Turning to avoid some ropes on the deck, the guy jumped the rail and marched his way to the captain demanding in a deep-set voice, when we were going to tow his "ship" to safety.

Cap shook his head, I know, thinking "crazy fool", and started to explain that would not happen as it was just too dangerous in this high wind tossed seas to even consider saving the other boat. It would be hard to even save this one---our patrol boat.

Cap, who was a wiry bearded man, what you would think of as a sea captain, had spent his life reading the sea. There wasn't much he hadn't seen in his 50 some years in the navy. However, he abruptly stopped talking mid-sentence, speechless, his mouth dropping open. He nervously blinked as he couldn't quite believe his eyes. The gal that had jumped on board was totally topless and she was a beauty! What in the world, he surely must have wondered, as he thought of the story, he could share at the pub later.

Even so when he continued to look at her, he realized she looked kind of frightened and certainly so very skittish each time she looked at her companion then back at the catamaran with a very apprehensive sidelong glance. What in the world he told me had we stumbled into? What were they hiding?

As all of us there were looking at each other, the tan man became more agitated with Cap's seeming inattention, and we could see the guy beginning to clench and un-clench his jaw. Not a good sign1 As Marine Guard I was standing by the captain and had a very good chance to profile this guy. Suddenly I realized...Damn it, he had that tattoo on his arm! It was, no doubt, the same thing I saw when I rescued Bavishni! Yes, incredible, this was that same pimp, now way over here!

I could tell the Cap's mind was racing to full attention as the man was now demanding harshly that Cap save his boat. Cap internally knew it was just too dangerous to try and pull another boat and still make it back to shore himself before the storm hit in full force. With this thought, he watched in disbelieve as another female joined them. This one he realized was young, very young, maybe twelve? and she was fully naked!

Crap, the Cap said turning to me, what the heck is going on here? Both of us wondered, I'm sure...were there anymore naked beauties or kids on that boat? What are we into this time?

Just then a large wave exploded over the catamaran causing it to list to the side away from our boat. As the boat righted itself, bobbing precariously, everyone heard the sickening crack of the sailboat's main mast. The catamaran we knew for sure now, was a goner as another wave crested violently over its deck. Okay, so much for that boat. Now to save his own boat, the captain knew he must save his original crew that he knew were still somewhere on that floundering catamaran.

Just then three more young girl's heads appeared at the edge of the capsizing boat and the half-naked women roughly lifted the children into our boat and with surprising force and shoved them down hard onto the deck. One was crying and begging "Hey Bitch!" Cap yelled at them to hold on, but the wind seemed to carry his protest off unheard. Moments later two young boys scrambled up on the deck of the catamaran. Their hands were tied!

All of them, these poor children, looked scared and stood there with their big wide brown eyes afraid to move. Then we finally saw our two seamen sent to help appear behind the boys, one of them carrying what looked like a 3 or 4-year-old that was not moving. Her hands were also tied.

Then looking back at the owner of the catamaran, there was a gun in his hand! Crap and double Crap, I thought as my adrenalin went into overdrive!

It seemed that pale eyed crazy man was now in control, as at that moment the only weapon handy was a shark gun and that was not within reach. The angry man looking out at his floundering catamaran, started shaking the gun at the sailor who was still holding the unconscious child, to set her down, and then to release the ropes that held the two boats together. When she complied, the catamaran quickly drifted away until the next white capped 6-foot wave hit it broadside, heaving it up and dropping it back down on its side. The boat's nose started to sink under each new wave as they with increasing strength claimed their prize.

As all this was roaring on, I saw Cap, looking at the ocean beyond over the shoulder of what we now knew was a slave trader. We both saw two great white shark fins as they broke the water and then slowly sank out of sight, only to appear moments later closer in to the patrol boat. Suddenly though, the man with the gun was on him, pounding Cap in the face and stomach, and yelling him to pay attention and to get the boat into land!

So now had to be the time. I took advantage of the disastrous sea and, naked woman and bound children, and grabbed hold of his hair and using the neck lock hauled him off Cap and tossed his violently, sending him sprawling onto the deck. A crew member grabbed a rope and he started towards the pimp's arms wanting to secure the man while the guy was off balance. He reached down to grab the guys arm, but the agile pimp, twisted out of his grasp and with unexpected grace got to his feet and slipping and sliding on the wet deck found himself propelled into the cold tropical ocean.

We saw him swimming with full strokes trying to get back, unaware of the visitors of the deep.

No one tried to help him as the white shark fins appeared silently behind him. No warning was shouted, no facial expression changed as suddenly the man was just gone. Nothing but a light reddish tint colored a wave where the man had been. Rapidly even the colored wave was also gone. I thought Neptune took revenge, ridding the world of an angry sore of humanity.

Back on board our patrol boat, the older women started to cry for the now dead man. Realizing she may have been helping him, even perhaps if it wasn't fully through her own initiative, the crew drug her over to the edge of the boat and she was lashed unceremoniously to the side railing and told roughly to sit down and shut up. She stood there glaring at them, then as a large wave put an end to the catamaran, she deflated onto herself, and sat with her head down in silent disbelief.

The captain had heard there was human trafficking going on in this bay, and he realized with the help of Neptune and the Greek wind Gods, "Anemoi", he had just helped put an end to one of the smugglers that had taken so many children. Now it was his crew's mission to see to those children; especially to that little one that had been tied up and not moving. All of us prayed that she was okay.

With the sea still beating us nearly to death, we headed into the cove and a lone beach house railing that still showed above the surging ocean. There, we hoped the water would not rise higher and we could tie up and last out the storm until the water started retreating.

Our radio operator called the coastguard and told them where we were, and that we were going to try and ride out the storm on the boat in the cove. They gave us a firm negative, to tie up our boat and then to abandon it and get as far inland as we could. They did this because there had been a fast cutter boat in that area earlier in the day that had taken shots at the coastguard when they had tried to approach it. They believed that same boat was now near lingering in the cove and would probably not take kindly to Cap's company.

Well of course this was a U.S. PT boat, well- armed and instead, this captain, never failed to challenge the seeming impossible and turned away from the mouth of the cove and raced under full power to the main dock, about one quarter mile further to the west. The coastguard was waiting there for the storm to ease up when waiting somewhat surprised when we pulled in. (Meanwhile I watched the topless lady trying to untie her bonds as we touched the dock.)

Once docked the coastguard officers boarded our boat and took control of the sad passengers. After it was all over, with the women removed in cuffs, Caps', me and his crew were taken into an office for questioning. First our identities were verified as being who we said we were, and then more gently, they were debriefed in detail about what the crew had found about the catamaran before it sank. The male owner of the catamaran was indeed a child smuggler that had purchased a 'load' of human cargo a few days ago and was going to sell them to someone on the faster cutter that had shot at them earlier in the day.

The half-naked women said, the guy had held her hostage as well and was going to transfer "the cargo" over to a faster cutter that was now in the cove. They didn't believe she had also been a hostage but couldn't prove it. Regardless they were going to hold her until their federal marshal arrived. Once the weather let up a little they would go back into the cove and see if they could find the cutter and put its occupants into custody as well.

The littlest one was taken by land to the nearest hospital where she was treated for a head wound and a broken wrist. The rest of the children and young ladies were handed over to the immigration departments human services to see where they had come from and see if they could get them back home to their families.

Of course, I was at once in awe at the curious power of coincidence but felt a very special satisfaction that the man that fed the sharks was the same one that I encountered in that war-torn county a few years before."

Chivonn, after telling the story to Samyak, said, "This time the 'slaves' won! It is a terrible shame on us all that normally they do not, this horror is repeated the world around!

Samyak said with sympathy, "Thank you for the account, Ms. Chivonn. And it was good there was justice for that evil man! I am sure the swelling oceans will tell of many other tragedies, more than we can possibly imagine as the future unfolds!"

~~~~~~~~~~~~~~

That night Chivonn's e-mail to her professor on their personal one-on-one mail, expressed a concern she had from her biology class.

"In class the Professor indicated he was watching a NOVA show on the beginnings of humans. In it he realized they were suggestion Climate Change is OK! They are finding out that the rapid climate change from dry to wet in Africa is one of the key reasons that humans evolved from the flat line brain growth that produced us. So, can you imagine what followed? "If this sharp climate changes in weather really caused us to evolve into a better and more intelligent human being, why should we try to slow down the climate changes here on planet earth? Would it be better to force us to adapt more rapidly by allowing the climate changes to become more sever instead of less?"

"Professor, I don't know if that argument he showed is substantiated by hard science. I couldn't find it! But it certainly ignores the evolution time scale! And, now we are a new differently formed human, and what we cannot forget is that the dry will continue into deserts that will kill, and floods that will drown and eventually freeze innocent people to death within the time of us, Homo sapiens."

The Professor responded briefly as follows. "Chivonn, of course, follow up on that but I am impressed with your ending comments the potential of exploring about the evolutionary time scale!"

Chapter 6

(OUR) DETONATION!

Or FACING NUCLEAR EXTINCTION

- Sharing with Samyak
- Samyak's Fourth Future Projection
- Sharing a Marine Nuclear Experience
- Prospectus Section Four
    - 4a. Do people think it will happen?
    - 4b. What did WWII look like?
    - 4c. The potential of WW III
    - 4d. The world after WW III
    - 4f. The age of Cosmoscide
- "Unavoidable" Blindside Causing WWIII

Sharing with Samyak

Now ten days into her stay, Chivonn completed prospectus sections on threats from artificial inelegance, overcrowding and global warming. An overwhelming concern that she wonders about is the ever-apparent danger of massive nuclear war.

Samyak's Fourth Future Projection

She wonders if Samyak has an experience on that! And he pulls from his shelves, several essays he has written on the subject...saying you may want to look through these in addition to your library research. However, let me give you an oral viewpoint this evening once you return for the evening meal.

Offspring - 95

A bit later with the rain finally ceasing Daya and Chivonn take a walk, and then it is back for tea and Samyak's lesson. He begins with a long review of the minor wars, then turns to what could happened in a Major one beginning with...

……... " And you thought the unbearable heat was a fantasy from say the movie "The Maze Runner", but no!

There is another real solar flare, like the one that narrowly missed us in 2020 which wiped out all our satellites (disabling Wi-fi and Cell Phone Service technology for a decade) and made it extremely hot. Remember, food became scarce, governments became scared, and gangs took advantage. You were lucky if you survived. But now the Flare is, indeed, real and it is here, from an Atomic Conflagration."

"Now though, with the loss of nature's immunity that destructive pathogen is let loose. Its' killed, totally wiped out millions of people in the first wave. There is no cure yet found and that is certain with the loss of the laboratories. And it continues to kill millions of people mercilessly. Populations are accelerating downwards so rapidly that families are gone before one knows what happened. The few left must constantly avoid all contact with others, for the disease does not begin to painfully so tortuously kill until about a month, and many have it already. Doctors are racing to find a cure, but most of them got infected too. It spreads through the wind and water. It destroys!"

"Those left face the Terminal Apocalypse!"

"Whether by nanobot regeneration and malfunction, disease evolution, or other, outcome from the world-wide wars-so belittling past human conflicts that the final the terminal apocalypse has begun.

You are hiding for your life sometimes in forests, sometimes underground. A few have escaped to Mars or the exoplanet colonies set up for escape. But the armored new nanobot war lords are almost invincible in their alloy suits. Although there are ways to kill them such as sudden large explosions, or for the millions of new diseased people, it would be just plain killing with a worse disease. And one alone simply hasn't the means.

Escape? That is, simply no matter for sentient life, it has been reduced to the virtual impossibility. Your only hope is not to be found, to live for a while longer…Clearly, all, even the hunters will expire, the vast nuclear infected winds will burn them into cinders."

Suddenly Chivonn feels her skin on fire, and batting all over her body in her half sleep, slapping hopelessly to kill some strange nuclear generated vermin she finally awakes, turning and writhing… finding herself against a wall near the door, in the cool air, with Daya crawling up to her.

When she seems fully together, now sipping a resting tea, Samyak comments the now familiar "Ms. Chivonn, that is a potential some experts express, what really is the threat? Write the reality in your prospectus!"

Chivonn Tells a Marine Experience

As it was, that request leads Chivonn to remember her training in "Nuclear". So, after that projection prompted by the teacher, she first shares the following with him and Daya.

"I have a bit, a tiny bit of a feel for the hell of it, that in your projection. After graduation from Boot Camp, I was chosen to lead an NBC that is Nuclear, Biological and Chemical" decontamination training site where we taught other troops how to help soldiers, which had just come out of an NBC environment in their methods of decontamination, clean up and medical assist.

 We also were trained on the signs and symptoms of a hazardous attack, how to react, and how to use the needle "ampules of life saving compound" that each of us carried on our MOPP gear which I will describe in a bit. We learned to treat ourselves first and then our team members if they needed the help. It was scary, but necessary training for all of us.

Warfare has changed from the WWII days and my time in service and now the rear lines were the lines first to be hit as without beans and bullets, the front lines couldn't fight. And as I remember, most in the rear lines at that time were female and were considered the weaker and easier target. Anyway, we were training in all ways to ensure this would not be the case!

After I became an E-5, that is Sargent, I received some "special training" that I will remember for the rest of my life.

For 8 hours our team sat in front of a larger view screen watching classified movies of actual footage of NBC attacks and the resulting terror that followed for the unlucky ones that survived. Then for the next four hours we watched old television war time movies of what the general public was shown.

The movies that the public were shown were terrible; but the real ones we saw, the actual footage of Hiroshima after nuclear attack were much worse and even more terrifying. And as it turned out the officers brought in colleagues, older retired marines who went on ground to survey and told of the unbelievable horror, the maimed and ruined children and the total devastation.

Yet the military was on orders to drive home the point that we could survive an NBC attack, so we were required to wear full gear called MOPP from head to toe.

Yes, Marines are trained to fight in nuclear war situations, but those damn impossible suits, I remembered training drills wearing those things what they called in military jargon "Mission Oriented Protective Posture" suits, but we called them simply MOPP!

No doubt they are the very highest-grade protective gear, designed to withstand fighting amidst chemical, biological and radiological hazards. But oh My! Those damn suits!

What we soon realized was there was no way of taking the gear off to go to the bathroom!

It was an unbelievably miserable and a very ripe 12 hours completely captured, enslaved in that suit!

Afterwards we each had to strip and were hosed down. There was no privacy from the ones with the high-pressure water hoses. That was how I knew what it was like for those that I had hosed down in our 'mock' decontamination site years before.

We were all just human beings. Not one of us was male or female at that time; we were simply Marines doing our duty and no one acted inappropriately in looks or comments. It was true training that would need to be completed if the real need was ever there. In many deployments, that training saved many Marines from illness, disease and death.

I remember my Master Sargent saying "In the instance where they do have to wear MOPP gear in a real-life scenario, it's not going to be a shock or surprise to you of why and how you are going to operate."

At that Chivonn opened her wallet, paging pictures and shows Samyak and Daya exactly what she looked like, that is, her and her MOPP. (That is the picture page 95).

Then she continued with the story.

"Here, however, is a bottom line, I took away in my mind after this training. I began to ask myself, how could mankind even dream up such a horrible weapon? How could they allow them to ever be used?

What terrifying creatures we have become! And, the next war, I believe, will most likely be chemical or biological in nature. Both are already being tested in certain parts of the world on the countries own poor people.

Uncaring, the statistics are quietly collected for the improvement of their deadly warfare tools. Our soldiers have come back from each new conflict with a previously unknown illness or disease.

Mustard gas in WWI, Nerve gases of all kinds now, jungle defoliants like Agent Orange, and now the strange after effect of something the troops are coming back with from the middle east are just a few of the insane tools of war that are currently in use today."

Daya listening intently to Chivonn's account shook her head and entered with "goodness how right you are!" And Samyak looking almost tenderly at his student, said "Yes Ms. Chivonn, as you said the military does see the possibility of a nuclear war!"

"It is certainly worth your research time to set down the realities and the possibilities!" So that day, Chivonn made even more fully aware of the potential hell of nuclear war from Samyak's

"Stimulated History" and her memory of Marine times spends many hours in the library and over the next several days completes the necessary additional section in her Prospectus. That is, Justification for Research, Section Four follows.

SECTION FOUR

ANNIHILATION ---

----WORLD WAR III?

4a. Do People Think it will happen?

She writes the following reflecting on her own time in the military. The United States and Russian relations have fallen off and on again frequently but now rise to their worst since the Cold War.

China is building a massively stronger military. The mixture is complicated with North Korea which has run hot and cold. Indeed, North Korea has conducted a 'sacred' nuclear war, with rockets able to reach the United States! Even if this is resolved by interaction of the President and North Korean leaders, it could simmer on for that country is obviously desiring to make clear its strength toward a demanding position among nations.

Unthinking bellicosity it is-the testing has already ignored for that selfish irresponsible purpose the tragic effects such explosions have on the earth. The tested explosions are many times that of the A bomb attacks end of WWII. As the potential conflict between North and South Korea show sighs of healing the "on going war" hopefully resolved by a handshake, evidence arises that Iran has been cheating on its Nuclear Disarmament agreement. And so, it goes in and out, the insane shaking of fists!

Although people in Nordic countries hedge, believing a world war is unlikely a great many people in the US predict a world war, while French, German and British people are also pessimistic. Some 64 per cent of Americans think the world is actually close to a major war, compared to just 15 who think world peace is likely. Britons are only slightly more hopeful: 19 per cent believe peace is possible but 61 per cent say war is a distinct possibility. For France, fears are linked more to the threat of terrorism. The French public are the least likely to see Russia as a hostile threat to the European Union, but by far the most likely to think that there would be another major terrorist attack on their country in the years ahead.

American fears perhaps reflect some people's uncertainly about the stability of the Presidency, an office that stands at the top of world power therefor demanding the utmost in understanding the horror that such a worldwide war would entail.

Headlines certainly have cause to worry people. "Russian military withdrawal from Syria is more of a political statement. Russia 'poses major threat' to US, intelligence officials tell Senate. Russia's foreign ministry proposes expelling 35 US diplomats. Syria ceasefire in doubt amid fresh clashes. The Russian confidence has grown to the extent that they feel comfortable in interfering with American Elections."

In short it is clear that the world is still massively unstable, not truly at peace... a World War, very likely Nuclear is one of the several major threats to peaceful and comfortable life felt by people the world over.

4b. What did a World War II look like?

There is essentially no way to capsulize the insanity of humanity charging into the inevitable horror and loss of these past world wars. The record is there if only it could reside to haunt-permanently in the minds of those who would dare to think the matter trivial.

A photo taken by Hitler's personal photographer (and later acquired by LIFE) shows a 1939 rally in which Hitler salutes Luftwaffe troops who fought with Francisco Franco's ultra-right-wing nationalist rebels in the Spanish Civil War. Soldiers-men so sunk in a deep weird charisma goose-step past the Fuhrer in honor of Hitler's 50th birthday, April 20, 1939.

Less than five months later, on September 1, the Third Reich's forces invaded Poland in the quest of a Thousand Year Reich! This Nazi idea totally based on inhuman premises perished with the loss of millions of lives throughout the world, a loss whose insanity is so clearly visible in the terrible tortured bodies in the Holocaust.

Alfred Eisenstaedt captured a private moment repeated in public millions of times over the course of World War II: a guy, a girl, a goodbye - and no assurance that he'll make it back. But, by war's end, more than 400,000 American troops had been killed. In a photo that reflects a very-very small piece of the horror, an American Marine cradles a near-dead infant pulled from under a rock while troops cleared Japanese fighters and civilians from caves on Saipan in the summer of 1944. The child was the only person found alive among hundreds of corpses in just one cave.

In the waning days of the struggle for the island, of Saipan in 1944 thousands of Japanese civilians and troops committed suicide, rather than surrender to American troops. Many leaped to their death from the top of sheer cliffs that fall 200 feet to rocks and surf below. How could their minds become so warped to ignore the precious sanctity of their bodies? On Iwo Jima, the degree to which the Japanese were willing to fight to the death, rather than surrender, is summed up in one remarkable statistic: Close to 20,000 Japanese soldiers were killed during the battle; only around 200 were captured.

There are statistics, that must have made daily life insufferable for the statisticians tracing the facts as they worked to report the final data. WWI took 37 million lives, this includes 10 million civilians! WWII killed upwards of 80 million, within which number there were an estimated 50-55 million civilians. These numbers reflect an inner horror which includes millions upon millions of people dying from disease and starvation.

We must stop and think of the horror and suffering placed upon the helpless children. There is no way to depict the absolute insane level of killing in these past wars.

Even so, the insanity bred and grown in these wars should be to all in the future unfathomable, but it seems largely forgotten by the press of human affairs.

And now arises the potential of a WW III!

4c. What is the Potential of a WWIII?

So-what would WWW III really look like as many people believe it will happen, why hedge on that question?

The following is suggested by the historian Houghton Harcourt. "Great power conflicts defined the 20th century: Two world wars claimed tens of millions of lives, and the Cold War that followed shaped everything from geopolitics to sports. But at the start of the 21st century, the ever-present fear of World War III seemed to be in our historic rearview mirror. Yet that risk of the past has made a dark comeback.

Russian land grabs in Ukraine and constant flights of bombers decorated with red stars probing Europe's borders have put NATO at its highest levels of alert since the mid1980s. In the Pacific, the U.S. and a newly powerful and assertive China are engaged in a massive arms race. China built more warships and warplanes than any other nation during the last several years, while the Pentagon just announced a strategy to "offset" it with a new generation of high-tech weapons. Indeed, it's likely China's alleged recent hack of federal records at the Office of Personnel. Management was not about cyber-crime but a classic case of what is known as "Preparing the Battlefield" and gaining access to government databases and personal records just in case."

"The worry is that the brewing 21st century Cold War with China and its junior partner Russia could at some point turn hot. "A U.S.-China war is inevitable" recently warned the Communist Party's official People's Daily newspaper after recent military face-offs over the rights of passage and artificial islands built in disputed territory.

This may be a bit of posturing both for U.S. policymakers and a highly nationalist domestic audience: A 2014 poll by the Perth U.S.-Asia center found that 74% of Chinese think their military would win in a war with the U.S. But it points to how the global context is changing. Many Chinese officers have begun to lament out loud what they call "Peace Disease," their term for never having served in combat."

So, it is the historian sets the stage, and here is the quite rational summary of a blogger unidentified…

"The Russians develop a missile that is undetectable, unstoppable by missile defenses, the trigger is hit by a surprise set of events and the nuclear armed thing hits New York, setting off the alarms as the city is destroyed and that with most of the eastern coast. Then are launched the thousands from US. holding sites, and as they cross the sky more from Russia, hitting not just the US. but its allies and the deluge of nuclear power explodes across the world. The Nuclear Armageddon arrives, in this singular event, most of humanity is obliterated, the few remaining destined to short horrible skin burned, starving unreproducible lives."

There are of course many other writings. P.W. Singer is Strategist at New America and August Cole is a Nonresident Fellow at the Atlantic Council. They are the co-authors of "Ghost Fleet: A Novel of the Next World War". Their description follows.

"Wars start through any number of pathways: One world war happened through deliberate action, the other was a crisis that spun out of control. In the coming decades, a war might ignite accidentally, such as by two opposing warships trading paint near a reef not even marked on a nautical chart. Or it could slow burn and erupt as a reordering of the global system in the late 2020s, the period at which China's military build-up is on pace to match the U.S.

U.S. and Chinese warships then battle at sea, firing everything from cannons to cruise missiles to lasers. Stealthy Russian and American fighter jets enter and dogfight in the air, with robotic drones flying as their wingmen.

Hackers in Shanghai and Silicon Valley duel in digital playgrounds. And fights in outer space decide who wins below on Earth."

Are these scenes from a novel or what could actually take place in the real world the day after tomorrow? The answer is both.

"Making either scenario more of a risk is that military planners and political leaders on all sides assume their side would be the one to win in a "short" and "sharp" fight, to use common phrases. It would be anything but.

A great power conflict would be quite different from the small wars of today that the U.S. has become accustomed to, and, in turn, others think reveal a new American weakness.

Unlike the Taliban or even Saddam's Iraq, great powers can fight across all the domains; the last time the U.S. fought a peer in the air or at sea was in 1945. But a 21st century fight would also see battles for control of two new domains. *The surface of the Earth and Space!*"

"To put it bluntly the lifeblood of military communications and its control now runs through space, meaning we'd see humankind's first battles for the heavens!

Similarly, we'd learn "cyber war" is far more than stealing Social Security Numbers or e-mail from gossipy Hollywood executives, but the takedown of the modern military nervous system and Stuxnet-style digital weapons. Worrisome for the U.S. is that last year, the Pentagon's weapons tester found nearly every single major weapons program had 'significant vulnerabilities' to cyber-attack."

"A total mind-shift is required for this new reality. In every fight since 1945, U.S. forces have been a generation ahead in technology, having uniquely capable weapons like nuclear-powered aircraft carriers. It has not always translated to decisive victories, but it has been an edge every other nation wants.

Yet U.S. forces can't count on that "overmatch" in the future. These platforms are not just vulnerable to new classes of weapons like long-range missiles, but China, for example, overtook the European Union in research and development spending last year and is on pace to match the U.S. within five years, with new projects ranging from the world's fastest super computers to three different long-range drone-strike programs."

"And now off-the-shelf technologies can be bought to rival even the most advanced tools in the U.S. arsenal. The winner of a recent robotics test, for instance, was not a U.S. defense contractor but a group of South Korea student engineers.

An array of science-fiction-like technologies would likely make their debut in such a war, from AI battle management systems to autonomous robotics. But unlike the ISIS's of the world, great powers can also go after high-tech's new vulnerabilities, such as by hacking systems and knocking down GPS.

The recent steps taken by the U.S. Naval Academy illustrate where things might be headed. It added a cybersecurity major to develop a new corps of digital warriors, and also requires all midshipmen learn celestial navigation, for when the high tech inevitably runs into the age-old fog and friction of war.

While many leaders on both sides think any clash might be geographically contained to the straights of Taiwan or the edge of the Baltic, these technological and tactical shifts mean such a conflict is more likely to reach into each side's homelands in new ways. Just as the Internet reshaped our notions of borders, so too would a war fight partly online."

"The civilian players would also be different than those in 1941. The hub of any war economy wouldn't be Detroit. Instead, tech geeks in Silicon Valley and shareholders in Bentonville, Ark., would wrestle with everything from microchip shortages to how to retool the logistics and allegiance of a multinational company. The new forms of civilian conflict actors like Blackwater private military firms or Anonymous hacktivist groups are unlikely to just sit out the fight."

A Chinese officer argued in a regime paper, "We must bear a third world war in mind when developing military forces." But there is a far different attitude in Washington's defense circles. As the U.S. Chief of Naval Operations worried last year, "If you talk about it openly, you cross the line and unnecessarily antagonize. You probably have a sense about how much we trade with that country, it's astounding."

"This is true, but both the historic trading patterns between great powers before each of the last world wars and the risky actions and heated rhetoric out of Moscow and Beijing over the last year demonstrate it is no longer useful to avoid talking about the great power rivalries of the 21st century and the dangers of them getting out of control.

World War Three is just around the corner and the planet is teetering on the brink of all-out conflict – according to people in major Western nations, at least. A new poll shows the public are somewhat gloomy about the future, fearing a 'worldwide conflict' is looming."

"With superpowers backing different sides in the bloody conflict in Syria, Isis continuing to fight in the Middle East, a spate of terrorist attacks across the globe and Vladimir Putin and Donald Trump both talking a tough game, the You Gov survey of 9,000 people across nine countries found popular opinion thinks world peace has rarely been further away."

So, following is a consensus as to what it will look like, if above is not enough. This is from Wikimedia Commons on what WWIII would look like.

"You've seen what a nuclear winter looks like, as imagined by filmmakers and novelists. Now you can take a look at what scientists have to say. In a new study, a team of four U.S. atmospheric and environmental scientists modeled what would happen after just a - limited, regional nuclear war.

To inexpert ears, the consequences sound pretty subtle— two or three degrees of global cooling, a nine percent reduction in yearly rainfall. Still, such changes could be enough to trigger crop failures and famines. After all, these would be cooler temperatures than the Earth has seen in 1,000 years.

However, Let's take a detailed look at what would be the more rational conclusions, from all out nuclear war.

To fix on this the team describes 100 nuclear warheads, each about the size of the atomic bomb the U.S. dropped on Hiroshima, detonate over the Indian subcontinent. That is an India-Pakistan nuclear war. It seems unfair to single out these nations, but they are

Offspring - 107

a reasonable model as they have relatively small nuclear stockpiles compared to countries such as the U.S., Russia and China. The idea is, if these lightweights can do this to Earth, imagine what the bigwigs can do!

So, after the Indian-Pakistani nuclear exchange…Five megatons of black carbon enter the atmosphere immediately. Black carbon comes from the massive burning of virtually everything and it absorbs heat from the sun before it can reach the Earth. Even so, some black carbon does eventually fall back to Earth in rain.

After one year, the average surface temperature of the Earth falls by 1.1 Kelvin, or about two degrees Fahrenheit. After five years, the Earth is, on average, three degrees colder than it used to be. Twenty years on, our home planet warms again to about one degree cooler than the average before the nuclear war.

Earth's falling temperatures reduce the amount of rain the planet receives. Year five after the war, Earth will have 9 percent less rain than usual. Year 26 after the war, Earth gets 4.5 percent less rain than before the war. In years 2-6 after the war, the frost-free growing season for crops is shortened by 10 to 40 days, depending on the region.

Chemical reactions in the atmosphere eat away Earth's ozone layer, which protects Earth's inhabitants from ultraviolet radiation. In the five years after the war, the ozone was 20 to 25 percent thinner, on average. Ten years on, the ozone layer has recovered so that it's now 8 percent thinner. The decreased UV protection must lead to more skin cancers in people, as well as reduced plant growth and destabilized DNA in crops such as corn. In short, the sustainability of living things on earth will be so vastly affected that it will resemble nothing at all as we know it."

And, in a separate study, published in 2013, International Physicians for the Prevention of Nuclear War estimated "2 billion people would starve in the wake of a 100-A-bomb war."

Well, those points made there is a central issue to all this doom and gloom, the modelers write in their paper. The scientists want to motivate countries to destroy the estimated *17,000 nuclear weapons* they still hold!

Will this work? Well, scientists and journalists have been imagining the dire consequences of an atom-bomb war for decades.

It is clear to virtually all thinking people that this insanity must stop, but it is in fact continuing.

4d. The World after WW III.

All around us, we see violence between nations and conflict between individuals. The Cold War is behind us, but fears of terrorism and global nuclear holocaust remain.

Will humankind destroy itself? Some say the Bible reveals that there will be a "World War III"-but offers a hope-filled message of our ultimate destiny. Yet realism fails. Humankind continues to invent and produce weapons of mass destruction. The weapons of World War I killed ten million people. The weapons of World War II killed 55 million. Will humanity be able to survive World War III, or will it regress to Stone Age conditions?

We in the Western world profess to value the life of each individual. But when we review the history of humankind, we count the millions of dead soldiers and civilians in the never-ending cycle of escalating war. Do we realize the numbers of casualties that nations have inflicted on one another, and on themselves? The United States' Civil War caused more than 630,000 deaths. World War I resulted in 10 million deaths; World War II saw 55 million deaths. The Iran-Iraq War caused nearly 1 million deaths.

Man's inhumanity to man bloodies our history with genocide. Millions have died in the Holocaust of World War II, under the Khmer Rouge in Cambodia, and as victims of atrocities in Rwanda, Bosnia and Kosovo, to name just a few.

Eventually, all nations will fight in World War III. That war would lead to total Cosmoscide-death to everyone and everything on the earth the earth and life on it will barely survive World War III. But of course, some believe God will intervene while evidence of the killing so far in wars contradicts this thought.

What will the earth be like afterwards? We need to know the good news beyond the bad. There is a new world coming:

tomorrow's world. What will it be like? What will the future be- beyond World War III?

4f. The age of Cosmoscide.

The nuclear age began during World War II. On August 6 and August 9 in 1945, the United States dropped the first-ever atomic bombs on the cities of Hiroshima and Nagasaki in Japan. The age of potentially instant global mass destruction had begun.

Has the danger of nuclear war diminished? We need only to read our newspapers to understand that terrorists and rogue nations still threaten our world. Then add the threat of nuclear nations themselves.

Many of us have heard about the "Doomsday Clock" kept by the Bulletin of the Atomic Scientists. It reflects the danger of living in the nuclear age. After years unchanged, the Bulletin in June 1998 moved the "minute hand" of its clock ahead five minutes to just nine minutes before midnight. This was a jump of five full minutes! Two more nations had joined the "nuclear club": India and Pakistan, which the Bulletin labeled a "failure of world diplomacy in the nuclear sphere.

Then, in February 2002, the Bulletin advanced the clock's minute hand from nine to seven minutes before midnight. They reported: "Since the end of the Cold War in 1991, this is the third time the hand has moved forward." The Bulletin warns of "troubling trends: More than 31,000 nuclear weapons are still maintained by the eight known nuclear powers, a decrease of only 3,000 since 1998. Ninety-five percent of these weapons are in the United States and Russia, and more than 16,000 are operationally deployed. Even if the United States and Russia complete their recently announced arms reductions over the next 10 years, they will continue to target thousands of nuclear weapons against each other." (Bulletin of the Atomic Scientists, February 27, 2002). In 2017 the clock was moved minute hand was moved again toward midnight. So, the notion, something of a consensus is 'World War is Coming'!"

We, the Offspring of the many centuries have set the stage. The ultimate war yet lies ahead of us. We created two world wars in the 20th century, and World War III looms in the 21st century! The next war will be catastrophic. The great scientist Albert Einstein once said: "I do not know with what kind of weapons World War III will be led, but the fourth world war will be fought with sticks and stones."

In the opinion of this author history documents the evil nature of some human beings, and their insane destructiveness in war after war. Where will it all lead? There are sadly too many dreamers.

There are dreamers who believe an overseer will aid the devastated world, the ruined cities will be rebuilt. The desolate farms will be revitalized. Indeed, some religion groups prophesize as follows after nuclear war." Then-you shall dwell in the land that I gave to your fathers; you shall be "My people", and I will be your God. I will deliver you from all your uncleanliness. I will call for the grain and multiply it and bring no famine upon you." *And I Chivonn say-then all the lost burned to death little children will be remembered?*

(When the forgoing section of the Prospectus was shared with the Professor, he called Chivonn into his office for a consultation. He became concerned that his student would be going into a state of depression, she was continuing to deal with matters far above the simple life in laboratory. What he discovered was the Marine trained-now academic was thus far only more firmly committed to her objectives!)

"Unavoidable" Blindside Causing WWIII?

Here the computers raise their "Voice". A cyberattack could lead to inadvertent nuclear strike!

Nuclear strikes could be launched by mistake because the aging and/or unsophisticated weapons systems are vulnerable to cyberattacks, an international-relations think tank has warned. "A hack could lead to false information being passed to decision makers during a crisis," the think tank, Chatham House, based in London, said in a new report.

"Nuclear weapons systems were first developed at a time when computer capabilities were in their infancy and little consideration was even given to potential malicious cyber-vulnerabilities" it stated. "At times of heightened tension, cyberattacks on nuclear weapons systems could cause an escalation, which results in their use. Inadvertent nuclear launches could stem from an unwitting reliance on false information and data."

"The report comes as U.S. officials grow increasingly concerned that North Korea might use cyberattacks alongside conventional weapons. Intelligence officials have long ranked the rogue regime among the world's most dangerous cyber actors trailing only Russia, China and Iran and have blamed it for the 2014 Sony hack that leaked sensitive company data.

The FBI also suspects North Korea was behind a $81-million cyber-heist of the Bangladesh central bank's account at the Federal Reserve Bank of New York. However, the U.S. is also using cyberwarfare to disrupt North Korea's weapons program in a campaign that began under the Obama administration — and was blamed for the April 2017 failure of a rocket that disintegrated seconds after being launched."

While digital espionage is appealing to leaders, it creates uncertainty for both sides, the report warns. "During peacetime, offensive cyber activities would create a dilemma for a state as it may not know whether its systems have been the subject of a cyberattack," it said. "This unknown could have implications for military decision-making, particularly for decisions affecting nuclear weapons deterrence policies."

The report also said "The likelihood of attempted cyber-attacks on nuclear weapons systems is indeed relatively high and increasing!"

"The potential weaknesses include also rudimentary components," the report said. The report cited the example of Britain's newest aircraft carrier, "which was reportedly using a customized version of discontinued Windows XP in its control room during trials. Most countries acquire computer chips from the global marketplace rather than from national defense units and laboratories," it said.

~~~~~~~~~~~~~~~~~~

The section completed...Chivonn according to her agreement before her journey to India sends the section to her Professor Dr. Jordyn... Then in the now usual note one containing her personal feelings she writes as follows.

Why can't mankind's good intentions be stronger. What is it going to take to turn humankind around to realize we are killing ourselves and the planet we live on?

"Nuclear is a very real threat dispensed from the bullies of the world. It seems only a country that will stand up to them and shows equal retaliatory threat level is the only thing that seems to keep the world in check. We can only hope that level heads may never need to use this destructive weapon.

"And there are already degrees of Nuclear Poisoning. Before coming to the University, on one of my many post service jobs I sat surrounded by what my fellow railroad train workers call 'dirty dirt'!

The dirt is radioactive from mill tailings and was at one time used as fill dirt in major cities in the creation of homes foundations and traffic streets. It is only now that its insidious face is seen. As for now, just as years later, the quest for the gold and silver riches desired by our ancestors has produced the deadly cancers and other ailments in their own children and grandchildren, we face that in our Nuclear World!

We are left to clean up the mess. There is no way to decrease the deadly life expectancy of the nuclear waste, so the children now call it 'dirty dirt' and transport it to deserted and desolate lands for long term storage. It comes into the government facilities, housed in sealed railroad containers that line the rail siding that runs through these government facilities to be buried in the land that no one wants, and hopefully may never want for many hundreds of years to come.

I have sat by those rail cars, at the landfills waiting for the next railroad crew to bring in yet another train with another deadly load of 'dirty dirt'. The crew van transport drivers that take the railroad crews back to their home terminal and the rail road workers themselves are never tested to see what kind of exposure they are receiving in their daily jobs.

"It is now as safe as our current technology can make it for all that work in and round the toxic dust and dirt, so why raise the concern they say? There are maybe better ways, but it would cost too much the bean counters whisper to the committees, so it remains the same.

The Government instead sets up permanent funds to treat those that get sick from the exposure and funds to the families of those workers that die the horrible and long-term death that might come their way.

It is just the way it is. Money talks! Not enough people seem to care, after all, it is not affecting them or their families; right? So, it is the callous- cynical minded nature of business continues!"

Sorry about spouting off so Professor, but what the hell has happened for our feelings for one another?

Professor Jordyn did respond to these comments by return e-mail. "Chivonn, I note in your Prospectus Sections, that you have tried to balance the fear aspects with the opinion of various experts. In the nuclear area the use of nuclear energy, if properly managed could provide us with a great many benefits. I have a peek at your outline for the future sections, and I do, indeed, encourage you to point to "Ways of Healing the Mess". And, do take some time out to enjoy the town there, it is quite remarkable! "

~~~~~~~~~~~~~~~

That night, feeling good after the message from her "Prof", and warmly comforted after a delicious Jain vegan dinner, student Chivonn, slept sound until about four in the morning when there arose within her perceptive mind a dream, a bending back, perhaps more aptly put a nightmare.

It was a curious dream mixing present and past with one of her struggles in the service. Her Company was in survival exercise a "Land Navigation Test". The substance of the exercise was that after a massive attack they would wind up in a swamp fighting against the mud and intensive rain stimulated by and carrying the product of the nuclear storm.

She first sensed the reality-the tightness of her body in what she indeed felt at the time in the past. The 3rd night of Land Navigation was underway as she struggled into the dream... survival actually loomed dark, dank & wet. The bog moss hung down from the branches swaying with ghostly tendrils over the forested floor of Paris Island's, SC. Marine Corps Recruit Depot.

She reflected...saw her-self, then private Chivonn...laying belly down in the mire of mud and decayed leaves under a knurled Cyprus tree.

The circadian Katydid mating calls and the frogs croaking blended with the rainy night. That pitch-black night enhanced the fragile earthy smelling drizzle dripping off the hanging moss above her hitting her helmet in a steady light drumming. The feelings were indeed imprinted, and she felt them now, fully!

Laying spread-eagle with one boot toe hook around a Cyprus knee for leverage she reached out with stick to her team mate who had stepped into a sink hole and was now waist deep in the sucking black bog! The more she tried to free herself, the lower she sunk.

Chivonn heard the whisper raising from her throat to her team mate again, to quit struggling and to be quiet! They were too close to the red team's encampment, and they couldn't be caught after coming this far. The waist deep private quieted and reached out and grabbed the offered stick. Slowly Chivonn started pulling the private towards her, and to safety, when all of a sudden, the ground shifted below Chivonn's body!

She wasn't in the swamp any more, but on a muddy bank in India, falling backwards from the mud-covered ravine where the bus lay broken below. Hands reaching for her. She again found herself back in boot camp. She had saved her friend then, but this time deep in REM sleep, her friend and team mate slowly slipped from her

Offspring - 115

hold on the stick, back into the muddy bog while holding a small child's head above the suffocating mud!

She woke with a silent scream on her lips, drenched in sticky sweat as she still saw the ghostly image of her team mate disappear slowly into the blackened muddy hole, followed by the beautiful brown eyed child.

Suddenly, damn, she said way-loud, likely waking the household, maybe the Professor is right, I may need some R&R!

But she cleared her mind recognizing that the intensity of the objective, the challenges to life she was exposing, even the "Corporeal Lessons" of Samyak were getting a hold of her deep reflexes…

Then, No More! She said full voice, that is not this woman! I don't stand down! And with that taken care of she jumped out of bed and looked out over the railing of the cozy patio in the Jain home into the Tarr, re-focused, and ready to continue that Prospectus!

The morning arriving is best described as "a soaking in" because of the humidity, though the area is fundamentally a desert, the Tarr- golden sand usually overriding the break of dawn, sans a wetting.

And, in spite of the nightmare our heroin was smiling. It was as she knew to be a day of learning, that in a somewhat unusual format, but still she looked forward to her times with the Samyaks!

She was aware how experience influences our dreams but at the same time how dreams can offer the challenge, the path for action when we meet each day.

About ten in the morning, the Samyak's-the best hosts, began a time with her in a detailed tour of the town. She saw the many ancient buildings, the unusual fort, and the way the town was built to shield out the unremitting sun were a tourist joy.

In the afternoon Chivonn was taken on a full very detailed library tour. This for Samyak the historian, was, after all, his office! And after all it was in those places where the "Prospectus" takes on its life. That term "Prospectus" was now locked in her mind as "The Objective"!

How fortunate she was here in this place, with libraries of massive shelves holding all the worlds history, and with rooms equipped for the "modern world", i.e., with the necessary computing gear!

Chapter 7

Our ABANDONMENT!

Or ADIOS EARTH!

- Samyak's Fifth Future Projection
- Prospectus Section Five.
    5a. Do People think it will happen?
    5b. What do various experts propose?
    5c. Humans must leave earth?
- When do we do it?

Samyak's Fifth Future Projection

    The night on the sixteenth day with the Samyak' was nearly blinding with stars seeming to reflect red and golden rays from the wet sand of the Tarr.

    Chivonn was quite comfortable settling in to her cozy bedding in the portico after a full day of library work in the city and taking some time to tour that remarkable city.

    During the day Samyak was given her prospectus thus far and gave her a warm smile and gentle praise with its progress.

    He said before she retired "that the next evening perhaps she might want to consider what is being said, given the problems people have made for themselves, the thinking on leaving earth for new homes."

    There followed thus, a night of restful sleep and with the new day-and a good time in the library she was going over her writing, smoothing out the language and cleaning up a typo here and there. Then back at the little Jain home dinner was a delicious

"Dal Makhani". This is a dish for good health with whole black lentil and kidney beans.

After dinner she settled in with Samyak and Daya who served the requisite tea while she listened to the wise historian as he reflected on the need's folks saw to move away from earth.

Even so Samyak chose to begin with a bit of a formal account and even provided pictures he had from the internet. He first said a quote from his source "Humans, you've met your match!"

"Unlike us, Tardigrades the world's most indestructible species will indeed survive until the sun dies", according to a new Oxford University study released Friday.

"Researchers found the tiny, eight-legged creatures, also known as water bears (picture pg.113), will survive extinction from all astronomical catastrophes, including supernovas, gamma-ray bursts and large asteroid impacts. The weird, water-dwelling critters should be around for at least the next 10 billion years---far longer than the human race."

For sure, given our behavior, Chivonn puts in! Samyak nods, not too patiently, and continues reading the account…

"Without our technology protecting us, humans are a very sensitive species," said study co-author Rafael Alves Batista, a physicist at Oxford University in the United Kingdom. "Subtle changes in our environment impact us dramatically." "For example, the effects of gamma-ray bursts, from collapsing or colliding stars, on humans would be disastrous, as the eradication of the ozone layer would leave us exposed to deadly levels of radiation."

"There are many more resilient species on Earth. Life on this planet can continue long after humans are gone," Batista said.

Study co-author David Sloan, also of Oxford, said: "We found that although nearby supernovae or large asteroid impacts would be catastrophic for people, tardigrades could be unaffected. Therefore, it seems that life, once it gets going, is hard to wipe out entirely," he said. "Huge numbers of species, or even entire genera may become extinct, but life as a whole will go on!"

"Tardigrades are the penultimate example. They live in almost every region in the world, are the toughest, most resilient life form on Earth, able to survive for up to 30 years without food or water.

The critters, which are only about 1/100th of an inch long, are best viewed under a microscope. Tardigrades are as close to indestructible as it gets on Earth", Batista said. "The creatures can endure wild temperature extremes, from 450 degrees below zero to 300 degrees above. They can also survive in the deep sea and even the frozen vacuum of space, the study said."

"So why bother about all this? The research has implications for life elsewhere as well: It is possible that there are other resilient species examples elsewhere in the universe," Batista said. "In this context, there is a real case for looking for life on Mars and in other areas of the solar system in general," he added. "If tardigrades are Earth's most resilient species, who knows what else is out there."

This discourse was remarkable and had Chivonn thinking. She said *"Are humans really structured well enough to first stay on earth and then even to leave earth and move elsewhere, the move which would take it seems a truly insurmountable effort! Are we good now, complete enough?"*

But Samyak's soft voice drifted in changing her thoughts as she drifted at first comfortably into that half sleep, she had become familiar with and then with a horrible jolt, she was into a nightmare insane! She was feeling, seeing as follows.

…She managed to get out of that doughnut-shaped habitation section used to provide an equivalent to gravity, with the 'floor' being the inside wall of the outer radius. She could see, looking into the support incubation chamber, the vegetables are wilting…and she already knew from the warning in the chamber, that the stores of chemical protein are very low.

But that was trivial. She rehearsed the situation. We've lost contact with the parent ship holding on to that pseudo orbit at half point. The Mars trip was to take just a year but the shutdown just off the parent at 10,000 miles left us without power holding, waiting for the right nanobot repair.

That ion engine was supposed to cut travel time to Mars from six months to a little more than one. But that is now a myth!

She then found herself screaming out loud to her fellow Mars spacemen! "We had to leave the hibernation chambers, because of the power failure, and Oh…my god! Look at the cosmic radiation gauge! Hell, we are being bombarded! That invention using a plasma shield, confined by a magnetic field, was supposed to, was it seemed reducing the energy of any incoming particles? Made no difference, that last bot must have melded to the shield, but where is it now, camera gone on the outside? Michael, I wonder, look at him he's pulling at that beard he refuses to shave, like he wants to rip it off, and shit! Marlene she… is she breathing?

Then the training raced through her head…. we've already gone beyond the spaceflight psychiatric issue adjusted reactions to the novelty of being in space, no transient anxiety or depression. But we know, astronauts on a long-term mission will find that there are more serious threats to their health and well-being created by the hazardous environment of space. Living in zero or negligible gravity for extended periods has a range of health consequences: from a puffy face and dizziness to muscle wastage and bone decalcification. And, in fact, the more serious effects really weren't mitigated with the program of exercise even with the artificial gravity because of the small size of the ship and simply because of the long term, the delay so far. But the main thing is the cosmic radiation we were warned, schooled again and again was the most serious, the bottom line. Around 90% of cosmic rays are protons, with the rest being made up mainly of alpha particles, the nuclei of heavy elements, electrons, and small numbers of antimatter particles. Long periods of exposure to radiation will trigger cases of cancer, while even short-duration exposure to extremely high levels, such as that generated by solar flares, can cause potentially fatal radiation poisoning. The High-energy particles also risk damaging a spacecraft's electronic components, which is clearly happening, and now though its' Us!

Cosmic radiation, energy-charged atom fragments can give astronauts anxiety, depression, and impaired decision-making. Mars-bound astronaut would receive 0.3 sieverts of radiation on a one-way trip—that's hardly close to the lethal dose of 8 sieverts or even the radiation sickness–causing dose of 1 sievert, but researchers think that amount (equivalent to 24 computerized tomography scans) is enough to cause irreversible damage to brain cells and other cells that aren't readily replenished.

And here we are blood and muscle effects already making us weak and what was I just thinking...what is happening to my eyes...Oh no my left eye is...and I'm...God help me...going blind! How am I...?

Then, pushing out with her arms as if to move a curtain to the side Chivonn finds her-self once again in the arms of Daya, who is gently holding a warm cloth over her eyes and saying...its OK Chivonn ...just a dream!

A bit later she is reviewing what she experienced with Samyak... who responds in a most serious voice. "Yes, Chivonn, travel into space, the effort to leave earth is a very serious matter, indeed! I let your research tell us all what is being said nowadays about that!"

After a night of peaceful sleep falling into it with Chamomile tea, Chivonn tackles the matter with intense research the result of which follows in Section Five of her prospectus.

SECTION FIVE

WE MUST LEAVE HOME
---Or ADIOS EARTH

5a. Do People Think it will happen?

Here is a "Folksy" conjecture for relocation, drawn from a comment posted on Facebook.

"The pressures have created a realm of folks saying we must escape to 'Other Worlds', leave our planet behind for the future of humanity. There are of course many fundamental questions: Why, is it necessary, is it possible, who would be candidates, what numbers would be possible? That is, this is a really big and relevant topic!

A basic question is where we go, demand some life, or if living ability is indeed there. The suggestion is out there, if there is life anywhere in the solar system, we might know about it by the time we have a human on Mars with projections about 2075.

So, we would have by then some idea of the true logistics, that is, a new home, a practical abode may be possible. Some of the ice-covered moons around the gas giants might have life in their waters. Might be small life, single celled maybe, but life!

If so, there are repercussions this discovery would have on human society that might have to be dealt with but one could imagine it would at least cause a major upheaval as religion, that is, a need to re-calibrate to allow for alien life and a different perspective about god.

So possibly all humans would not be on board, but surely some would and would want to go.

But in the same vein as those basic concerns, what would be the status on earth by then, that is the ability to support our kind on another world? Even now there is potential for massive effects of global warming, possibly nuclear war. Those life ending ideas aside there are other possibilities.

Nonetheless, 'AI' it is said by that point would be very significant, with robotics capable of most everything, in which case it is argued, the apparent problems on earth would all be corrected.

And even if extra-planetary existence has many questions without answers there being so many variables there is popularity that says what the heck…"Let's Go!".

5b. What Do Various Experts Propose

The long-term proposition from the astrophysicists, one most of us have likely heard many times is---in a universe aglow with 2 trillion galaxies, you'd be supremely smug to think that Earth alone hosts clever creatures. One 2015 poll showed that 54 percent of Americans feel confident that intelligent aliens are out there, based upon this oft repeated argument.

Maybe that optimism came originally from science fiction. Here is that often stated and entertaining proposal on that.

"After all, if there are no extraterrestrials, there isn't much of a mission for the Star-ship Enterprise or job openings for "Vulcans". Fiction aside, many scientists agree that the cosmos is undoubtedly sprinkled—perhaps liberally sprinkled — with life. Even sentient life."

But on a rational basis, can we say anything about that sprinkling? Can we hazard a guess as to how close the nearest aliens might be? This is an uncertain business but not a new one.

Perhaps it is best to state the source who has real experience behind his comments. In 1961 astronomer Frank Drake devised a simple equation for estimating the number of "technically active" societies in our galaxy. That bit of easy math is known as the "Drake Equation", and it's often said to be the second most famous formula in science (the first, of course is Einstein's $E = mc^2$).

If you look up the formula online, you'll see that it considers the odds that there are habitable planets around other stars, the likelihood that life will arise, and the probability that biology will occasionally evolve to produce clever beings. But even without wrestling with the Drake Equation, we can use similar reasoning to gauge the plentitude of alien societies and how close the "Klingons" might be.

Continuing to follow Drake rational logic. "We start with recent research showing that one in six stars hosts a planet hospitable to life. No, not one in a million. One in six. So, let's take that number and run with it. Next, we have to make a few assumptions. In particular, if you were given a million Earth-size worlds, what fraction do you think would ever beget technically sophisticated inhabitants?

Life on our planet began quickly: random chemical activity in 350 million trillion gallons of ocean water spawned a reproducing molecule within a few hundred million years. So maybe biology doesn't need much of a prod to get started. It is not unreasonable to figure that at least half of all planets suitable for life actually produce it.

Of course, being rational we must stipulate intelligence is less certain. The dinosaurs were a good design but didn't do well in school. But let's say that one in 100 biology-encrusted planets eventually coughs up some thinking beings. And, as per Frank Drake, let's also assume that any Klingons out there continue to hang out for 10,000 years before self-destructing (nuclear war, anyone?) or meeting some other woeful end. Someone said I heard we just beamed a signal at space aliens. Was that a bad idea?

Do the arithmetic, and you'll find that one in 100 million-star systems has technically adept inhabitants. That's not much different than the fraction of jackpot tickets in this week's Powerball lottery!

So how close are the nearest signaling extraterrestrials? If we're going to pay good money to fire up the warp drive and visit some bumpy-headed aliens, how far do we have to travel?

Well, the average distance between stars in our part of the galaxy is 4.2 light-years (the distance to Proxima Centauri). That is, for every cube of space that's 4.2 light-years on a side, you'll find (on average) one star. Now imagine a bigger box, 2,000 light-years on a side. It will contain 100 million-star boxes, and possibly one sophisticated civilization.

By this rough and ready calculation, the nearest aliens are probably between one and two thousand light-years away. In other words, no closer than the three bright stars of Orion's Belt. Sure, alien neighbors might be farther—or closer. But this order-of-magnitude estimate tells us that they're not next door. They haven't heard our news reports, and they're not likely to have any incentive to visit. They simply don't know we're here.

By the way, we probably aren't going to visit them either. Today's fastest rockets would take at least 20 million years to get there, by which time you're going to be awfully tired of on-board pretzels.

Yes, the aliens are likely around, and 10,000 societies could inhabit our galaxy (not to mention those other galaxies!) They're not close. But they may be discover-able.

That's why we continue to search the sky for radio signals launched into the ether long ago by our cosmic brethren."

And, to the crux of the matter, the idea of life elsewhere continues to serve as a foundation for us, for us to find new homes in the cosmos! That is to leave Earth, to say Adios! So, to address that more specifically, and formally open the argument. The following amplifies what the premier physicist Stephen Hawking had in mind when he said, shortly before he passed on, "The species needs to colonize other planets in the next century to survive".

And it is all such arguments and postulations that have prompted developers as Elon Musk to unveil his plans to build a Mars habitat in 40 to 100 years.

5c. Strong Arguments-Humans Must Leave Earth!

The following are commentaries by experts and/or practiced analysts on the subject of human beings leaving earth for new horizons.

"After Earth: Why, Where, How, and When We Might Leave Our Home Planet." This is relayed from "Humans Must Leave Earth to Survive, Says Hawking." (Tree Hugger, Web. 18 Nov. 2016)

"Impetuous and sometimes uncontrollable progress in all spheres of science, the growth of population around the world, ecological problems, wars, and many other crises modern humanity faces nowadays raises a question about whether Earth will remain capable of being home for us as a species in the "nearest future."

"There are measures taken to soften, slow down, or even negate the effects human civilization causes to our planet, but some of the problems seem to be unsolvable.

One of them is population growth. People can discover new energy sources, learn how to grow food from nothing, or invent thousands of new appliances to improve the efficiency of everything, but it is not a fully effective way to stop the global population from growing.

For a long time, the solution was to expand the territory on which this population is living. However, it is not enough; measures such as constructing artificial islands, "Terra Forming" is relatively effective, but unfortunately the various measures cannot impact the situation with overpopulation on a global scale. Besides, some of these solutions affect the environment in destructive ways.

There is, nevertheless, yet another way to deal with overpopulation: an ambitious and daring project, which, in case of its success, can start a new era in humanity's history: exploring and colonizing distant planets. Space colonization is a controversial, debated, and expensive method, but it is probably the best we have for now, for a number of reasons."

(This Prospectus author notes that this relates no information on the numbers so "luckily escaping".)

"First of all, there is always a danger of a cataclysm that humanity will not be able to predict or defend itself against. Every year, the media publishes messages about "killer asteroids" approaching Earth, but all of them have been missing our planet so far. One day, humanity could be less lucky; be it an asteroid, technological catastrophe, or some kind of ultra-intensive sun flare, one day there could be something we will not be prepared for—like it happened to the dinosaurs more than 60 million years ago. "The dinosaurs died out because they were too stupid to build an adequate space-faring civilization. So far, the difference between us and them is barely measurable," says Tihamer Toth-Fejel, a research engineer at the Advanced Information Systems division of defense contractor General Dynamics (Popular Science). Since it is impossible to be prepared for everything, setting off from our planet and traveling to other planets seems to be a more efficient choice in terms of preserving human culture, gene pools, and civilization in general from total eradication, in case something goes terribly wrong. As the saying goes, it is better to not keep all eggs in one basket."

(This Prospectus author notes that as a valuable notion. Planning for cataclysm is certainly sensible, but of course, cost must be faced!)

"Another reason might seem a bit far-fetched, but it is neither less strong, nor less significant to human civilization.

Leaving Earth and colonizing new planets and star systems will probably become the greatest achievement of our species. The Universe is not just huge, it is fact endless, at least in relation to that tiny piece of space humanity occupies in it; as such, it would be naive to assume there were or are no other sentient civilizations we could one day come in contact with. And even if we do not, would it not be great or even sublime to leave a trace in the history of the Universe, even if we, as a species, will disappear?

So that when some alien archaeologists would visit a distant planet somewhere on the outskirts of the Andromeda galaxy, they would find the remains of our architecture, art, technology, history? So that those alien scientists of the future would study us as we study the ancient civilizations of Babylon or Greece, and would admire our achievements, the great expanse of our genius? I know it sounds probably too solemn and proud, but is it not what the purpose of a civilization is: to leave a legacy? Would it be better to reach the population of 100 billion people in the next two centuries and choke on our own toxic emissions, crowdedness, fight for free space, and starve to death? Because this is what awaits humanity if it does not venture to space."

This Prospectus author notes, full agreement with the notion of preserving the distant future, but for all our children, and not just as a legacy but as continuing reality for all humans, for the species. That is a central matter in this Prospectus!

This (meaning a drastic finale for human civilization) is confirmed by several influential scientists.

Stephen Hawking in particular has said. "Our only chance of long-term survival is not to remain inward looking on planet Earth but to spread out into space. We have made remarkable progress in the last hundred years. But if we want to continue beyond the next hundred years, our future is in space," Hawking says (Tree Hugger).

"In addition, colonizing other planets would solve not only the problem with overpopulation, but would also create additional working places, establish brand new economic systems, such as space tourism, and finally solve the ever-existing problem of natural resources."

There are numerous opponents of this motive for colonization, mostly among "green" citizens. "Why do we need to move to other planets to excavate even more resources? Why do we need to exhaust other planets beyond our own?" they ask. Because, first of all, colonizing other planets would prevent us from sucking Earth dry and completely destroying it. Because, secondly, too many people in a tiny space (and Earth is already becoming tiny in terms of available living space) will inevitably lead to conflicts over whatever becomes precious in the following years: oil, free space, clean water and air, and so on.

And thirdly, because there is no guarantee that a civilization that is advanced enough to fly around space will, by that time, treat ecology the same way it does now.

Colonizing space is perhaps the only "win-win" solution humanity can come up with in order to solve the problem of overpopulation."

It would not only insure our civilization from oblivion in case of any kind of global catastrophe (be it total war or giant asteroids), but would also solve the problem with natural resources, create working places, stimulate the economy, and contribute to the overall scientific, cultural, and industrial progress of humankind. And, which is the most important, it will help humanity leave a trace in the history of the Universe; instead of remaining and probably disappearing as a small local civilization on the outskirts of the Milky Way, it will become a galactic phenomenon, leaving its relics all over the explored space, a legacy for future generations. Whatever happens to humanity, this would be its grand finale!"

So, when do we do it?

The forgoing is representative of the strong arguments that we venture as soon as possible out into the cosmos. Following expresses the fears that prompt the drive to indeed say Adios Earth.

"After Earth: Why, Where, How, and When We Might Leave Our Home Planet!" The following article by Ben Austen in March 16, 2011 addresses that matter.

"Humanity may have millennia to find a new home in the universe--or just a few years.

Earth won't always be fit for occupation. We know that in two billion years or so, an expanding sun will boil away our oceans, leaving our home in the universe uninhabitable—unless, that is, we haven't already been wiped out by the Andromeda galaxy, which is on a multi-billion-year collision course with our Milky Way. Moreover, at least a third of the thousand-mile-wide asteroids that hurtle across our orbital path will eventually crash into us, at a rate of about one every 300,000 years.

Why? Indeed, in 1989 a far smaller asteroid, the impact of which would still have been equivalent in force to 1,000 nuclear bombs, crossed our orbit just six hours after Earth had passed. A recent report by the Lifeboat Foundation, whose hundreds of researchers track a dozen different existential risks to humanity, likens that one-in-300,000 chance of a catastrophic strike to a game of Russian roulette: "If we keep pulling the trigger long enough we'll blow our head off, and there's no guarantee it won't be the next pull."

"Given the risks humans pose to the planet, we might someday leave Earth simply to conserve it.

Many of the threats that might lead us to consider off-Earth living arrangements are actually man-made, and not necessarily in the distant future.

The amount we consume each year already far outstrips what our planet can sustain, and the World Wildlife Fund estimates that by 2030 we will be consuming two planets' worth of natural resources annually.

The Center for Research on the Epidemiology of Disasters, an international humanitarian organization, reports that the onslaught of droughts, earthquakes, epic rains and floods over the past decade is triple the number from the 1980s and nearly 54 times that of 1901, when this data was first collected.

Some scenarios have climate change leading to severe water shortages, the submersion of coastal areas, and widespread famine. Additionally, the world could end by way of deadly pathogens, nuclear war or, as the Lifeboat Foundation warns, the "misuse of increasingly powerful technologies."

Further, "Given the risks humans pose to the planet, we might also someday leave Earth simply to conserve it, with our planet becoming a kind of nature sanctuary that we visit now and again, as we might Yosemite."

None of the threats we face are especially far-fetched. Climate change is already a major factor in human affairs, for instance, and our planet has undergone at least one earlier mass extinction as a result of asteroid impact. The dinosaurs died out because they were too stupid to build an adequate space-faring civilization," says Tihamer Toth-Fejel who is a research engineer at the Advanced Information Systems division of defense contractor General Dynamics and one of 85 members of the Lifeboat Foundation's space-settlement board. "So far, the difference between us and them is barely measurable." The Alliance to Rescue Civilization, a project started by New York University chemist Robert Shapiro, contends that "the inevitability of any of several cataclysmic events means that we must prepare a copy of our civilization and move it into outer space and out of harm's way—a backup of our cultural achievements and traditions."

In 2005 then–NASA administrator Michael Griffin described the aims of the national space program in similar terms. "If we humans want to survive for hundreds of thousands or millions of years, we must ultimately populate other planets," he said. "One day, I don't know when that day is, but there will be more human beings who live off the Earth than on it."

Regarding this section of her Prospectus Chivonn e-mails two comments, really concerns to Dr. Jordyn.

Reviewing the available comments on "Leaving Earth", I noted that in addition to worries about war, etc. the common proposition, the idea, the main impetus for leaving earth was "relieving overpopulation! That is the big leave earth warning! And in connection I note that the matter of hyper-urbanization, which is the crux of the problem, was not mentioned!

Dr. Jordyn wrote back simply. "Then the matter should be addressed as you move into your next section, right? I will be very much interested in how you handle that!"

Note: A look at some other of Chivonn's e-mails to her professor can be seen at the end of Chapter 11. They are in a file folder together with her finished Prospectus.

Tracing the story so far and pointing to the next...

In chapters 3-7 Chivonn has addressed in her Prospectus five major problems facing Human Kind.

Of course, there are more! Around the world there is horrible cruelty to children for various political miss-directions, and the matter of misogamy continues. Women are suppressed and abused in too many societies.

Dictators and politicians still rise to power even in governments that should have sufficient checks and balances, due as the following in the Prospectus notes to the fundamental lack of empathy in populations.

So, it is in chapters 8-10 following she turns attention to the underlying human cause for these tragedies and then with focus attends to what could be, i.e., that "Empathy makes Cures Possible".

Chapter 8

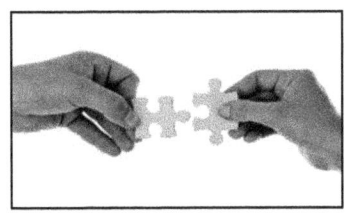

WHAT WE ARE!

Or at least...WHO ARE WE MOSTLY?

- Chivonn's Thoughts
- Section Six Prospectus
    - 6a. Personalities we believe are ours!
    - 6b. What makes personality?
    - 6c. Why are we what we are?
    - 6d. The "Charisma Trap"!
    - 6e. Who We Are Then and Now?
- The Party at Skellan's

Chivonn's Thoughts

Chivonn thanked the Samyaks courteously for allowing her to stay as she realized the sessions with the mystic were the stimulus, indeed, the flames that helped her to focus on creating the first chapters of her Prospectus!

She expected problems on the trip home, however, except for wrestling with customs regarding a small token given her by her new Jain friends the journey was uneventful. On the flight she was warmed with the thoughts, taking all else away, about her getting home and hugging Tayler. She let all the other responsibility fly away as she rehearsed her time to come-the two of them together after her trip to India.

Home again, and just in the door she found his kiss as it always was, so sweet to her, and as it had been from their very first kiss, she found it was still so overpowering that again it took her breath away. Taylor was a big man, a good six foot five and he lifted her gently, swung her around in a gleeful greeting and carried her into their bedroom. They lay there together, easy reviewing events since their last time together. Then later, together in each other's arms within the tangled bed-sheet, they drifted off into a blissfully deep sleep.

In the morning, she awoke alone in their bed, Taylor off to work at five am. and as her sleep filled mind drew in the glow through blinds, the memory of the familiar sounds and the aroma of India styled pancakes drifted in-awaking all her senses, and her mouth started to water as she hurriedly made the bed!

The reason was clear. From her trip to India, she had discovered the wonderful and spicy tastes of the far east. A few she hadn't cared for but most others she truly loved. The pancakes she mixed and smelled-cooking were one of her favorites. She could hardly wait!

As it was, on the way down the stairs from their bedroom to the main floor and the kitchen, she remembered how she had begged Daya into giving her the recipes of her favorite dishes. The "Chocolate & Apple Pancakes" were simple enough to make. "Put together 1 c. plain flour (maida), ½ c. peeled and grated apples, ¼ finely chopped dark chocolate, ¾ c. milk, 2 tbsp. castor sugar, ½ tsp vanilla essence, ¾ tsp baking powder, 1 tbsp vegetable oil, and little of that for cooking. Mix all ingredients with a little water and wisp well making a smooth batter. Set aside while heating a little oil in a pan and spread about 3 to 4 tbsp of batter (1/4 c.) to make a thick pancake of about 100 mm. (4") diameter. Cook on both sides on medium heat until golden brown, using a little oil if needed. Serve hot with pure maple syrup." It always amazed her how every Jain recipe she was served with Samyak was filled with taste and no matter what the meal not one creature's life was tragically interrupted!

Life was good, she realized, even with all the horrors that were present, life was still good. Her mind had settled, and she was ready, confident that her ideas forming up to complete the prospectus-later to be defended before her committee-would surely lead to the needed funding for her research. If not, she felt secure in the knowledge that something better would soon be coming her *way! **Her path, her destiny was absolutely set, and she would not deviate from it!***

And after several days of home and bliss with her partner, she was warmly welcomed back in the lab and spent a good week helping with the projects there.

The Prospectus sat on her desk almost smoking every time she looked at it, worrying about where to go next with her ideas.

Then one day looking out the large window in the room off the stairs where she often ate her lunch, she saw the mass of people milling around here and there seeming to her they were just hoping for an idea of how to get to the next challenge in their lives, how to get the perks to enjoy their days.

At that moment it came to her just as powerful in emotion as Samyak stimulated in his "Future Predictions". It was as clear as a vision she once had of the cresting pure white waves on a sunlit beach! It had to be held in mind and addressed. What is behind those matters I have reviewed and so many others, the killing of children in schools from senseless lack of vigilance on guns, from the world-wide overbearing misogamy and so much more.

Of course! we are all the "Offspring" creating this mess! The next chapter and future ones must address clearly "Who Are We (really)" that have brought this about? Then what is in us to help us out of it, and where should we be going from there. And that later part coupled with the foreground will defend what I am proposing for my research! So that evening the writing was there well formed in her mind and the Prospectus continued in Section Six as follows...

SECTION SIX

WHO ARE WE MOSTLY?

Then and Now

----- in Good Part!

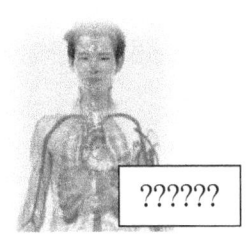

??????

Obviously, we must be a function of our personality! The multiple species threatening situations as of this time have been created by mass action following on our own inner selves but prompted by this or that leader.

That is there is a resultant background to us. I choose to coin a terminology, I will call it our *"Net Personality"* or these things would not have been possible. This then begs the question what do the people within that "Net" think they are themselves

6a. Personalities we believe are ours.

In her Prospectus Chivonn argues as follows. "The outcomes we are facing are surely from a loading factor, that is-our resulting population personality, or in short our "Net Personality"! This is because, in the end, an outcome involving all of us is focused on all of us-because of our permission for it in mass or our acceptance of it in mass.

Then what kinds of personality have there been or are there contributing to this-as people see themselves-as surveys show?

In fact, Chivonn discovers today with the extensive internet connectivity there are popular surveys for just that purpose, so she records in her Prospectus the following.

A very popular survey proports to place the personalities of individual people in one of 16 types. These are as follows. Percentages are estimates of that part of the general population-personality distribution one "belongs to" after entering the survey. (The data source is the "MBTI Manual" published by CPP.)

The Sixteen Personality Types

1. The Duty Fulfiller. 11.6%.
Serious and quiet, interested in security and peaceful living. Extremely thorough, responsible, and dependable. Well-developed powers of concentration. *Usually interested in supporting and promoting traditions and establishments.* Well-organized and hardworking, they work steadily towards identified goals. They can usually accomplish any task once they have set their mind to it.

2. The Mechanic. 5.4%.

Quiet and reserved, interested in how and why things work. Excellent skills with mechanical things. Risk-takers who live for the moment. Usually interested in and talented at extreme sports. Uncomplicated in their desires. *Loyal to their peers and to their internal value systems,* but not overly concerned with respecting laws and rules if they get in the way of getting something done. Detached and analytical, they excel at finding solutions to practical problems.

3. The Nurturer or Caregiver. 12.3% (alternate estimate 13.8%).

Quiet, kind, and conscientious. *Can be depended on to follow through.* Usually puts the needs of others above their own needs. Stable and practical, they value security and traditions. Well-developed sense of space and function. Rich inner world of observations about people. Extremely perceptive of other's feelings. Interested in serving others.

4. The Artist. 8.8%.

Quiet, serious, sensitive and kind. Does not like conflict, and not likely to do things which may generate conflict. *Loyal and faithful.* Extremely well-developed senses, and aesthetic appreciation for beauty. *Not interested in leading or controlling others.* Flexible and open-minded. Likely to be original and creative. Enjoy the present moment.

5. The Protector. 1.5%.

Quietly forceful, original, and sensitive. Tend to stick to things until they are done. Extremely intuitive about people and concerned for their feelings. Well-developed value systems which they strictly adhere to. Well-respected for their perseverance in doing the right thing. *Likely to be individualistic, rather than leading or following.*

6. The Idealist. 4.4%.

Quiet, reflective, and idealistic. *Interested in serving humanity.* Well-developed value system, which they strive to live in accordance with. Extremely loyal. *Adaptable and laid-back unless a strongly-held value is threatened.* Usually talented writers. Mentally quick, and able to see possibilities. Interested in understanding and helping people.

7. The Scientist. 2.1%.

Independent, original, analytical, and determined. Have an exceptional ability to turn theories into solid plans of action. Highly value knowledge, competence, and structure. *Driven to derive meaning from their visions.* Long-range thinkers. Have very high standards for their performance, and the performance of others. Natural leaders. Will follow only if they trust existing leaders.

8. The Thinker. 3.3%.

Logical, original, creative thinkers. Can become very excited about theories and ideas. Exceptionally capable and driven to turn theories into clear understandings. Highly value knowledge, competence and logic. Quiet and reserved, hard to get to know well. *Individualistic, having no interest in leading or following others.*

9. The Doer. 4.3%.

Friendly, adaptable, action-oriented. "Doers" who are focused on immediate results. Living in the here-and-now, they're risk-takers who live fast-paced lifestyles. Impatient with long explanations. *Extremely loyal to their peers*, but not usually respectful of laws and rules if they get in the way of getting things done. Great people skills.

10. The Guardian. 8.7%.

Practical, traditional, and organized. Likely to be athletic. Not interested in theory or abstraction unless they see the practical application. Have clear visions of the way things should be. *Loyal and hard-working.* Like to be in charge. Exceptionally capable in organizing and running activities. "Good citizens" who value security and peaceful living.

11. The Performer. 8.5%.

People-oriented and fun-loving, they make things more fun for others by their enjoyment. Living for the moment, they love new experiences. They dislike theory and impersonal analysis. *Interested in serving others.* Likely to be the center of attention in social situations. Well-developed common sense and practical ability.

12. The Caregiver, 12.8%.

Warm hearted, popular, and conscientious. Tend to put the needs of others over their own needs. Feel strong sense of responsibility and duty. Value traditions and security. *Interested in serving others.* Need positive reinforcement to feel good about themselves. Well-developed sense of space and function.

13. The Inspirer. 8.1%.

Enthusiastic, idealistic and creative. Able to do almost anything that interests them. Great people skills. *Need to live life in accordance with their inner values.* Excited by new ideas but bored with details. Open-minded and flexible, with a broad range of interests and abilities.

14. The Giver. 2.5%.

Popular and sensitive, with outstanding people skills. *Externally focused, with real concern for how others think and feel.* Usually, dislike being alone. They see everything from the human angle, and dislike impersonal analysis. Very effective at managing people issues, and leading group discussions. Interested in serving others, and probably place the needs of others over their own needs.

15. The Visionary. 3.2%.

Creative, resourceful, and intellectually quick. Good at a broad range of things. Enjoy debating issues and may be into "one-up-man-ship". They get very excited about new ideas and projects but may neglect the more routine aspects of life. Generally outspoken and assertive. They enjoy people and are stimulating company. *Excellent ability to understand concepts and apply logic to find solutions*

16. The Executive. 1.8%.

Assertive and outspoken - *they are driven to lead*. Excellent ability to understand difficult organizational problems and create solid solutions. Intelligent and well-informed, they usually excel at public speaking. They value knowledge and competence, and usually have little patience with inefficiency or disorganization.

The population percentages suggest that the rarest personality types are The Protector followed by The Executive and the Scientist. That is the fewest number of people fell in those leadership or driven to be inquisitive groups.

It is noteworthy that all of these groupings are...shall we say...kind with no grouping of violent, narcissistic or other less friendly categories. That is at least when challenged to think about their personality most people "feel' they are "kind".

And most noteworthy just 20% if the "general population" are of the type that resist following along, because of independent, analytical thinking.

To check into the idea in this study suggesting that we each will fall into a singular type, this researcher arranged to have the test for a sociology class of 115 students.

The result was that only one person felt that they belonged into just one group, most evaluated themselves as belonging in three or four of the categories.

It is somewhat troubling that the rarest types are those that have leadership, deep thinking and protective characteristics which few in the survey felt were personality types to which they belonged!

Nonetheless, the main message in this survey would appear is that people think they are basically good though largely followers, without a great drive to think, lead or protect.

This suggests that the Net Personality while good, is open to, indeed, needing leadership. That is what we think of ourselves and that is what (statistics valid) has opened the door to a floor level cause for us allowing or creating our dilemmas!

6b. "What Makes Personality?" (Essential to Who We Are)

Clearly a part of our behavior is centered around our personality. Asked what propositions are worthy of wider debate, Dan McAdams a professor of psychology at Northwestern University wondered how humans arrive at their personalities.

He wrote: "I am in personality a life-span developmental psychologist. Thus, my main activities are teaching, writing, and research. In my field, there are many ideas that are widely and vigorously debated. But it is not clear to me that the public at large is aware of these debates. Actually, "debate" is not quite the right word, because it suggests two diametrically opposed sides who take each other on. A better way to characterize it would be simply "conversations" among psychological scientists, ones of different persuasions and inclinations, all of whom study the phenomenon of human personality."

"We may think of personality as the distinctive set of psychological characteristics that distinguish one person from the next. The back-and-forth among psychologists regarding the nature of human personality draws mainly from scientific research and theory, but it is also informed by ideology, culture, and personal experience."

A central question in the field of personality psychology today is this: To what extent is our personality given to us, and to what extent do we make it ourselves!

Here to this question are Ideas put forward in 2016. These are dispatches from the Aspen Ideas Festival/Spotlight on Health...

"It seems pretty clear that certain foundation features of human personality –such as our basic dis-positional traits feel as if they are given to us.

For example, as people move through life, from one situation to the next, they do not typically choose to be, say, "extroverted" or "anxious" or "especially kind and considerate.

"This is just how I am," an especially extroverted person might say, regarding her tendency to be outgoing and socially dominant. "I can't help it, I am just a very nervous person," an individual with high levels of the trait neurotic-ism might conclude.

People do tend to feel that their disposition traits are given to them (introvert, extrovert, shy, etc.) by genes, past experiences, luck, whatever. *And research does support the claim!*

At the same time, there are other features of human personality that feel chosen or made, such as one's life goals and values and, especially, the story that a person has constructed about life. Life stories–or what psychologists call narrative identities–are a very hot topic today in the psychological sciences.

A person's life story is an internalized and evolving narrative of the self that reconstructs the past and imagines the future in such a way as to provide life with some sense of meaning and purpose.

The story provides a subjective account, told to others and to the self, of how I came to be the person I am becoming. With respect to human personality, people's stories about their lives (their Narrative Identities) layer over their disposition traits.

To understand a person well, even if that person is the self, one must understand the basic traits that inform everyday social behavior and the inner story that gives meaning to the person's life. The traits are given, it seems; but the stories seem to be made!"

Human beings, therefore, are simultaneously social actors whose behavior is shaped 1.) by given traits and 2). autobiographical authors who make meaning out of their lives through narratives!"

Then following on that, do circumstances determine human behavior more than character or personality

On this subject the following was reported 2016 from C. E. Clark, et.al (University of North Texas).

"This is a very controversial issue in the world of psychology, and I'm going to tell you that right up front. There are psychologists who believe it is personality that determines a person's behavior more than anything else, and there are psychologists who believe it is circumstances that influence behavior more than anything else---more than character and/or personality.

If a choice must be made, circumstances get my vote, and here is why. The Stanley Milgram Experiment (among others) showed that what are considered normal, ordinary, stable, dependable, decent people, who were not known to be violent or radical in their behaviors, could and did under certain conditions do unspeakable things."

(Note this relates to "Net Personality", as we have seen there are cases where the masses have done so.)

"Here "Situation Psychology "is the subject. It is looking into what makes people behave the way they do. To clarify, the "Stanley Milgram Experiment" tests "Obedience to Authority".

The Milgram Experiment was created and carried out in order to determine if German people were more inclined to be obedient to authority than most people in the world. Clark's comments continue as follows.

"During the "World War II Nuremberg War Crimes Trials" many of the accused gave the reason for their unthinkable behavior as obedience to authority. They said they were just following orders.

Stanley Milgram, a Yale University psychologist and professor, set out to determine just how much influence authority really played in the behavior of people in general.

Milgram's Experiment initially resulted in 65% of participants from all walks of life, complying with the orders of authority figures. The experiment was repeated hundreds of times after that with a result of 62-67% of research subjects complying with the orders of authority figures.

The authority figures requested that the research subjects do a terrible thing, which is administer electric shocks to people they did not know and who had never harmed them in any way. On average, 65% of the research subjects from all walks of life complied, mostly without protest or question.

The Milgram Experiment tested people from all walks of life. It is because the research participants administered the shock. were from all walks of life, with many different characters and personalities, that I side with the psychologists who believe circumstances more than character or personality influence a person's behavior. The Milgram Experiment is only one of many different experiments that have been conducted and that have achieved the same results every time on this subject of how authority affects human behavior."

Milgram repeated his experiment several times, making small changes to the way he conducted the experiment. For example, he changed the location of the authority figure and that did make a difference to many of the participants administering the shocks.

However, "it was argued" if it was the location of the authority figure that changed it was not the participant's personality or character that changed. But, by changing the circumstances of the situation and keeping the participants the same, Milgram proved that circumstances rather than personal traits make the difference in a person's behavior. What Milgram proved was that changing the circumstances changed the outcome. In other words, the circumstances determined the change, personality and or character of the participant did not." Clark continues following.

"Here is an example that may help you to better understand what I am trying to say. John usually goes straight home from work. One night he decides to stop in to a neighborhood bar where several of his coworkers like to relax after work. There is a very attractive woman he has never seen before in the bar on the night he stops in. The woman flirts with John and after a few drinks, he flirts back. Eventually John and the woman have a conversation and she let him know she is attracted to him. John is married, but he finds this woman very tempting. He doesn't tell her he is married because he enjoys the attention, she is giving him and fears she might change her mind about him if she knew he was married.

Normally John would be a model husband, but this night he is away from his wife and family and has had a few drinks that lower his inhibitions, like alcohol usually does with most people. He likes the attention this strange woman is giving him, and it brings back memories of before he was married. The woman in the bar makes him feel attractive and desirable in a way his wife does not. After a few drinks and a couple of hours later, John goes home alone to his family, but he was sorely tempted to accept the woman's invitation to stop by her apartment for a night cap.

Basically, John behaved out of character because he was "under the influence of alcohol" and he was in a different atmosphere than usual. What if he had been away from home in another city and state at a convention? What if the woman he met at the convention was from a different state hundreds of miles from where John lives? Might John have given in because he felt more confident, he would not be found out? Might he have stayed in the bar longer and drank more, thus causing the alcohol to lower his inhibitions even more?

Hopefully you can see how as each of these factors of the circumstances change, so might John's behavior, but his personality and character remain the same, *(do they?)*. These same circumstances might very well apply to a woman who is married and away from her family for a few hours and drinking alcohol, or at a convention many miles from home.

The point I am making is that often people behave the way they do more because of the circumstances they find themselves in, external factors, than because of their personality type or their character. Most of us believe, at least hope that everyone wants to make sure other people take responsibility for their behaviors, and ultimately a person does make their own decision to do something or not to do it. Yet Milgram's Experiment shows over and over again that sometimes people act out of character. Milgram's Experiment shows that the reason people most often act out of character is because of circumstances they find themselves in."

(This Prospectus Author's Critique: The arguments above can be classified as "What if's" and are not necessarily proof of the premise. One can place on this a question, do all people necessarily have to behave in this way? Does it not in the end depend on how well grounded a person is, how secure in their own skin and hold against the influence, the exciting enticement that might make them follow a certain path? And to a great degree we often choose our circumstances! Further, it is important to insert here those percentages of people that are quite rationally thinking, though in a minority. In addition, the caring for others, in example the wife, hangs heavily on the sense of empathy the "miscreate" has within.)

It is important to note that other psychologists will say, but people do choose their circumstances and they choose particular circumstances because of their personality. To some degree that is true. The question unresolved is to what degree!

The final note on this is that a part of human behavior is due to their susceptibility in some challenging circumstances.

This brings to bear again that 20 % which included people who indeed are the (our) Protectors, Thinkers, Inspirers, Visionaries, Executives and Scientists. This says there is hope, there are a set of people who can and will discern and act within their own informed action!

6c. So, "Why Are We --What We Are?

In net so far, personality is a part of us. It is under argument- partly given and in some cases, circumstance driven.

But why are we what we are what makes us act evil, what makes us for example participate in "Mob Behavior". And that, of course, relates to "Net Personality". That most assuredly is behind many of the drifts in history that have created our sacrificial dilemmas!

What then is the reason normally decent law-abiding responsible people sometimes get caught up in a group think situation and participate in unspeakable behaviors, and later regrettable actions?

How often have we heard of children going along with a friend, or group of friends, who did something that, surely, they knew was totally unacceptable? Maybe the children were at a party where drugs were being circulated and that situation will persuade them to go along with what everyone else is doing. They do not want to be the only person at the party who is not going along with what most other party goers are doing. They do not want to draw attention to themselves by saying no.

To address this there are the "Solomon Asch Experiments" on conformity. How important is it to you, or to people generally to fit in? Why do many people choose to fit in? Here are thoughts gathered from the literature on this.

The Solomon Asch Experiments show that most people want to fit in more than they want to do the right thing! This is even if doing the wrong thing will hurt them. They also point to circumstances having more influence on behavior than personality or character.

Many people disagree that circumstances play such a big role in human behavior, but most of them will readily admit it is because they are afraid people will not be held accountable if it becomes widely accepted that it was the circumstances rather than the individual's decision and judgment that caused the problem.

This is sort of like people not wanting to accept that sometimes people really are insane when they commit certain crimes, and they really were not responsible for what they did because their brain was not functioning normally.

Here is an example put forward to bring us deeper into the argument about our self-decision strength. Think about this. "If you are a chocolate lover and there was a decadent delicious brownie, renowned for its superior quality from an exclusive restaurant, just one brownie of that sort, sitting in your pantry, would you eat it? Let's say you brought it home from a luncheon at that exclusive restaurant with friends ostensibly for your roommate who loves chocolate, but she is at work and does not know you have a brownie for her. You plan to surprise her with it when she gets home. She will never know if you eat the brownie unless one of the friends you had lunch with tells her and asks her if she enjoyed it. It's those little details that people often overlook that get them into trouble." Given these circumstances will you eat the brownie? Obviously, life is full of decisions, relating to "Fitting In".

Most of us (80% is the estimate) seem to want to fit in. Is this the undercover driver that prevents far future insight? That is do we follow situations and particularly leaders, who are by nature charged to drive us to fit in. If their programs do nothing for us in later years, do we too much of the time now accept the proposal and go along with it at our future detriment?

What goes wrong that so often in our history has led to the creation of the threats or drives the absence of will to remove them? This then delves deeper into the psychology of people, and what makes them the way they are? Fortunately, there has been some pretty good thinking on this.

The fundamental psychology of that is defined in a fair and sensible way in the work of George Kelly. Kelly was an American psychologist, therapist, educator and personality theorist. His proposal on behavior is critical for analysis of what we are and why we behave in certain ways. The following proposal is extracted from Wikipedia.

"He is by many considered the father of cognitive clinical psychology and is widely known for his theory of personality, personal construct psychology. It was at Oklahoma State University that Kelly developed his major contribution to the psychology of personality." This is specifically "The Psychology of Personal Constructs".

"Kelly saw that current theories of personality were so loosely defined and difficult to test that in many clinical cases the observer contributed more to the diagnosis than the patient!

If people took their problems to a Freudian analyst, they would be analyzed in Freudian terms; a Jungian would interpret them in Jungian terms; a behaviorist would interpret them in terms of conditioning; and so on."

Kelly acknowledged that both the therapist and patient would each bring a unique set of constructs to bear in the consulting room. Therefore, the therapist could never be completely "objective" in construing his or her client's world.

Personal construct psychology and Personal construct theory were the outcomes of his thinking. Kelly's fundamental view of personality was that *"people are like" naive scientists" who see the world through a particular lens, based on their uniquely organized systems of construction, which they use to anticipate events."*

"Personal construct theory explores the individual's map they form by coping with the psychological stresses of their lives. But because people are naive scientists, they sometimes employ systems for construing the worlds that are distorted by idiosyncratic experiences not applicable to their current social situation."

Kelly would say, a system of construction that chronically fails to characterize and/or predict events, and is not appropriately revised to comprehend and predict one's changing social world, is considered to be that which underlies psychopathology or varieties of mental illness

It is clear from this viewpoint that "personality" is susceptible to circumstances and attractions. And personality is us and must contain both benevolent empathy and even evil self-defensive capacity.

Then what are the circumstances outside that born in instinct (or genetic imprint) that make the decisions both individually and subsequently for people who are acting in concurrence. From either in-born or circumstantial development what is the deep end influencing who we are in Net?

There are certainly reasons as yet not understood, but a central question must be...is it a history that reveals a misdirection or overemphasis of some personality characteristics arising in leaders such as a "Narcissistic Personality"? This type of personality is, many believe, embedded in the minds of many who drove the circumstances creating our dilemmas. A review of those kinds of people brings this point to the forefront.

Following is a short record of those afflicted in history. This is abridged from a report "Some Important Narcissistic Leaders in History" by Alexander Burgemeester.

"To be included under the title are Mahatma Ghandhi, Franklin D. Roosevelt (these guiding the Net Personality most to the good), then there are Muammar Qaddafi, Adolf Hitler, Pol Pot, and Stalin, indeed most dictators." Here following are comments about other leaders with Narcissistic Traits.

"Napoleon: Napoleon was considered a tyrant with grandiose beliefs and overly aggressive behavior, allegedly to make up for feelings of inferiority (origination for the term 'Napoleon Complex'). He was so feared that a nursery rhyme was written to scare children into behaving ("the Bogeyman"). 'It was precisely that evening in Lodi that I came to believe in myself as an unusual person and became consumed with the ambition to do the great things that until then had been but a fantasy.' Napoleon Bonaparte, on 'Thoughts'.

That being one example, what more specially makes a leader a "Narcissist"?

Narcissists have vision; but then again so do people in psychiatric hospitals. The basic definition of a leader is someone whom other people will follow; narcissistic leadership is a leadership style in which the leaders' main goal is serving self-interest at the expense of their people or group members. Narcissists tend to be appealing and quite adept at attracting followers. They often do so through language and believe that their inspiring speeches can influence people."

From Maccoby (Productive Narcissist, 2003), the following helps to clarify. "Narcissistic leaders are accomplished and charismatic speakers. Indeed, anyone who has seen narcissists perform can attest to their personal magnetism and their ability to stir enthusiasm among audiences.

Although most people think that followers need their leader, it is also true that narcissistic leaders need their followers. A narcissist seeks and indeed, needs praise and admiration from his admirers.

Think of Winston Churchill's wartime broadcasts or JFK's "Ask not what your country can do for you" inaugural address. The admiration that followed these speeches reinforced the self-confidence and beliefs of the speakers. *Typically, as the narcissist becomes increasingly self-assured, he or she becomes more spontaneous and feels freer from previous constraints.*

They not too uncommonly begin to think they are invincible. Their stronger confidence and increased energy further increase their followers' enthusiasm.

Unfortunately, the admiration that a narcissist demands can have a negative effect. As she or he (let's call that one "N") grows in power, N listens even less to words of caution or advice from his subordinates or from his people. N does not try to persuade those who disagree with him but instead N ignores them (or their advice) or in the case of some dictators, has them deposed or otherwise gotten rid of. The result is sometimes brazen risk taking that can lead to catastrophe of historical proportions. In recent history is the breaking down of respect for all people, the rise of a new bigotry in the United States under what many feel and evidence supports the misogynist and racial misdirection produced by the lies and deceptions of a President current in the times of this Prospectus.

There are in fact a number of weaknesses of the narcissistic leader, and populations following along experience the end result of actions too frequently by that leader.

They will try to dominate meetings with subordinates as well as equals. One of the significant weaknesses of a narcissistic leader is that his faults become even more magnified the more successful he becomes.

Due to their extreme sensitivity to even the slightest comment that they view as negative, narcissistic leaders tend to shun all emotions. Narcissistic leaders typically keep others at a distance and can become quite emotionally isolated. They can put up a wall of emotional armor as thick as Fort Knox. Given their difficulty with knowing or acknowledging their own feelings, they are most uncomfortable with other people expressing theirs, especially if theirs are negative feelings."

So, it is most centrally the Narcissists critically lack empathy! Narcissists, in general, demand empathy from others yet they are characteristically lacking in empathy themselves.

To continue from the afore mentioned book. "Lack of empathy is a defining trait of some of the most charismatic and successful narcissistic leaders. But a lack of empathy in themselves did not prevent some of history's greatest narcissistic leaders from knowing how to communicate and inspire. They find the weakness in populations, extract and magnify it.

That is, they play on empathy, raising up ideas that are charismatic, attractive presentations to enlist populations in a directed way of "feeling sorry for their own plight. The outcomes can be positive sometimes but often cruel and devastating. Neither Churchill, de Gaulle, Stalin, nor Mao Tse-tung was empathetic. Yet they inspired people due to their passion and conviction at a time when people longed for certainty."

In other words-they seized on presentation, the attraction. That is, to put it clearly, they put it on "Charismatic Appearance"!

"The leaders who fall in this category are numerous. Examples include Alexander the Great. His unending record of war mongering and conquests, attracted followers and was then at the great expense of his generals and soldiers, is an indication of Alexander's lack of empathy for those he led. Another example is Henry the Eighth who was famous for his six wives and his quest to have a son for political reasons and from personal vanity. Yet he was considered one of the most charismatic rulers in England, even with his reputation of being harsh, insecure and egotistical. History suggests that he exhibited grandiosity and entitlement and of course the total lack of empathy is clear in his beheading "the inconvenient wife.

Narcissists do have an emotional cleverness, but it is rooted more in exploitation than empathy. They tend to provoke opposition, and yet often people are only willing to tolerate a narcissist as a leader at times of turmoil.

There is evidence that narcissistic personality disorder (NPD) is heritable, and individuals are much more likely to develop it if they have a family history of the disorder. Studies on the occurrence of personality disorders in twins determined that there is a moderate to high heritability for narcissistic personality disorder.

And it is in individual cases sometimes argued whether the leader is truly narcissistic (has NPD) or is simply hyper-attractive in a charismatic way. In this regard there are evaluated several types of Narcissist."

However, this author notes the specific genes and gene interactions that contribute to its cause, and how they may influence the developmental and physiological processes underlying this condition, have yet to be determined.

To be complete on narcissism Theodore Millon suggested five sub-types. However, there are few pure variants of any sub-type. The Millon sub-types are as follows.

"Unprincipled Narcissist. This one includes antisocial features: deficient in conscience; unscrupulous, amoral, disloyal, fraudulent, deceptive, arrogant, exploitive; a con artist and charlatan; dominating, contemptuous, vindictive.

Amorous Narcissist. This one includes histrionic features, is sexually seductive, enticing, beguiling, tantalizing; glib and clever; disinclined to real intimacy; indulges hedonistic desires; bewitches and inveigles others; pathological lying and swindling and tends to have many affairs, often with exotic partners.

Compensatory Narcissist. This one includes negativistic and avoidant features seeks to counteract or cancel out deep feelings of inferiority and lack of self-esteem and offsets deficits by creating illusions of being superior, exceptional, admirable, noteworthy; self-worth results from self-enhancement.

Elitist Narcissist. This one is a variant of the pure pattern, feels privileged and empowered by virtue of special childhood status and pseudo-achievements, entitled façade bears little relation to reality; seeks favored and good life and is upwardly mobile; cultivates special status and advantages by association.

Normal Narcissist. This one is absent of the traits of the other four. Least severe and most interpersonally concerned and empathetic, still entitled and deficient in reciprocity, bold in environments, self-confident, competitive, seeks high targets, feels unique, and has talent in leadership positions expecting of recognition from others."

6d. The Charisma Trap!

In reality, the susceptibility of people to persons of strong personality narcissist or gradients of that or just with attractive ideas causing populations to join in, going along with the flow, for reasons-the leader argues benefit them-can be evidenced by a number of well documented and very telling examples!

Two such are the tragedies from a summary by James K. Knoll, M.D. (knollj@upstate.edu).

He performs forensic psychiatric evaluations for the courts and private sector. He has special interests in the areas of suicide, violence and cultural criticism. Especially supporting the idea of "Charismatic Influence and Power" from his and related studies are both the David Koresch and Jonestown Tragedies discussed as follows.

"Why? Over the last several decades, the new religious groups or cults promise the individual a closer and more direct contact with the ultimate divine power by mediation via a charismatic leader. They are taught to believe that they are the possessors of absolute truth, which leads them to condemn all those who hold different ideas. The sect is also seen as a solution to existential difficulties by individuals who, in periods of crisis, have more acute feelings of disorientation and solitude and feel that society cannot adequately fulfill their needs.

The sect promises its members a sense of belonging and shared purpose, which overrides the existence of the individual. The sect unites the need of its members to submit to a higher power in the form of a charismatic leader who exerts a dominative force, which gradually becomes absolute. The functionality of the sect is dependent on this dynamic interrelationship.

Members are promised eternal life. Then, the charismatic leader makes the promises tangible by ensuring contact with supernatural powers and even interrupting future events and revelations via the hidden massages of the scriptures. One typical aspect of the sect's conception of life is a hostile attitude towards the outside world, perceived as vacuous, chaotic, aggressive and evil. The apocalypse is seen as bringing the millennial fight between good and evil to a definite end.

The outcome of both of these examples was death shared by the followers, even in the case of the Jonestown tragedy, where the members of the society voluntarily took a poison drink and watched each other suffer and die until all were dead."

So, to be rational, there is a fundamental problem in "Who We Are". We are for many, and for the most part susceptible to charismatic influences from people and their ideas (or products).

There is in us a tug of war between charismatic attraction and empathy.

The Narcissist is driven to obtain and hold attractants, in effect developing a charisma---a trap into which many people fall. But this charisma is deeper and more wide spread, from writings on the internet, from social media, from products, all which makes us non-evaluates of wrong influences and to turn away from this issues that will insure our future, destroy the threats.

Clearly within most of us, within our genetic makeup, perhaps from survival history, there is a need to follow wherein the impetus is a charismatic influence. The following provides a necessary description of this "Trap".

Charisma as defined in Wikipedia, the free encyclopedia follows. "The term charisma or as an adjective 'charismatic has two senses. The first is that compelling attractiveness or charm that can inspire devotion in others, a divinely conferred power or talent. In the second, scholars in sociology, political science, psychology, and management reserve the term for a type of leadership seen as extraordinary; to describe a particular type of leader who uses values-based, symbolic, and emotion-laden leader signaling.

Since the 1950s, the term has become widely used, with varying meanings, in religion, the social sciences, the media, and throughout Western societies. Contemporary charisma maintains, however, the irreducible character ascribed to it by Weber: it retains a mysterious, elusive quality.

Media commentators regularly describe charisma as the 'X-factor'! The enigmatic character of charisma also suggests a connection - at least to some degree – to the earliest manifestations of charisma as a spiritual gift."

In the collection of Max Webers works, "Economy and Society" edited by his wife, he identified the term as a prime example of action he labeled "value-rational," in distinction from and opposition to action he labeled "Instrumentally rational."

Weber introduced the personality charisma sense when he applied charisma to designate a form of authority.

To explain charismatic authority, he developed his classic definition as follows.

"Charisma is a certain quality of an individual personality by virtue of which he is set apart from ordinary men and treated as endowed with supernatural, superhuman, or at least specifically exceptional powers or qualities. These as such are not accessible to the ordinary person but are regarded as of divine origin or as exemplary, and on the basis of them the individual concerned is treated as a leader."

The sociologist Paul Joosse examined Weber's famous definition and found that through simple yet profoundly consequential phrases such as "are considered" and "is treated," charisma becomes a relational, attributable, and at last a properly sociological concept." For Weber, the locus of power is in those led, who actively (if perhaps unconsciously) invest their leaders with social authority.

In other words, Weber indicates that it is followers who attribute the individual with powers, emphasizing that "the recognition on the part of those subject to authority" is decisive for the validity of charisma.

So, Charismatic authority involves a specific type of organization or a type of leadership in which authority derives from the charisma of the leader.

This stands in contrast to two other types of authority: legal authority and traditional authority. Each of the three types forms part of Max Weber's tripartite classification of authority.

"Charismatic authority is often the most lasting of regimes because the leader is seen as infallible and any action against him will be seen as a crime against the state. Charismatic leaders eventually develop a cult of personality often not by their own doing."

Len Oakes a well-known Australian psychologist had eleven charismatic leaders fill in a psychometric test, which he called the adjective checklist, and found them as a group quite ordinary. Following the psychoanalyst Heinz Kohut, Oakes argues that "Charismatic leaders exhibit traits of narcissism and also argues that they display an extraordinary amount of energy accompanied by an inner clarity unhindered by the anxieties and guilt that afflict more ordinary people."

Hitler and Charisma

Laurence Rees is an acclaimed historian and filmmaker and the author of "The Dark Charisma of Adolf Hitler".

In 2006 he won the British Book Award for history book of the year for "Auschwitz: The Nazis and the Final Solution."

He has written as follows "As we see economic events unfold in Europe today, it's scarcely possible to imagine a greater warning from history.... I think, from the story of Hitler's appointment as chancellor of Germany in January 1933.

We discover that Hitler could be an instinctive and extremely powerful politician–light years away from the broken and crazed man portrayed in Downfall.

Above all, we can see the power of the situation to change perception.

Hitler was dismissed as a peripheral figure in 1928 yet lauded by millions in 1933.

What changed was not Hitler but the situation. Economic catastrophe made huge numbers of Germans seek a 'Charismatic Savior.

It's a view confirmed by Konrad Heiden who heard Hitler speak many times in the 1920s: "His speeches are daydreams of this 'Mass Soul'." *Developing- in the terminology this prospectus author calls a "Net Personality"!*

"The speeches begin always with deep pessimism and end in overjoyed redemption, a triumphant happy ending; often they can be refuted by reason, but they follow the far mightier logic of the subconscious, which no refutation can touch.

Hitler has given speech to the speechless and certainly terror for the modern masses!"

Nazi leader Adolf Hitler sits at a table facing a group of young and uniformed National Socialists crowded into a small room in the 'Braune-Haus'-(Brown-House). This picture was taken in Munich Germany c.1935. (Photo: Hulton Archive-Getty Images)

Does it really need clarification? This man Hitler was a demonic narcissist who produced one of the most significant and terrible of human tragedies in all of history-and it cannot be denied that his use of charisma in targeted propaganda-creating unbelievable mass action - was the root cause of it all!

~~~~~~~~~~~~~~~~

Note: Columnist David Brooks points out that "Meritocracies" do arise in societies. These could be potentially good but may too often result in awarding individual treatment of members of their "Class", i.e. You will have, will go high up". That is, they can fall into a charisma trap which endangers building a society high in narcissism but low in social connection, empathy for others.

6c. In Net: Who Are We Then and Now!

In summary, who we are then and now in good part follows along the below listed lines.

1. We are personalities, a part in-born and a part formed by circumstances.

2. Within our populations most of us simply want to fit in, i.e., follow along with the crowd, but also there is a small percent who grow up destined to set models, be leaders and some protectors.

3. Within us also are personalities who move toward narcissism characterized by the ability to capture the feelings of disappointment by the masses and create mass action using charismatic exhortations. It is likely that a good many of us today hold as part of our personality a degree of narcissism.

4. The most of us use these charismatic presentations as *naive scientists* who see the world through a particular lens, based on our uniquely organized systems of construction, which we use to anticipate and act on events forth coming.

5. In net we are susceptible to charismatic presentations which can build to mass action or mass inaction depending on the leadership and presentation we accept to fit in with and find levels of comfort in.

6. History proves the many developments to end our species clearly point to the need to buffer in some way those impulses that drive the charismatic-narcissistic (join in, not rational) trap in cataclysmic directions.

To put it bluntly- is their harboring in our minds, embedded there through parental hereditary transmission contradictory, saving impulses? If that is so, then should that not be understood and protected for saving the future of human kind?

The Party at Skellan's

The sixth section in her prospectus thus completed, targeting the matter of "Who We Are" Chivonn "gathered up her companion "Tyler" saying as she pulled him out the door...common my love we are going to that party... and I know that break with great people will feel so...good!

The spring semester about over, and their friends so much "University Bred, Tried and True" Skellan and his wife Angelei who was Technical Recorder in Dr. Jordyn's lab-- decided to have a party at their home to help them all loosen up for the summer. And there were some remarkable surprises for Chivonn during the revelry!

Almost at the beginning, with everyone gathered around new Lab Assistant Jamie King asked Chivonn the nagging question that many of her fellow students had in mind when they met and/or interacted with her "I hear you were in the Marines. Is that real?"

Of course, Chivonn proud of that experience seized on the opportunity, not surprised about the surprise because of the news that always seemed to highlight the negative ideas of women in the military, to include sex abuse, the weaker sex, etc. But for her it was no problem to comment. She was proud of her service, and she knew of the many female heroes, so she responded straight away..."Yes, that's true and I was fortunate to be one of the first female Combat Reconnaissance Marines". But that was following, shall we say on a progression of others...the fact is that the first female Marines enlisted in the 1940's. Most folks don't know that."

Now Jamie's curiosity was up and running. What do you mean by "Combat Reconnaissance Marines"?

"The distinction of this honor, for me is that up until the times of my duty assignment there had never been a female assigned to a combat "Rec Unit"! It had not been allowed due to the overall Marine Corps policy banning women from combat and recon service. I should note here that there are two distinct and different types of service, as not all Combat Marines are Recon. members. Both of these assignments provided a key element and step forward in the women's 'equal rights' movement as it allowed for the first time ever, women's role as Combat and Recon members alongside their male counterparts!

You see, up until 1975 women were not allowed to serve in any combat units within the Marine Corps. I believe other branches were allowing it...but not the Marine Corps which held to the old-fashioned values. The motto of the female Marines at that time in history was, "To free a man to fight"!

With this first female Marine assignment, (that I was granted the privilege of holding); this started the process of ending the female gender bias and stigma within the US. Marine Corps forever. This first acceptance and assignment into what had been an all-male Marine combat unit is something that many current and future female Marines now can take for granted. This assignment started the overall military equal treatment of their female personnel and that is why it was so important!

Although the change is real, it is slow but is steadily growing. For male Marines to accept the females as their equal may still be being sorted out due to ongoing old-fashioned values that are still well entrenched into our modern society (both male and female). I believe my combat and Recon. assignments became a key turning point in the history of the Marine Corps treatment of women. This is why I feel so privileged to have been a part of the change leading to how all military women, not just the Marine females, are now treated today, and as a result, will be treated into the future!

Now Jamie, actually quite taken aback by the little seminar, was looking hard as Chivonn." Well, what about you know-all the killing?" And the answer was straight away but not expected. "Yes, I did, and I still have nightmares and deep regrets for that, and I was treated, probably due to memories of that, for PTSD. But that isn't of course a female thing, it is a feeling of humanity deep in some of us, and you know it happens very much to the guys."

Just as she said that a tall man, very buff, quite handsome joined and said simply, "She is right on all accounts!" which, perhaps because of the great looking handsome man, left Jamie with glowing eyes and no further utterance.

Then the second remarkable party event occurred! Chivonn knew with great surprise who he was, and he surely knew her! My god, "Gabe" she exclaimed! This was in such volume that almost everyone in the party looked their way. It was Gabriel -Skellan's son, who most at the time of Chivonn's service thought had been killed on a raid to save some children in a Muslim school from an improvised explosive device (IED).

So there started between the two a tour of military memories, She, of all her Marine times, the ins and outs of seeming impossible adventures and He his times as Corpsman tending the wounded and destitute. It was of course a perfect teaming, because the Corpsman is the medic to the Marines. Gabe did tell her of his attempt to save those school children, where he failed and was wounded, but where his memory was now and forever locked in the fact that saving them was impossible! And, of course, Chivonn described the last of the life of the pimp she encountered in her time in the dark alley and on board the Navy Patrol Boat.

Even so, as dusk came and the party wound down, Chivonn could not escape from Gabriel's story, the tragedy, so many children sucked up in the stupidity of adult selfish agenda.

Consequently, she left the party, even more resolved to pursue her goals...and once at home began immediately to outline the next section of the Prospectus.

Thanks to Taylor, coffee and snacks were provided to keep her going. It succeeds in being a late-night mission but an outline with possible reference sources was set up for the next section she chooses to call "What Promise is Inside".

Reflecting on this Chivonn thinks for the first time firmly on what must be said later in the prospectus.

To get out of this mess we are in, doesn't there need be a new population of humans, an upgrade so to speak, that is evolution is not complete, we must evolve further and rapidly?

She slept the rest of that night, this idea rolling around in her head, proposing different ways that needed to occur. Thinking I would be pretty darned nervy to suggest this with my prospectus and committee defense! I don't think anything like that has ever been done!

Although it was a restless and somewhat short night she followed as always-the way to awake and enter the day that she saw every day in India and learned from the Jains'-the Samyaks.

Wake up early (she was up at 5:30 a.m.). As you rise put your palms together with your back straight, take three deep breaths, and say your prayer (Her Jain friends did the Namokar Mantra three times).

Start your day with respect. As she observed, take shower for seven minutes do not leave water running, turn off lights, save energy. Then do three minutes of meditation (The Jain coupled this as she recalled with a prayer/suti).

Then back into marine fashion from that truly entrenched military habit she made her bed tight and neat, hospital corners, a quarter dropped on it must bounce!

In the kitchen she continued her "Jain" routine. Breakfast was soy milk, natural grain cereal, whole wheat bread as toast, Jain style fruit Jam she made. and fresh squeezed fruit juice (no grocery store juice with all the preservatives and fructose).

Somehow the routine (she was used to that as a marine) felt good as now she was entering her days as a civilian but wanted the solid feelings of a great start. It placed a sense of cleanliness, economy and very important order on the start to the day!

At work, so armed to push on she spent every minute she could find to cap off Section Seven and then push ahead on research for Section Eight.

A great convenience was the University Library right down the hallway for that research.

Chapter 9

BUT ISN'T PROMISE INSIDE?

OR --- WHO WE CAN BE!

- The "Documents on the Wall"
- Prospectus Section Seven-Items
    - 7a. What leads to success?
    - 7b. What is Empathy?
    - 7c. Is caring linked to Empathy?
    - 7d. Can Empathy be taught?
    - 7e. Do Empathy degrees cause loss?
    - 7f. Can reasoning help?
- Hoping for "Best Little Scientist's Constructs"

Documents on The Wall-

The day continued with Chivonn back at the lab double checking the prospectus-section six for errors and section seven's research so far was piled on her desk, crying out to be written!

Even so, when six pm. came, wanting anything else but to dig into more research, her eyes dry and tired, Chivonn closed out the day- returned home and found a lovely dinner prepared by Taylor. It was a "Bakri Pizza" from her Jain recipes.

The time together discussing their plans for next August relaxed her. After all the conversation was about their forth coming wedding. Later Taylor serving desert and somewhat surprising Chivonn asked "Was it hard to meld into the "Academic and Lab World" after your "Military Background"?"

She thought for just a moment and responded "Well, I was accepted pretty quick because of that profile on me I wrote and my

Offspring - 167

scores on the graduate test. But, Oh! You mean acceptance in the Lab. Well, the orientation (Dr. Jordyn's Protocol) was to read "The Words on the Wall" out loud with anyone of the Lab assistants. "Words on the Wall" I don't get it, what are you talking about?

Well, there are three framed documents rather large on the wall up and behind the bench with the analytical instruments.

They are very professionally presented, and the text is large enough, so it is easy to read, which I did with Dr. Bean as my witness, you know Tim?

I took pictures of them on my Smart Phone! Want to listen as I read, I don't mind doing it again, it helped me and him bond over comments!

Taylor acquiescing, she read them as follows saying "I will read them in their left to right order 1-3. This is what number #1 entitled "Existence" says...

EXISTENCE!

We recognize that our lives are dictated by the causes and effects, the power of the Cosmos. That is the final Karma, directed, unavoidable, and described following.

1. We live in an unbounded Cosmos. The outer limits are as a box or a sphere but have "walls" that are zero in thickness.

2. The principles of Einstein's relativistic field theory apply to all matter.

3. Matter can be interchanged to energy and vice–versa but the net is always the net.

4. Everywhere is a space-mass-time continuum.

5. A Governor for humankind's future, that entity, should it exist must be capable of altering the laws of mass-energy.

6. Each creation of the worlds in the cosmos and all creations within these worlds occur by chemicals coalescing-each formation dictated by its order of mass-energy.

7. The possibilities for these creations are so vast that they are infinite. Change in their order occurs only as dictated by the forces within the Cosmos; mass-to energy, energy to mass that is the only constant.

8. Life on our planet is derived from an earth conditioned association of mutate-able nucleic acid base arrangements named DNAs and RNAs.

9. This same life type could occur elsewhere by probability theory, but it is also reasonable that with billions of possible chemical associations one and only one intelligent, self-knowing organic-DNA based life structure developed on our planet. This unique species-the Hominid gave rise to our human form the Homo sapiens.

10. Given that progressive mutation is an allowed mass-energy change we Homo sapiens are, thus, through our progressing brain DNA the only creatures in the Cosmos likely capable of analyzing the source of existence. We think of it now, and as our minds improve, given time, we will eventually recognize it in complete knowledge.

11. As thinking creatures, allowed within the limits of this Karma, we have choices. We could accept our existence in a selfish way feeding always on our individual desires or take a stand in defense of our species, protect and provide for our young, throw down our dissimilarities and develop our societies for the greater goal; the acceleration of our thought processes to be the governors of this incredible unbounded Cosmos, to be those who finally understand the genesis of existence.

It is the latter objective, the natural mandate, the just inclination of our species that we choose.

We recognize first that the Cosmos is our real home! The reality of life and death, substance to energy, and rebirth of energy to substance demanded by the forces in the Cosmos dictates an overarching action to preserve our species! It is impossible to circumvent this because the future of Humankind matters to us for the sake of our children.

Survival for our kind is in turn, dependent on our ability to resolve our existence with each other. To this end we will develop the empowering conviction that we all are together ultimately–the record and extension of our own lives.

What we do today, for our needs will be through and thorough in the lives and future of our children.

Looking at Taylor warmly she could tell he was captivated. Indeed, he said "My...Oh my God- those are some '*Words*"!

Well let me continue...I will read the words on Number 2.

It is called rather appropriately "Realization".

REALIZATION!

Rationally, we realize that all things, all feelings and experiences are impermanent. Except for One's record of life there is no one thing or possession that lasts forever. We can, however, in the time occurring behave in a benevolent way, enjoy life immensely, its challenges and frequent rewards and achieve a sense of mental peace.

This we obtain through our Self Control, which will lead to compassionate behavior practiced to each other. Therefore, the troubling part of life; the conflicts between us are put aside, and we can enjoy all the other aspects of existence, the thrill of creating, of loving, of raising our children, of building for the future. We can strive to change ourselves in this way. This we know will increase the life span of our awesome species into the far distant future.

Above all, we can fix an essential. That is, we believe there can be a future for Humankind. We believe that each human being is precious and important, and all have the potential to develop into perfect human beings by replacing hatred, anger, spite and jealousy with love, patience, generosity and kindness.

We know that no one saves us but ourselves! Even if higher power prevails, that is expected of us. We are governed by our Karma, that personally through our actions recognizing that they have consequences and the inevitable cause and effect through the Cosmos.

We know that those are the realms and irrevocable principles in which we, but most importantly our future exists!

Finished with reading that, both she and Taylor held hands as he said "I see! And what you are trying to do recognizes that." Chivonn said quietly "Yes, my love. and then there is that Third set of "Words on the Wall." I will read."

MISSION!

If our eyes are truly open the mind recoils at the terrible fate of children around the world. Used as shields on tanks, tortured, starving, disease ridden- -thousands die every day with no hope. These children are surrounded by adults, buried in selfishness, who have lost the sense of empathy!

One cannot help but reflect on the fate of those children and their children's-children. What kind of future, which is-the long- term future can be developed for the continued existence of humans?

Around the world we are imprinted in truth books, steeped in superstitious hope of individually lasting forever, thereby deflecting our attention to our brethren, those children even in the here and now.

Yet our ability to think, to be at first mindful, is a gift so incredible-gifted by the forces in space and time---it would be the most terrible of all crimes ever-to lose that potential, through aberrations of greed and inhumanity.

If there is an answer, a way to survive the species, it seems from the long history of failure-that it must come from a change in the way we view ourselves, the way the Minds-Eye functions.

Clearly, we must develop a new Mindfulness, one that leads to mental security for each person who is then progressing in a universal mind set, as a member of the whole species!

This will be an individual who recognizes that we can evolve; if we plan as one mentally expansive world community, we will see an awesome future. These people are needed now- Future Navigators with whom you stand!

~~~~~~~~~~~~~~~~

Taylor as he listened intently, looked at Chivonn with absolute admiration. Then he said "And reading those words in the Lab, so very much your own mind-set made you immediately recognize that you were a companion, a soul mate for all the team in that lab".

Chivonn said simply, absolutely! And, she said there was more available in the lab, its character and other documents. So, she continued…

The folks there are bonded very much like a family, they are indeed working as "Future Navigators". Then pulling out two documents from the desk she sat with Taylor opening them for display.

Offspring - 172

They share, and now I do too, as it is so essential, so important these two guides.[1] The first here is called "A Declaration of Light for the World". It lays down a manifesto containing sets of values and behaviors to provide security and mature development for all the world's children.

The second teaches 50 steps for developing a free and rationally based mind, which is a "Healthy Mindfulness". Each member of the Lab is trained in and supports these ideas.

Taylor browses, states "This is really solid... and what do each of your colleagues do?" "Well briefly Dr. Jordyn and the techs are working on ways to repair damaged tissue. Yes, it is indeed true in the base lab research they are constructing cells from biochemicals off the shelves, goal to prolong life.

Dr. Bean is an environmentalist-impact on living tissue, Dr. Pi is inquiring into ways to secure the reality and our physical need for us moving into the Cosmos, Dr. Jehan teaches the Principles of the Mind', now that is largely to medical students, Skellan as you know disarms the weapons of war to help children from being killed or injured (all the left-over land mines, for example). But he also helps in the lab. He inputs information on damaged tissue gathered from medical records.

Angelei teaches classes in the U.S. where she describes the benevolent foundations of the world's religions. This is to lay the foundation that killing for religious reasons is contradictory and destroys children, the hope of all faiths and philosophies. And others in the lab have a wide variety of interests that are designed to support Dr. Jordyn's research and the development of programs aimed at securing the future.

For example, Jane is in charge of guiding the establishment of the "Skies" program which is based on and contains among other critical information the two documents you have in your hand.[1]

---

1. The central philosophy operating for all of these documents is termed "Objective Humanism". That is described in Chapter Eleven, along with details of a program called "Skies".

You know Tyler, I am so glad we got into this!

The people I work with have so much "Promise Inside" and that helps me to see what is important as I write this next chapter of my Prospectus.

So, with the added stimulation, her lab colleagues and Tyler's interest Chivonn focused each day coming on that part of her document. She knew it would be central and must be very thorough and carefully presented. And to help, Dr. Jordyn temporarily relieved her of her lab assignments...with return in three weeks. By this time the doctor was himself very much into her communications to him via the Prospectus, finding it a very informative traverse through issues of importance.

The Prospectus continues as the completed Section Seven following.

SECTION SEVEN

WHAT PROMISE

IS INSIDE?

7a. (First) What traits lead to success?

Here is a particularly relevant description by Thomas Koulopoulos the founder of the "Delphi Group". "We all have our own definition of success. For many of us it's measured primarily in terms of money and wealth, but there are clearly other important aspects of success.

Some people value the freedom to spend their time as they want, others value the ability to help those in need. Yet, whatever the metric, there are a core set of personality traits that are common to all successful people.

I have seen these traits first-hand in a diverse set of successful people I've worked with and known over the years, from billionaires to budding entrepreneurs. Each one was very different and yet they all shared much of the same DNA when it came to the traits that made them successful.

Take a look and see how many of these are reflected in your own behaviors. I'd venture a guess it's more than just a few. By the way my favorite is #15. When I think of the greatest success stories, from Disney, to Oprah, to Jobs it is this trait that most allowed them to overcome the past and build the future.

1. A Need to Compete--I've yet to meet a successful person who does not have a deeply rooted competitive streak. Being successful is fundamentally about needing to win; the reasons vary, but the determination doesn't. Successful people obsess over creative ways to get a leg up on their competition. And they hate losing with an abiding passion. People often confuse this with work ethics. But working hard isn't the objective. It is the competitive drive to do more than anyone else in pursuit of your dream that paves the pathway to success.

2. The Capacity to Let go--There is an important corollary to #1 above. I don't care how successful you are, holding onto to the past or your latest mistake will only serve to slow you down. Successful people are not anchored by the past. They learn from it--fast--and move on to a bigger challenge.

3. A Passion for Improvement--Successful people are perpetually trying to improve themselves. They are their worst critics--never satisfied; always striving to be better. The person they most need to best is themselves.

4. Obsessive Attention to Detail--Yeah, this one drives everyone who surrounds a successful person crazy. But it also drives excellence. This seems to fly in the face of the popular mantra, "Don't sweat the small stuff," but most successful people got there by doing just that when they were the ones doing the small stuff.

5. Keeping an Inventory of Accomplishment--Successful people keep track of their achievements, not because they necessarily want to put them on display, although many do, but because it reminds them, and those around them, of how overcoming the impossible is often just a matter of dogged perseverance.

6. Compulsively Working their Network--One of the most consistently common traits of successful people is their ability to relentlessly work their network. All success is built on a network of human connections that needs to be nurtured and reinforced.

7. Rewarding Themselves--When you're running at full throttle you need to take time to take care of yourself. Emotionally and physically. That may be as simple as a short meditation or a full-on workout, a hobby that indulges you, a philanthropic contribution, or a spontaneous getaway. Whatever it is, the purpose is to avoid burnout, stay centered, and remind yourself of why you're making the sacrifices you're making.

8. Being Grateful--I recall doing a series of interviews with space shuttle astronauts, incredibly successful people who had every right to be arrogant, and yet they were the most incredibly grateful people I'd ever met. They realized how fortunate they were to be where they were and weren't shy about sharing it.

9. Not Wavering in a Crisis--One of the greatest determinants of success is the ability to keep your head in a firestorm. Successful people do not lose their sense of purpose or direction in a crisis, and by doing so create a reliable compass setting for those around them.

10. Striving for Authenticity--It's nearly impossible to achieve any degree of success without being trustworthy. For successful people being authentic means that they are clear in expressing their opinions and consistently truthful and transparent. You don't have to agree with them, but you'll never be confused about where they stand.

11. Taking Responsibility--Inevitably even the most brilliant successes will falter. Owning the failure is a trait that not only engenders trust but also demonstrates to others that failure is not something to be hidden or passed on to the next person in line.

12. Advocating for Their Customers--Even the most hard-nosed and callous CEOs become models of charm and deference when they are in front of their customers. They realize that the only reason they are where they are is because of the loyalty of their customers.

13. Discounting the Praise of Others--Successful people find that their jokes get funnier and the number of people who agree with them rises exponentially. I've sat in conference rooms with CEOs and EVPs of F500 companies who are treated like deities. Successful people do not let it get to their head. They realize that agreement does not constitute infallibility.

14. A Desire to Give Back--One of the most rewarding things about achieving any degree of success is opportunity to encourage and motivate others. Successful people realize that they have the power to help others increase their confidence in themselves. In doing so they create life-long loyalty that comes back many times over. Personally, nothing has amazed me as much and been as fulfilling as the support I've received from colleagues I've helped find their own success.

15. Refusing to be Defined by Their Failures--Nobody is 100% successful. Success is a net positive outcome that always includes an abundance of failure, experimentation, and learning. Scientists tell us that the universe itself exists only because there was an incredibly slight margin of matter over antimatter, amazingly just one particle per billion; it took a lot of destruction to create what's left. If you fear failure, then, by definition, you are avoiding success. Get over it; the universe leans towards success!

And your success is based on other people, your attention to their needs as you work on your own! "

In brief, if one really analyzes this...success occurs in people who think-who have a strong internal (to self) and external (to accomplish good goals) sense of empathy.

And, their success is counterbalanced as it also belongs to people who ward off wasteful charismatic influences through their guarded reflexes based on critical comparisons.

This empathetic rational guarded persona, the successful leader is critical to what would solve many of our problems in the future.

This begs the question about their emphatic side, what is it? Is it simply a learned characteristic?

It is easy to find accounts showing people are concerned about its origin as in this touching example from the "Open Journal of Philosophy" (2014).

"Twenty-three years ago, my husband and I were strolling with our toddler on the steamy streets of Yogyakarta, Indonesia, where we were taking a time-out before diving into our careers.

At eighteen months, Zai was toddling ahead of us, and I watched as an elderly woman approached her, cupped hands outstretched, in the universal request for food or money.

I held my breath as Zai offered the woman her most precious possession: her stuffed kitty! I did not want to interfere with Zai's gesture of compassion—but the kitty was her security object.

As for Zai and her kitty, the old woman responded by gently guiding Zai's laden hands back to her chest as if to say, "Thank you. I appreciate your offer, and I see that you are just a child. You keep your treasure."

Children's kindness often brings out the best in adults!"

It seems to us in the very young at the start of life we may have a sense of concern for others, a sense of empathy.

To clarify this idea, first is definition, then source, how developed, and finally how can it be lost. To the later this Prospective author will bring forward "The Kelly Effect".

Then finally there must be addressed the need to preserve it-that sense of empathy which is detailed beginning in Section Eight (In this book Chapter 10).

Section 7b. What in more detail is Empathy?

Antonio Guillem provides this analysis. "We know much about empathy. We are born with a sense of empathy.

Empathy is the bedrock of intimacy and close connection; in its absence, relationships remain emotionally shallow, defined largely by mutual interests or shared activities.

Without empathy, we could live with other people, and remain as clueless about their inner selves and feelings as we are about those of strangers on a crowded subway car.

Empathy isn't just the engine for closeness and pro-social behavior; it also puts on the brakes when we are behaving badly and become aware of the pain we're causing.

Those of us who've had the misfortune of being intimate with someone high in narcissistic traits, combined with impaired empathy, know the devastation that can ensue. When there are no brakes and an excess of self-interest, you end up with scorched earth."

Yet for all the emphasis and value our culture places on empathy-especially as an antidote to bullying and other anti-social behavior there's real confusion about what it is and isn't.

There are several descriptions from experts as to what it is- are we born with it and can it be taught.

This is followed up by what it is related to-and how it could be affected.

The first discussion is drawn from articles by V. Manning-Schaffel, V. Jarret, J. Orloff, and D. Sauvage.

First though, according to Dictionary.com, "empathy" is described as "the psychological identification with or vicarious experiencing of the feelings, thoughts or attitudes of another."

Roman Krznaric, author of "Empathy: Why it Matters and How to Get It," describes the fundamental difference between empathy and sympathy: "Sympathy is feeling pity or sorry for someone, but without that extra step of grasping what that person is going through, or how they are experiencing the world," he says. (The difference is refined further below.)

And, indeed, empathy is variable, and felt at various levels. Some folks are able to watch the latest racist incident or school shooting unfold on the news late at night, roll over and go right to sleep. Yet, plenty of others can't watch the news past dinnertime, for the pain and agony they witness seeps too deeply into their skin and all hope for sleep is lost.

There is also a difference between feeling empathy for others and being an actual 'Empath'."

Judith Orloff in "Life Strategies for Sensitive People," identifies the empath and describes them as "emotional sponges who are so sensitive, they tend to take on the stress of the world."

"The gift of feeling empathy, or being an empath, is that you care deeply for others and want to help, says Orloff. Obviously, the downside of empathy is it can be mighty exhausting if one borders on the "Empath Side". "Empaths have an extremely sensitive, hyper-reactive neurological system," she explains. "We don't have the same filters that other people do to block out stimulation. As a consequence, we absorb into our own bodies both the positive and stressful energies around us."

"Nonetheless, empathy is an extremely important part of human personality. Orloff says the ability to feel empathy is, if you will, a little bit psychological tendency and a little bit neurological wiring."

"It is hypothesized that empaths may have hyperactive mirror neuron systems (the compassion neurons in the brain) and they work on overdrive feeling compassion," she says.

Even so, according to Krznaric, "Your capacity for empathy is likely a question of nature and nurture.

"Research (examples below) suggests that about 50 percent of our empathic capacities are genetically inherited and the rest we can learn, because empathy is not simply a matter of wiring, he explains, adding that adversity can also lend itself to the development of an empathetic nature.

I recently met a stand-up comic who has lived with cerebral palsy all her life. She has an amazing empathy with people who not only have physical disabilities, but who get marginalized by society in other ways," he says.

Orloff also mentioned how adversity contributes to an empathetic nature: "A portion of empaths I've treated have experienced early trauma such as emotional or physical abuse, or they were raised by alcoholic, depressed or narcissistic parents, potentially wearing down the usual healthy defenses that a child

Offspring - 180

with nurturing parents develops. Their lives lacked both sympathy and empathy."

People often use the words empathy and sympathy interchangeably, but they are, in fact, separate processes. When you feel sympathy for someone, you identify with the situation that the person finds him or herself in. This can be a perfectly genuine feeling; you can feel sympathy for people you've never met and for a plight you've personally never experienced, as well as for people you know and scenarios that are familiar to you.

But feeling sympathy doesn't necessarily connect you to the person or what he or she is feeling. You can be sympathetic to someone's situation while being completely clueless about his feelings and thoughts. Sympathy rarely compels you into action except, perhaps, writing a check when you see heartrending photos of abused dogs set to weepy music on television commercials. Sympathy doesn't build connections!

The emotional process called empathy is something else; it involves identifying with what someone is feeling and, additionally, *actually* feeling those feelings yourself.

This isn't a metaphor like walking a mile in someone else's shoes, but more literal than not, as neuroscience has shown. Sympathy is feeling for someone; empathy *involves feeling with them.*

Further to clarifying what empathy is, research shows that most people think of empathy as intuitive, more of a gut reaction than a function of reasoning, somehow connected to feeling or associated with the popular term "mindfulness."

Psychologists Jean Decety, and Claus Lamm, suggest that "empathy consists not just of emotion sharing (a largely unconscious process), but executive control to regulate and modulate the experience. Both are supported by specific and interacting neural systems.

Research shows that mimicry is part of human interaction, and it happens on an unconscious level; we mimic the facial expressions of those we interact with, along with their vocalizations, postures, and movements. Talk to a frowning person and you'll probably end up with a frown on your face too. This unconscious mimicry probably helped early humans communicate and feel kinship; it's the component that precedes empathy. Neuroscience also confirms that seeing someone in pain activates the parts of your brain that register pain.

Being able to take on the perspective of someone else-a cognitive function-is also part of empathy; it's thought that children begin to see how others see them around the age of four and, in turn, they are able to see others by shifting perspective.

Finally, the ability to regulate and modulate emotion is part of empathy. Since science knows that moods can be "contagious," the ability to self-regulate stops us from going down for the count when we empathize with someone who's suffering. Clearly being thrust into the depths of emotional turmoil yourself would be a deterrent to empathizing with anyone."

Then, to put a cap on the matter with its unquestioning importance in human behavior, where do we turn to find direct indications that we are born with Empathy. Here attention must be turned to studies that have involved children.

Until recently, researchers believed that true empathy doesn't emerge in children until the second year of life, after 12 months of age, when a more separate sense of self begins to be consolidated. Psychologists believed that to accurately appraise how another person feels requires greater cognitive complexity. Children needed to be able to separate what others might be feeling from their own internal experience.

But three researchers were interested to see whether true empathy might actually be evident earlier, in the first year of life. These are Ronit Roth-Hanania at The Academic College of Tel Aviv-Yaffo, Maayan Davidov at The Hebrew University, and Carolyn Zahn-Waxler at the University of Wisconsin, Madison.

Roth-Hanania, Davidov, and Zahn-Waxler went in to the homes of thirty-seven middle, and upper-middle class infants from eight to 16 months and set up three distressing situations:

"The mother pretended to hit her finger with a toy hammer and be upset for one minute (and she avoided eye contact with her child in this minute so as to not bias the child's response). The mother walked toward the baby and pretended to bump her knee, again showing distress for one minute (and again without making eye contact). And, the baby was shown a video of another baby crying for one minute.

The result was that all of the infants showed genuine empathy in emotional and cognitive ways. The younger babies' feelings of concern for their mothers' pain registered on their faces, from a fleetingly furrowed brow to sustained looks of sadness. Many cooed or made other sympathetic sounds. As the babies tried to figure out what had happened, their glances bounced from the hurt body part up to the mother's face and back. Some made questioning sounds, or they looked to the face of another adult for interpretation.

In the first two scenarios, the older babies, who were more mobile and physically coordinated, added behavioral attempts to comfort and help, softly patting their mothers and making soothing sounds. The 16-month-old made the most physical attempts to help, by far.

In comparison, the video evoked very few responses in all of the babies, showing that they no longer have the reflexive, contagious upset of the newborn, and that they are beginning to tell the difference between situations they can do something about and those they cannot!"

Although the exact central nervous system locus for empathy or it's inherit-ability is not yet known, it is clear empathy is within us, at least from the start.

~~~~~~~~~~~~

So, is it a struggle for empathy to be shown in today's world? Of course, it is as currently shown! Around the globe it fails. There are so many examples, but just consider we allow children to suffer the terror of chemical war in Syria!

But even at the daily level we see it's loss. David Sauvage, an empath performance artist who consults with corporations and entrepreneurs on building more empathetic cultures, says "The basis of empathy is emotional self-awareness -which isn't a skill fostered by today's popular ideas on achievement (i.e., winner take all)".

"The average person in our culture doesn't have much empathy toward others because we prioritize everything other than emotional well-being," he explains. 'How often are boys told to 'suck it up?' How often are girls told they're 'Acting crazy?' "How many times during the course of the day do we feel like we shouldn't feel a certain way, so we hide our sadness only to feel shame around that sadness? There's no healthy balance between the negation of people's feelings and the acceptance of people's feelings. The only way to cope is to disassociate," explains Sauvage.

Simply put, the average person in our culture (He is referring to the "civilized develop country") doesn't have much empathy toward others because we prioritize everything other than emotional well-being!

A meaningful and directed way of stating this is that we are attracted to presentations that serve us personally. Those "Charismas" sink into our being thus staying away our empathetic sense, which could mean the absence of deep feeling we feel inside us, for others.

So, that raises a number of fundamental questions. These are as follows: 1.) Is empathy actually a part of "Caring"? 2.) Can it be taught? 3.) Does it come in worrisome degrees causing its loss? 4.) How else could it be lost? 5.) Is it "reachable" by our sense of reasoning, and central to a fundamental concern in this Prospectus 6.) *Where is empathy embedded in the genome and how does that influence parent to child?*

7c. Are Caring, Altruism and Moral Sense linked to Empathy?

Taking that empathy is inborn as recognized by a good population of experts, the next question that arises naturally is caring for others, altruism and our "Moral Sense" linked to empathy.

Marilyn Gisk-Walker addressed this in 2014. The following quotes from her article published under the auspices of Scientific Research Publishing Inc.

"Recent neurophysiological research has identified areas of the brain involved in caring behavior. Evolutionary biology, in conjunction with neuroscience, seems to have an agreed-upon hypothesis on how to care; i.e., bonding behavior evolved via natural selection."

"Where does it come from? What are the manifestations? How and when is it a force for good, or not? Does caring behavior necessarily imply a moral sensibility?

First, what does 'Caring' mean? It is generally believed that caring behaviors in the human species are built-in; they are part of our evolutionary heritage and are often unconscious. The automatic identification with others, what Pfaff calls "the blurring mechanism", frequently results in moral behavior; e.g., a mother caring for her crying infant. But there is a distinction between caring and moral behavior.

The first is a given; the latter is not. For we are also capable of heinous behavior; just watch the news or read the newspaper. Moral behavior can result from both unconscious impulses and conscious decision making. It is easy to be moral when the impulse is not thwarted, or better yet-reinforced; e.g., a mother cares for her new infant. It is not easy when social forces or personal needs interfere; e.g., a teen-ager is part of a crowd whose approval he wants; and the crowd is bullying a kid on the playground.

Increased conscious awareness allows for more choice in difficult moral situations. Both top-down and bottom-up processing are involved. The lower level, which is automatically activated by perceptual input, the 'blurring mechanism', accounts for emotion sharing, the implicit recognition that others are like us."

Decety & Lamm commented, "The top-down regulation, through 'executive functions' modulates low levels and adds flexibility, making the individual less dependent on the automatic external cues. The possibility for reappraisal of a situation and increased exercise of control seems to be dependent on the development of the prefrontal cortex, sometimes called the 'executive suite', which continues to mature through adolescence."

So, we are created as human creatures to care about others! And we have the capability of using that caring for moral ends: "To do unto others as we would have them do unto us." That is, we can be 'Altruistic'."

It seems that altruism is not just a self-serving way of expressing self-interest but may be a part of human nature. And we also have the capability of emotional reconsideration, so that the initial impulse need not prevail. We can review, rethink and then act.

And Empathy must be what fires it up!

Also, recent work in evolutionary biology indicates that both socialization and care for others are part of our evolutionary heritage via natural selection. "We are born as proto-moral, social beings." Proto-moral in this context is the human capacity for morality as "a biological adaptation, having perhaps conferred a selective advantage on our hominin ancestors by enhancing social cohesion and cooperation" This is noted by Fitz-Patrick, 2012.

"Each newborn only survives to adulthood if given adequate care; groups only survive through cooperation. "Homo sapiens…as well as such closely related species, such as chimps possess instincts and emotions that are proto-moral. We didn't create the relevant instincts and emotions, natural selection did."

"A genetic disposition toward fellow feelings for one's kin is more conducive to survival and reproduction than a disposition toward complete selfishness. Individuals possessed of at least a modicum of fellow feelings will do better at dating, mating and child rearing" (Flanagan, 2002).

That is "Caring Behaviors", are an essential in good and healthy well lived human life!

It is generally recognized that these caring behaviors include altruism, emotional contagion, empathy, and empathy induced altruism.

So, what about altruism and why is it sometimes linked to empathy. Donald W. Pfaff (2007) describes altruism as "The 'Golden Rule', i.e., unselfish behavior to do unto others as you would have them do unto you." He claims it "to be both universal among humans and also manifest in other species".

Others define altruism differently. For Verplaetse (2009) for example, "An act of altruism requires not only unselfish behavior, but behavior which "reduces the evolutionary fitness of the doer and increases the fitness of the receiver".

Pfaff sees altruism "as a neurological adaptation of the mechanisms that support maternal-infant bonding that then are adapted for more general social relationships. Plaff's thesis is that many of the "brain mechanisms which evolved to facilitate reproduction have subsequently become available to support a much wider variety of friendly, support behaviors that have nothing to do with sex or parenting".

"They are at the service of more complex social relationships needed to maintain the Golden Rule. That is, of course, a prime example of altruism. We follow the Golden Rule; i.e., behave in an ethical manner toward others as a transference of the evolutionary mother-child bonding behavior to more general and expansive uses." He continues, "the brain does not have a signaling circuit dedicated to ethics. Rather it has mechanisms to make use of circuits that are already there." (Pfaff, 2007)

And according to De Schrijver, "the circuits that support moral intuition, like most of the structure and function of the human brain are innate, guided by subconscious modular processes that are the result of natural selection." (De Schrijver in Verplaetse, 2009).

Pfaff hypothesizes that "the mechanism at play in altruism is a blurring of identity between the self and the other, which takes place in the cerebral cortex. The loss of information, the blurring, causes the other's identity [to become] less easy to discriminate from oneself. The merging of the self with the other through, according to Pfaff, the blurring of the other's face is critical in empathy, identification, altruism. "When we recognize another as non-threatening, then it is decreased social recognition that someone is led to obey the Golden Rule. A person momentarily forgets the difference between himself and the other, and as a result he complies with a universal ethical principle" (Pfaff, 2009).

That is of course, in a universal vision of it is <u>an aspect</u> of right directed empathy.

7d. Can empathy really be taught?

Because it matters toward recovery of our future this has been argued as example the following.

Krznaric says "empathy is a skill that you can learn, like riding a bike or driving a car, and that some learn it really early in life. It's easier to develop the cognitive capacity to make that imaginative leap into someone else's perspective," he says.

To help her patients relate to each other, Orloff puts them into an empathy training program. "It can be as simple as getting people into the habit of asking others how they are and actually listening to the answer," she says.

That is in a sense, empathy is a skill that you can learn, like riding a bike or driving a car, and that some learn really early in life.

However, and this is a most important detail, Sauvage says teaching empathy is rarely a straightforward process! "If someone both doesn't understand what it means to be another person-and they don't care-you can't just ask them to close their eyes and do it. They will shut off," he explains. "You can't feel for others if you're shut off from your own emotional experience."

Although empathy is necessary to forge a better understanding between people of different cultures and belief systems, science says our brains may be wired to empathize more with people who look like us. A recent study published in Trends of Cognitive Science examined brain scans to better understand how the brain works in relation to racial bias and empathy. Consistently, people had increased neural responses to the perceived pain of the same-race compared with other-race individuals in many areas of the brain, at different times.

Such evidence suggests that there is good reason for empathy to be taught at a very young age! (To recognize we are all Human Beings)

As a leading example, Krznaric mentioned "Roots of Empathy", a Canadian-based global non-profit that teaches young, school-aged children to empathize with each other. According to their research summary, "children who participated in the program were approximately 50 percent less lightly to fight."

Clearly, empathy is a concern for others and is present in children from the beginning but not much has been known about how it unfolds or is affected early or later in life.

Studies of newborn babies show that they cry more to the sounds of other babies' cries of distress than they do to equally loud sounds of other types or even to recordings of their own crying. Psychologists believed that while this reaction foreshadows later empathy and suggests a hard-wired orienting to other people's feelings, empathetic distress throughout the first year of life was a more contagious, reactive, egocentric kind of response. Upset in others simply triggered, or got merged with, a baby's own feelings of anxiety or fear. (This somewhat disagrees with child studies noted above, yet still admits that babies do have empathetic feelings.)

While present in children, where is it located. Experiments in neuroscience, using MRI imaging, provide physical evidence that bolsters the theoretical understanding of empathy by pinpointing the parts of the brain involved. That's what research by Boris C. Bernhardt and Tania Singer showed in an extensive review of the scientific literature, including their own work. "Mimicry and mirroring the key parts of the theoretical understanding of empathy—actually take place in specific areas of the brain as well.

However, relevant to the underlying theme in this prospectus, this does not address the DNA function, i.e., the super sub-cellular location. Nor does it clarify the extent of transfer parent to child.

Even though the capacity for it is inborn can it be influenced and "adjusted" later in life.

This is a critical and a central question regarding human deep future. To lead into the future those involved must have a true sense of empathy, to feel the pain of the child there, to know ways to avoid it.

The best way to think about empathy is an innate capacity that needs to be developed, and to see it as a detail in a larger picture. It can, indeed, be influenced. The individual personality part of this is discussed later via Kelly's Set of Corollaries.

Various studies show infants learn to identify and regulate their emotions through successful dyadic interactions with their caretakers, primarily their mothers. An attuned mother who's receptive to her child's needs and cues is one who permits her baby to thrive and develop emotionally. By having his or her emotional states recognized and responded to, the groundwork is laid not just for the child's sense of self but sense of other. In time, that seed grows into empathy and the capacity for intimate connection. This is called secure attachment.

Children who don't experience this kind of dyadic interaction have a diminished sense of self, difficulties managing and regulating emotions, and sometimes an impaired capacity for empathy. Such an individual isn't comfortable in intimate settings, and has trouble recognizing his or her own emotions, as well as those of others. The anxiously attached adult may lack the ability to moderate emotions and may end up being swept up in someone else's emotions. That isn't empathy.

And, the capacity for empathy varies from one person to the next. Not surprisingly, the extent of your own emotional intelligence-your ability to know what you're feeling, to accurately label and name different emotions with precision, and to use your emotions to inform your thinking-will make it easier or harder for you to be empathic.

Perhaps this is why Orloff describes empathy as "the medicine that will save the world."

"When someone feels like you are empathizing with them instead of judging them, the communication between you will be dramatically improved," she says. Or, as Sauvage points out, "We could shift well-being to the forefront of our priorities. If we want to build a culture of empathy, we have to have a culture of emotional literacy," he says.

Further, of course, this requires actually listening to the answer when you ask how someone is. It is important, also, to note that some babies were more empathic than others, and those personality differences were fairly stable from ten months through 16 months. And all of us wanting to know, in this study, there were no sex differences in expressions of empathy. Other studies have found mixed results in babyhood, and more consistent differences seem to show up later in middle childhood when more girls than boys express their concern for others."

As an associated concern what is the role of parents in the development of empathy.

Carolyn Zahn-Waxler at the "Dx-Golden Gate ED Conference" in 2011 addressed this matter. Zahn-Waxler, who has studied children's emotional lives for decades, says that "parents often miss expressions of kindness in their babies, even in the presence of the experimenters who are recording the child's empathic expressions at that very moment.

In the flow of everyday life, tantrums, conflicts and other demands can obscure more gentle behaviors, and adults may start reinforcing achievement-related skills over helping behaviors in the preschool years."

"As it is teaching empathy and compassion has become a big focus among progressive schools. These studies suggest that perhaps kindness doesn't need to be taught anew as much as supported more continuously from an early age!"

However, as opinion from the author of this prospectus, I don't think evidence supports that everyone, every teacher or their organizations will do this, at least as we currently understand what deflects us.

Even so, children's empathy seems inborn, a gift that is ours as a society to lose depending on how we react to these earliest overtures!

7e. Does Empathy come in worrisome degrees causing its loss?

We all realize that there are levels or degrees in which we feel or act empathetic. This leads to consideration of something called "Emotional Contagion" and its influences.

Emotional contagion, as defined by Decety and Lamm, "is a form of somatic mimicry; i.e., the tendency to automatically mimic and synchronize facial expressions, vocalizations, postures and movements with those of another person, and consequently to converge emotionally. The mimicry is typically not conscious.

Emotional contagion may also exist in other species; and it is manifest in infants and children. Macaca mulatta monkeys observed a fellow monkey in pain from electric shock. They could turn off the shocks by pressing a series of levers. Presumably, they read the pain in their fellow's face, shared his distress and physiological arousal, and thus learned to act to reduce his suffering." In other experiments monkeys saved themselves and other monkeys from electric shock with equal alacrity" (Hatfield, Cacioppo, & Rapson, 1994).

The authors speculate that "emotional contagion was the major factor. Infants, from a few months after birth through first year of life, react to pain of others as though to themselves. When they see another child cry, the subject child cries. From around fourteen months to two plus years, children feel their own fingers to see if they hurt when someone else hurts his fingers. By two and a half years toddlers realize someone else's pain is not theirs."

"It is a puzzling incongruity that "people…are able to 'feel themselves into' others emotional lives to a surprising extent" (empathetic-ally) while being "oblivious to the importance of emotional contagion in social encounters, and unaware of how swiftly and completely they are able to track the expressions of others" (Hatfield et al., 1994).

It can readily be argued that this function is an element of Empathy. But while generally a good factor of personality, as is empathy. It can sometimes have worrisome outcomes. In emotional contagion the emotion of the other is catching, it is transferred and becomes the subject's own. For example, you can be infected by cheerfulness or hilarity, without knowing what it is about" (Decety & Lamm, 2006).

Decety and Lamm, however, see "primarily positive effects of emotional contagion." They point out "that from an evolutionary perspective it may have had survival value by helping humans to communicate. That is, it leads to more smooth interactions and increased liking. And further that it also seems to contribute to our ability to perceive and understand others' pain. Emotional contagion allows one to feel oneself into the emotional life of the other". This it is noted is a property of Empathy!"

But "given that emotional contagion frequently occurs without self-awareness, does it typically lead to awareness and action on behalf of the other? And, if so, will the action taken be appropriate to the other's needs since you can be infected by the mood of others without even being aware of them as distinct individuals?" (Zahavi & Overgaard, 2012).

"In some circumstances non-conscious awareness of another's pain could cause an adverse reaction in the observer that will result in retreat. In Freudian terms, can this experience evoke "defense mechanisms that allow the conscious mind to shield itself from painful unconscious information? There are those who may just want to flee!" (Hatfield et al.,1994).

"One 'MRI' study showed that observing fearful body expressions not only produces increased activity in brain areas associated with emotional processes but also in areas linked with representation of action and movement. Thus, the mechanism of fear contagion automatically prepares the brain for action" (Decety & Lamm, 2006).

Another and most significant potential negative impact of emotional contagion is that it may lead a person infected by other's reactions to more easily be caught up in a mob situation; e.g., bullying a kid on a school yard. It can cause the individual to lose her identity and join the crowd.

As Gustave Le Bon wrote (1896) in discussing crowd behavior, "feeling of membership within a crowd…contributed to an enlargement of the ego (a sense of power), that is more specifically a release of impulse...a sense of contagion, and a heightened suggestibility. Individuals in the crowd mimic the actions of the leader, and this mimicry, once initiated, infects all in attendance." That is why "The Leader" is so important!" (Hatfield et al., 1994)

The critical nature of empathy as a mark of maturity and in decisions is found in this description. "But that does not entail that the other's experience is literally transmitted to you. In basic empathy the focus is on the other, on his thoughts and feelings, and not on myself. The emotion of the other differs from the way you would experience the emotion if it were our own. Empathy is and is not first-hand experience; it is both like and unlike perception. It is like perception in being direct, unmediated and non-inferential. Unlike perception it is not being able to offer the fullest presence of the empathized experience—that presence is only available to the subject of the experience. Whereas emotional contagion is self-centered, empathy is essentially other-centered." (Zahavi & Overgaard, 2012).

Further to this subject, Zahavi, and Overgard, give a phenomenological account of empathy. *"Healthy Empathy requires that Individuals must be able to be mature enough to disentangle their own feelings, which is to attribute mental states to the target.* Self-awareness is a necessary condition for making inference about the mental states in others. It denotes a basic, form of intentionality, directed at experiencing subjects as such! *To have empathy with another person is in short to experience the psychological life of that person."*

According to Decety & Lamm (2006) "in the case of empathy, affectional sharing must be modulated and monitored by the sense of whose feelings belong to whom, and thus, agency is a crucial aspect that enables a selfless regard for the other rather than a selfish desire to escape aversive arousal. If emotion regulation does not maintain the separation necessary for effective evaluation and action, the cost might be too high and the identification with the other too painful. Then the empathetic observer might direct her attention elsewhere so as not to "pay attention to another's emotional state".

"The idea, however, that empathy can induce altruism is indeed recognized. Recent arguments are more compatible with the view that true altruism-acting with the goal of benefiting another-does exist and is a part of human nature." (Batson in Decety, 2012).

There are some possible consequences to this. Batson cites both good and bad potential impacts of empathy-induced altruism. "The good potential consequences are as follows. It can produce more sensitive care for those in need. It can improve attitudes toward action on behalf of members of stigmatized groups. It can increase cooperation. But empathy-altruism can also be used with negative effects. People can be motivated to avoid experiencing empathic concern; if it is too hard."

Batson cites the extreme effort involved; "e.g., pedestrians confronted by homeless people may want to avoid fellow feeling; People can violate their own standards of fairness and justice by showing favor to those they feel empathetic toward against the common good; It can lead to inappropriate responses." Batson particularly cites" paternalistic response that does not empower the receiver but keeps her in an inappropriate dependent position." Batson does support the generally accepted thesis that "empathic concern evolved as part of the parental instinct among higher mammals" (Batson in Decety, 2012).

Our sense of fear plays into this a working that can be counter to pure caring empathy. "Fear is an evolutionary adaptation in humans for self-preservation. Fear can change what a person sees or thinks he sees, and it can act as an inhibitor of action. We may be afraid before we know it. Sensory stimuli reach our sensory receptors value free; we know we are afraid only when the fear-producing stimuli reach the amygdale" (Pfaff, 2007).

Confirmation of the role of the amygdala in fear is cited by Pfaff in a study of monkeys. "Rhesus monkeys are afraid of both snakes and human intruders. Scientists injected "a small dose of a toxic chemical into the portion of the monkeys' amygdala called the central nucleus destroying this group of nerve cells". After the injection, the monkeys were much less afraid under the same circumstances" (Pfaff, 2007).

Pfaff cites a study of fear in two-year old children "When in distress, the children's tendency to freeze in place in mid-task was tightly correlated with their bodily reactions such as speeded-up heartbeat and elevated levels of stress hormones" (Pfaff, 2007). Pfaff suggests that the reaction of freezing in place in response to fear 'stems from the innate fear response that in nature…saves their hide from time to time; a stiff immobility would, for example, make small animals harder to detect against a visual background. Fear-producing stimuli may act upon us without our knowledge and prevent either awareness of another's need or effective action on her behalf' (Pfaff, 2007).

Berns cites an experiment in which fear seems to change 'what a person sees or thinks he sees' (Berns, 2008). "A subject successively was given a series of cards, each with a single line on the left and three lines to the right. The subject was asked to identify which of the three lines on the right was the same length as the one on the left. When alone, 95% of the subjects performed without a single error. The experiment was repeated with a group of people in a room. Only one was the subject; the others were plants unbeknownst to the subject. Answers were given out loud and the plants answered incorrectly much of the time. In that situation only one-fourth of the subjects answered correctly 100% of the time. Most subjects caved to group pressure about one-third of the time. Obviously, the subjects were influenced by others' judgment. Did the subjects perceive the lines differently or did they perceive them and then change their decision?"

As Berns asks, "Can other people change what you see?" Subjects were given a new task: To turn two 3 dimensional figures around to see if they were the same. Alone 86% of the subjects did so correctly; in a group, with the others giving incorrect answers, 59% correctly identified the congruent figures. An MRI study showed that the visual processing areas; i.e., in the visual, parietal and temporal regions were very active when the person looked at the screen. When the subject "capitulated to the group and the group was wrong [there was] more activity in the parietal cortex, as if it were working harder" and less activity in the frontal lobes."

Berns' hypothesis is that the subject worked harder to see differently and that "the group's answers took some of the load off the decision-making process in the frontal lobe. In the case of conformity, the virtual image beat out the image originating from the subject's own eyes."

When the subject gave the correct answer against the "unanimously wrong group" there was increased activity in the amygdala.

Berns' speculation from this is that *"nonconformity underscored the unpleasant nature of standing alone*-even though the individual had no recollection of it." (Berns', 2008).

As an additional note on loss of empathy to the rarer extreme, one needs to recognize how it could be affected by Psychopathy.

This is fundamentally categorized by "Mind Sickness" and includes, Paranoia, Schizophrenia, Hallucinations, and Delusions (believing things unsupported by experiences to be true).

To clarify, Mind Sickness damages your ability to think, feel, imagine, maintain your sense of proportion, control your emotions, and understand reality. Imagine what it would be like to have one part of your mind either not working at all, or working against you, affecting your ability to think, feel, and understand.

Any breakdown in one or more of your mind's workings can create enormous difficulties, but what happens if the part of your mind that is damaged is your ability to feel or understand others' emotions?

And, this being of such great importance and the existence of empathy fundamentally critical there have been efforts to consider the extent and loss of empathy in nations around the world.

An effort to rank 63 nations by empathy gives the top spot to Ecuador followed in order by Saudi Arabia, Peru, Denmark, United Arab Emirates, Korea, the United States, Taiwan, Costa Rica, and Kuwait.

The least empathetic country was Lithuania. In fact, seven of the 10 least empathetic countries were in Eastern Europe.

The researchers analyzed the data from an online survey on empathy completed by more than 104,000 people from around the world. The survey measured people's compassion for others and their tendency to imagine others' point of view. Countries with small sample sizes were excluded (including most nations in Africa).

While a top 10 finish for the United States isn't bad, says William Chopik, lead author of the study, he notes that "the psychological states of Americans have been changing in recent decades leading to a larger focus on the individual and less on others."

And, indeed, there is evidence that empathy gets lost. "These changes might ultimately cause us to leave our close relationships behind," says Chopik, assistant professor of psychology at Michigan State University. "People are struggling more than ever to form meaningful close relationships. So, sure, the United States is seventh on the list, but we could see that position rise or fall depending on how our society changes in the next 20-50 years."

Chopik says, "he was surprised that three countries from the Middle East—Saudi Arabia, UAE, and Kuwait—ranked so highly in empathy considering the long history of aggression and wars with other countries in the region. That could be because the study did not distinguish between feeling empathy toward people in other countries vs. people in one's own country."

The study, published online in the Journal of Cross-Cultural Psychology, was coauthored by Ed O'Brien of the University of Chicago and Sara Konrath of Indiana University. Konrath and O'Brien in 2011 published research suggesting that "American college students had become less empathetic over a 20-year span. Potential factors included the explosion of social media; increases in violence and bullying; changing parenting and family practices; and increasing expectations of success."

The latest study is the first to look at empathy on a country-by-country level. And while it "only grabbed a snapshot of what empathy looks like at this very moment," Chopik notes that "cultures are constantly changing. This is particularly true of the United States, which has experienced really large changes in things like parenting practices and values," Chopik adds.

"People may portray the United States as this empathetic and generous giant, but that might be changing. Certainly, there are evidences that emanating from the behavior at the political top, our sense of empathy, and caring for others is depreciating."

(Chivonn reflected in an e-note, sharing with her professor that the America she knew as the nation of immigrants, racial equality and tolerance, appears to be in process of being buried by loss of empathy. More of her e-mails are at end Ch.11).

That is a central issue. Just how susceptible in the end are Americans and for that matter those in any other nation's people to the ever-growing inhumanity proffered through the massive cyber world propaganda?

And so, in a nut-shell critical to holding empathy, the empathy that you were supposed to have can be diminished or gone or even carried in a way that takes one well off course.

Clearly on the basis of the forgoing arguments, there is reason to understand the genetic basis of empathy and ways to buffer it!

7f. Is Reasoning a buffer for Empathy?

In the vein of the last thought, can individuals argue in or out of empathy? Is there a counter-balance in the way we think? And, if so, how powerful is it? The following is summarized from Wikipedia.

Highly important is a rational mind indigenous to us or easily gained by people that could "Save the Day"? First discussed following regarding that question, is the subject of our "Reasoning".

"Reason is the capacity for consciously making sense of things, establishing and verifying facts, applying logic, and changing or justifying practices, institutions, and beliefs based on new or existing information.

It is closely associated with such characteristically human activities as philosophy, science, language, mathematics, and art and is normally considered to be a definitive characteristic of human nature.

Reason---or an aspect of it is sometimes referred to as rationality and reasoning is associated with thinking, cognition, and intellect.

Reasoning may be subdivided into forms of logical reasoning (forms associated with the strict sense): deductive reasoning, inductive reasoning, abductive reasoning; and other modes of reasoning considered more informal, such as intuitive reasoning and verbal reasoning.

Along these lines, a distinction is often drawn between discursive reason, reason proper, and intuitive reason, in which the reasoning process, however valid, tends toward the personal and the opaque.

Although in many social and political settings logical and intuitive modes of reason may clash, in other contexts intuition and formal reason are seen as complementary, rather than adversarial as, for example, in mathematics, where intuition is often a necessary building block in the creative process of achieving the hardest form of reason, a formal proof.

Reason, like habit or intuition, is one of the ways by which thinking comes from one idea to a related idea. For example, it is the means by which rational beings understand themselves to think about cause and effect, truth and falsehood, and what is good or bad. It is also closely identified with the ability to self-consciously change beliefs, attitudes, traditions, and institutions, and therefore is associated with the capacity for freedom and self-determination.

Psychologists and cognitive scientists have attempted to study and explain how people reason, e.g., which cognitive and neural processes are engaged, and how cultural factors affect the inferences that people draw."

Then what is 'Being Rational?' Is There Such a Thing as 'A Rational Person?' (This is a question asked and commented on by Prudy Gourguechon).

"Is there such a thing as a rational person? One opinion in a short answer is no. The harder you try to be purely rational the less likely it is you'll get there.

What people have is the capacity for rational thought. This capacity exists on top (literally) of a large neuro-biological apparatus that is driven by emotion. And to complicate matters further, we all have the capacity for thought that doesn't appear to be emotional but is very far from rational 'fantastic thought' let's call it."

"Finally, there's a fourth factor that comes in to play which is neither thought nor emotion—I'll borrow the term "self-state" from psychology. This refers to underlying individual mental patterns of inherent personal reactivity to the environment. (*Reaction to Charisma*). How much stimulation do you need? What happens when you are tired? When and how do you get overloaded? What leads to under-stimulation or boredom, and what effect does that have on your capacity to think?

If you are a leader, you are constantly making enormously consequential decisions. If you can't count on yourself to be rational (and you can't) what can you do? In each of us there is an ongoing mental minute where rational thinking, fantastic thinking, self-states and emotion dance with one another and exert mutual influence in ever increasing complexity. At any given moment, some of the thought and emotion is unconscious as well."

"There is nothing to be gained by trying to eliminate emotion and fantastic thinking. Even if it were possible, you wouldn't want to. They are the source of vision, motivation, energy and creativity. When operating outside of our awareness, they are also the source of big errors in judgement."

The cure is to practice, develop and keep developing self-knowledge. (*And a portion of it is your level of empathy.*)

When is my capacity for rational thought most likely to be overwhelmed by emotion? What direction do I typically go when it is? What fantastic thoughts do I hang on to? How do these lead to specific emotions and/or interfere with rational decisions? What are the various self-states I experience, what triggers them, and what happens to my thinking? In an earlier Forbes post, I wrote about practicing the capacity for self-awareness, the analytic process that leads to self-knowledge.

The idea of the rational human started to take hold in the 1600's, thanks to the Scientific Revolution when, among other events, Newton defined the laws of gravity and Galileo promulgated Copernicus' sun-centric vision of the heavens.

Recommended by Forbes; In 1632, Rene Descartes gave birth to modern Western philosophy with his famous statement "I think therefore I am", establishing that the capacity to doubt proves that there is a thinking entity-and this defined what it meant to be a person. The scientific revolution gave birth to the 18th century Enlightenment also known as the Age of Reason.

Time went on and we all came to count on the idea that we humans had a refined capacity for rational thought.

This despite the contribution from Sigmund Freud in the early 20th century, unearthing the very irrational and emotional unconscious mind as a primary motivator of human action. Nevertheless, the preference for a rationalist theory of who we are persisted.

Famously, it led economists to develop the theory of "the rational market" where a rational consumer makes informed calculations about cost and benefit and arrives at a rational conclusion. The idea of a rational market was exploded by the wave of observations generated by behavioral economists, who demonstrated that unconscious, non-rational cognitive biases played an enormous role in decision making.

The now well-known cognitive biases illuminated by behavioral economists are one type of fantastic thinking. Let's take the "gambler's fallacy" as one example. If I've flipped a coin five times and gotten heads each time, I'm sure I'm finally going to get tails on the sixth try, even though the probability remains 50/50.

These are automatic, more or less universal cognitive sets (fantastic thoughts), having nothing to do with emotion.

Another set of fantastic thoughts are highly personal. They too seem devoid of emotion: they are thoughts not feelings. But they are distorted thoughts, part of one's personal narrative, forged in childhood and reinforced by later experiences. "Everything I do has to be perfect. "I'm responsible for everything going right." "Nobody gets it but me." These non-rational thoughts are usually semi-conscious-lurking just below the surface of our thinking-and very powerful influences on our overall thinking process.

A final word about self-states—those phenomena that are neither thought nor emotion but nevertheless strong determinants of our actions. I pay a lot of attention to these when working with clients. Restlessness, uncertainty, boredom, over-stimulation, under-stimulation, excitement, flatness-we each have different tolerances for these states and different needs to achieve internal equilibrium and optimal functioning. For example, I tend to get anxious when faced with uncertainty, but paradoxically always seek and need the excitement and stimulation of new ideas and projects. One of my investor clients found it hard to hold a position because of innate restlessness. An organizational leader wanted a new position but needed a familiar social group to feel confident. A business owner selling the company he built from nothing thrives on the adrenaline rush of making critical decisions. How could he take on a role that was less intensely stimulating and still feel vital and engaged?"

Prudy Gourguechon is a psychiatrist & psychoanalyst who advises leaders in business and finance on the psychology of critical decisions, irrational behaviors as well as key business relationships. He says "knowing how you personally integrate emotion, self-states, fantasies and rational thought on an ongoing basis leads to the best possible decision-making process for people."

The term "self-state" is from psychology. This refers to underlying individual mental patterns of inherent personal reactivity to the environment. (*Charisma influences*) How much stimulation do you need? What happens when you are tired? When and how do you get over-loaded? What leads to under-stimulation or boredom, and what effect does that have on your capacity to think?"

French social and cognitive scientist Dan Sperber, with his colleague Hugo Mercier, describes the idea that there could have been other forces driving the evolution of reason.

Sperber points out that "reasoning is very difficult for humans to do effectively, and that it is hard for individuals to doubt their own beliefs. Reasoning is most effective when it is done as a collective-as demonstrated by the success of projects like science." *(A reason for Future Navigators, and groups like Skies!!!)*

Sperber says this could suggest "that there are not just individual, but group selection pressures at play. Any group that managed to find ways of reasoning effectively would reap benefits for all its members, increasing their fitness. This could also help explain why humans, according to Sperber, are not optimized to reason effectively alone. *They also claim that reason may have more to do with winning arguments than with the search for the truth."*

Alone? How do we face the world and circumstances around us? To this is best addressed the hypothesis of Kelly.

Hoping for "Best 'Little Scientists' Constructs"!

Kelly's ideas show the underlying complications of reasoning hence the challenge and need to deeply understand our inherent empathy!

Kelly believed that each person had their own idea of what a word meant. If someone were to say their sister is shy, the word "shy" would be interpreted in different ways depending on the person's 'personal constructs" they had already associated with the word "shy".

Kelly wanted to know how the individual made sense of the world based on *their* constructs.

On the other hand, Kelly's fundamental view of people as "naive scientists" was incorporated into most of the later developed forms of cognitive-behavioral therapy that blossomed into the late

70s and early 80s, and into "Inter-subjective" psychoanalysis which would lean quite heavily on Kelly's phenomenological perspective and his notion of *schematic* processing of social information.

Kelly's personality theory was distinguished from drive theories (such as psycho-dynamic models) on the one hand, and from behavioral theories on the other, in that people were not seen as solely motivated by instincts (such as sexual and aggressive drives) or learning history but by their need to characterize and predict events in their social world!

As she wrote this Chivonn was thinking are some too weak in this, on moral decisions, on deciding what must come to survive?

Constructs provide a certain order, clarity, and prediction to a person's world. "We step and do not step in the same rivers." Experience is new but familiar to the extent that it is construed with historically derived constructs.

Again, Chivonn contemplates as she reviews this. Persons interested in preserving the future must work to let people see the "Same Rational Humane River"!

Kelly defined constructs as "bipolar categories-the way two things are alike and different from a third-that people employ to understand the world.

Examples of such constructs are "attractive," "intelligent," "kind." A construct always implies contrast. So, when an individual categorizes others as attractive, or intelligent, or kind, an opposite polarity is implied! This means that such a person may also evaluate the others in terms of the constructs "ugly," "stupid," or "cruel."

In some cases, when a person has a disordered construct system, the opposite polarity is unexpressed or idiosyncratic.

The importance of a particular construct varies among individuals. The adaptability of a construct system is measured by how well it applies to the situation at hand and is useful in predicting events. All constructs are not used in every situation because they have a limited range (range of convenience).

Adaptive people are continually revising and updating their own constructs to match new information (or data) that they encounter in their experience. They are capable of reasoning to optimal output!

Future thinking people, which is in a term "Vistaviens" follow "Principles of the Mind". This is a fifty- step protocol that helps develop an unbiased mind, free of unsubstantiated dogma. See the Skies program in chapters following, for an introduction."

Kelly's theory was structured as a testable scientific treatise with a fundamental postulate and a set of corollaries. These are reproduced following in pointed quotations.

The Fundamental postulate: "A person's processes are psychologically channelized by the ways in which they *anticipate* events."

The construction corollary: "a person anticipates events by construing their replications." This means that individuals anticipate events in their social world by perceiving a similarity with a past event (construing a replication).

The experience corollary: "a person's construction system varies as he successively construes the replication of events."

The dichotomy corollary: "a person's construction system is composed of a finite number of dichotomous constructs."

An organization corollary: "each person characteristically evolves, for his convenience in anticipating events, a construction system embracing ordinal relationships between constructs."

The range corollary: "a construct is convenient for the anticipation of a finite range of events only."

The modulation corollary stating: "the variation in a person's construction system is limited by the permeability of the constructs within whose range of convenience the variants lie."

And the last of the set, focusing critical attention, are as follows.

The individuality corollary: "persons differ from each other in their construction of events."

The choice corollary: "a person chooses for himself that alternative in a dichotomized construct through which he anticipates the greater possibility for extension and definition of his system."

The commonality corollary: "to the extent that one person employs a construction of experience which is similar to that employed by another, his psychological processes are similar to the other person."

The fragmentation corollary stating: "a person may successively employ a variety of construction subsystems which are inferentially incompatible with each other."

<u>*The sociality corollary*</u>: "to the extent that one-person construes (sees) the construction processes of another, he may play a role in a social process involving the other person." That residing, holding within this last corollary is Empathy!

"Disordered constructs are those in which the system of construction is not useful in predicting social events and fails to change to accommodate new information."

Transitional periods in a person's life occur when he or she encounters a situation that changes his or her naive theory (or system of construction) of the way the world is ordered. They can create anxiety, hostility, and/or guilt and can also be opportunities to change one's constructs and the way one views the world.

The terms anxiety, hostility, and guilt had unique definitions and meanings in personal construct theory (The Psychology of Personal Constructs, Vol. 1).

Anxiety develops when a person encounters a situation that his or her construct system does not cover, an event unlike any he or she has encountered.

An example of such a situation is a woman from the western United States who is accustomed to earthquakes, who moves to the eastern United States and experiences great anxiety because of a hurricane.

While an earthquake might be of greater magnitude, she experiences greater anxiety with the hurricane because she has no constructs to deal with such an event. *She is caught "with her constructs down!"*

Similarly, a boy who has been abused in early childhood may not have the constructs to accommodate kindness from others.

Such a boy might experience anxiety in an outstretched hand that others view as benevolent.

Guilt is dislodging from one's core constructs. A person feels guilty if he or she fails to confirm the constructs that define him or her. This definition of guilt is radically different from other theories of personality.

Kelly used the example of the man who regards others as cow-like creatures "making money and giving milk." Such a man might construe his role in relationship to others in terms of his ability to con favors or money from them. Such a man, who other psychologists might call a ruthless psychopath, and see as unable to experience guilt, feels guilt, according to Kelly's construct theory, when he is unable to con others: He is then alienated from his core constructs."

We develop core constructs of ourselves, ideas out of that are refused, so if our core construct has no empathy, then we would behave non-empathetic!

Hostility is "attempting to extort confirmation of a social prediction that is already failing."

"When a person encounters a situation in which s/he expects one outcome and receives quite a different one, s/he should change his/her theory or constructs rather than trying to change the situation to match his/her constructs. But the person who continually refuses to modify his or her belief system to accommodate new data, and in fact tries to change the data, is acting in bad faith and with hostility."

Hostility, in Kelly's theory, "is analogous to a scientist "fudging" his or her data. An example might be a professor who sees himself as a brilliant educator who deals with poor student reviews by devaluing the students or the means of evaluation."

Because *the constructs people develop for construing experience have the potential to change* Kelly's theory of personality is less deterministic than drive theory or learning theory. *There are, in short, options for our behavior.*

So, on the positive side, if on common oriented impulse as that of empathy -people could (may) conceivably change their view of the world. And in so doing that could change the way they interacted with it, felt about it, and even manage others' reactions to them and change.

Thus, there is theory regarding humankind as having a choice to "Reconstrue Themselves" or this is a concept Kelly referred to as "Constructive Alternativist".

Clearly Empathy can be made to dissipate in some and for various reasons (as fantasy reasoning) and find deviations from benevolent core construct. And it is true that too many people have less drive to run their scientific adjustments than others. Nevertheless, the opposite is in potential, which is to construct deeper empathy.

That can be further influenced as to how they see themselves, when washed with a plethora of charismatic influences. These, however, when negative for society can be countered by what else is inside-our ability to reason or construct our views back to a rational point. But that to occur we must exercise our promise---we are creatures with an inborn sense of empathy and caring!

This description of what is inside as individuals, most likely applies also to us in mass, i.e. our Net Personality. We are susceptible at the empathy level, which is critical to our ability to work together, to remove the threats we have created.

Unfortunately, while this is the case, we do not know the genesis of our empathetic selves, and how much of that is transferred parent to child. Since it is clearly capable of influences in wrong directions (example, inhuman self-construction), sadly, we have-currently no way to understand the genetic mechanisms through which its higher empathetic purposes can be protected!

Chapter 10

CAN PAST BE TURNED?

OR WHAT COULD HAPPEN?

- Chivonn's Contemplation
- A Preface
- Section Eight of the Prospectus
    - 8a. Save the Alien
    - 8b. Find Everyone a Home
    - 8c. Love your Mother.
    - 8d. Change Bellicose Actors
    - 8e. Reality in Space-Time
    - 8f. Hinting Evolution Need

Chivonn's Contemplation

Chivonn wakes up after writing her entries on the subject of "Is Promise Inside", that is "Who We Can Be" with a million questions in her mind. However, again she sees the weaknesses that got us into our fixes and wonders whether our present level of maturity (evolutionary speaking) is sufficient to overcome the limitations.

With coffee in hand she looks out the window of her "four flights upstairs apartment", sees the mass of folks rushing by struggling to get to work, the vendors setting up on the street corner and reflects on the need for more people caring for those around them, but also the need to respond to what could really happen! She says out-loud, "It is truly very challenging!" Taylor comes up giving a hug reaching around her and she comments with an emotional voice.

"My love, it is so frustrating for me to watch and observe, as so many people do really care! But there seems to be no real interlinking unified force, no team work to correcting all the problems that humankind has bestowed upon itself."

"The problems are so varied and diversified, that the ones that want to do good and make it right are fractured and seem to have no team work or leadership guidance. In the main there is no real universal sense of empathy that will pull the various fractions together in one common goal that really gets positive results that can happen only through the synergy of all."

"We have made some head way, but it is so slow that is not readily recognizable. The problems of man's cruelty to man are not new and we seem to be continuing this same pattern over and over again. Our elders remember similar things that they faced, and found the answers for, but we as their children and grandchildren have developed an attitude of disregarding their knowledge and advice."

"Because of it we are having to reinvent the answers all over again and as a result of reinventing the wheel we are not advancing to the next stage to better understanding and growth."

"Currently our work force is younger, and many seem to have the attitude that older workers should be forced out as they are becoming a burden, and that the older workers do not understand the modern technology that is currently in place. But we need to start learning what a wealth of knowledge and experiences our seniors possess."

"There is a lesson there, namely that is in their lifetimes they have evolved! They have succeeded because of their inward focus of empathy for self and their outward empathetic analysis of others."

"That is needed globally. And to start they need to know how experience could resolve the problems.

Charisma is "Presentation" we are like flies to the light! We seem too often not able to resist. It has been taking hold and could in the future be the downfall of the species!

Even so, a careful examination of the problems reveals avenues of rescue! What could happen, the past created rising calamities for us that could be turned, given that we pay attention, stand up and focus!"

With that she decides to address each one of the worries facing us humans, and working the next several days includes the following in her prospectus section eight.

SECTION EIGHT

CAN PAST BE TURNED?

OR WHAT COULD

         HAPPEN?

A Preface: First, following are some thoughts from non-scientists on the various perilous problems discussed in this Prospectus[1].

To begin the following is from Blake Emerson; "Dramatic environmental changes are already taking place.

The climate has changed drastically for the past couple of years. Global warming causes extreme weather conditions in both summer & winter seasons. It looks likely that 80% of land will be either deserts or prairies in 2075.

With that being said, people SHOULD migrate more than ever to find a fertile soil. There MUST be alteration…so that not just the richest 1% profit from this situation and the difference between poor and rich people will be greatest (as the poor become poorer even in current times)."

~~~~~~~~~~~~~~~~

1. These first are from various established social media and internet forums author giving name..

From Gustavo Muslera: "Global warming and climate change is really screwing up things, and we will have at our back famines, revolutions, disappeared countries and a political global map different enough from our own one, in good part that is fueled by it.

Public-anonymity will be thing of the past. We will go around able to know most about everyone we meet or cross in the street. And we will think that it is all OK. Being surrounded by information will make pretty accessible today events but will make it harder to follow big trends."

'Corporation Aristocracy' will be a thing in most places. And we will accept it!"

From Jeff Wilsbacher: "In 60 years, at the accelerating pace of technology we've seen since the early 1980's (Information based technology has been accelerating at about 8% per year.) we would see about 3800 years of technological progress at today's rate (20 years ago cellphones were rare and big screen TVs didn't exist and the internet was dial-up only for most people so in 60 years today will look like the bronze age). It seems possible that we could disconnect our consciousness from our physical form well before that time.

Part of the concerns regarding Artificial Intelligence are that it could accelerate its own development so rapidly that we humans would be incapable of understanding the change. If this is feasible it's very likely within the timeframe you've given. Robotics, now in the first stages, which is infancy, will probably be ubiquitous. Biotechnology and (molecular manufacturing) nanotechnology will be fully developed. Given the massive technological changes we'll be seeing, the path of environmental destruction that we're on now is not a foregone conclusion (we might still have bees and birds and flowers then).

The atmosphere could be an apocalyptic 4C+ warmer than pre-Industrial times, leading to the death of 90%+ humanity. The survivors would probably eke out savage lives in the higher latitudes."

From Earnie Moe of the Baltimore City Police Dept: "In 2075 the age of 81will most likely be considered middle aged. Living beyond 100 will be expected. The genome would have been altered to the point that congenital abnormalities would be removed and replaced or "edited" thus eliminating genetic problems that expiring prematurely would be a thing of the past. Parents will be able to choose their babies eye color, body type, height, etc. in other words 'Designer" people!'

From Diana Hockley: "Author of Australian crime novels, granny of three, animal lover. "I would be surprised if there is a world in 2075. The rate we're going now it's deteriorating as fast as our friendships with other countries. Once we have killed off all the animals-and we're doing an excellent job of that, BTW-we will be following them because we can't stop killing each other. The biggest surprise would be if I were here in 2075, LOL I am glad I won't be."

From Irina Ostapets, Moscow, Russia: "While we can't know what will threaten our bodies in the future, cures and vaccines for current diseases and illnesses will surely improve by 2075. In the coming decades, some scientists hope to upload the contents of human brains into computers, allowing people to live forever inside a robotic body or even as a hologram."

From Nandan Choksi (Optimist): "I like technology, but I don't always trust it. Particularly if you're talking about a time roughly 60 years from now. Take a look at what has happened in the last 60 years, and you will get some idea. Certain things have peaked, such as population. So, in 60 years, population growth will have more or less stabilized. In 100 years or so, the rate of growth of population will be negative (hope).

Technology development has also more or less peaked. Sixty years ago, there was no Excel, Quicken, Photo-Shop, Internet, etc. Now, all we have is variations on those things.

The only really big change I can see coming is travel. I don't mean speed of travel or beam-me-up technology. I am talking about currencies and borders. I think we will have fewer currencies and fewer borders.

There is another massive change coming but I have no idea how it will turn out, and that is the switch from manual labor to robots.

My personal feeling is that money will decline as a means of controlling capital and labor. Whoever controls technology will 'rule the world' just as people with plenty of money rule the world today. I don't see a 'Matrix 'type of world. But still, it is inevitable that technology is power---the technology that controls production of goods and 'delivery' of services.

We already have books on demand---books that are printed and shipped only after they are ordered. We also have 3-D printing. So, why not cars on demand, guns on demand, homes on demand, etc.?"

Megan Meg (Optimist with Balance): "I hope my great-grandchildren have more sense than I do. But the way I see it is that world in 50 years will be full of robots. Robots who will do everything from washing dishes to working in mega factories (like they're doing right now, but lower scale).

Here's what will it look like: Robots will wash dishes, Robots will serve dishes. Robots will do laundry, Robots will babysit. Robots will cook and Cars shall drive themselves!

People will have the same needs and wants fulfilled by more sophisticated tools. Computers are going to melt into the clothing, walls, floors, and ceilings.

Almost no one will own a smart phone. You just talk into the air. Directional sound technology will work to keep voice calls as private as you want them to be in terms of decibels. You will not own anything since the computer will be everywhere. Instead, you will have a monthly subscription fee to the cloud to access all technology presented through aerial delivery. It will be a literal cloud experience in a pure hands-free world.

(There will be "Have-Nots") The Have-Nots include those that cannot afford the subscription which will be much higher than you can imagine. Physical labor jobs will be almost extinct. Part of the cause will be the evolution of eCommerce into an advanced predictive system. Periodically, the ever-present computer will ask you to simply confirm verbally or with a wink and nod replacement supplies and items of potential interest. Robotic arms will pick the product and drones will drop it at the doorstep. The have nots will increase until you have a new underclass known as the Subsidized Society of the World.

Climate change will be solved through geo-engineering. You can count on that. Developments there will not encourage heavy carbon producing industries. Green technology will still be more lucrative as it assuages guilt in the destruction of middle-class lifestyles.

The absence of workers, even for green tech, does not eliminate an economy. Those with means will simply switch from a consumption-based economy to a business to business economy. The margins will be higher and the circulation of money more predictable. Meanwhile, people will be so enthralled with the entertainment medium that succeeds Amazon Prime as to care less about the actual loss of freedom.

On the other hand, a few can take the opportunity to evolve higher with all the free time on their hands. Evolve art, science, literature, and making things. At least that is the hope that with so much advanced artificial intelligence we will become better people because of machines."

These examples show what some people wish, even propose for the distant future to overcome what is actually now happening. Unfortunately preventing the problems in some of these propositions is a major overriding problem, discussed later. Although it would be fascinating 100 years from now to see who was the best predictor- predictions do have limits!

On that subject, Tom Foale at Cresa-tech proffers these bits of fundamental wisdom. "Looking back at the world 60 years ago, most predictions of the future had more in common with the Jetsons or Mad Max than the way the world is actually today!

The primary reason for this is that we can only extrapolate into the future from what we know today.

Computers were monolithic, so we imagined ever smarter but still monolithic, computers. We expected to have space colonies, house robots, nuclear fusion, nuclear Armageddon, etc. Much of what looked achievable turned out to be much harder than we thought, and much of what happened, like the mobile phone, world-wide-web, obscene salaries for some professional athletes, was not predicted even though, with hindsight, probably predictable.

One of my favorite failures of prediction is that you probably own a supercomputer way beyond the wildest dreams of governments in 1955-and almost all of that power is not being used to calculate anything 'useful' like the GDP of a country or the weather next year. Almost all of the software on it was developed to make it easy for you to interact with the computer, rather than calculating something. Quite telling really-progress is about making our lives easier and more productive.

Extrapolating from what we know today will lead us down the same rabbit hole. We know more about prediction than we did back then, particularly about the power and dangers of exponential growth.

However, on what we already know about what is happening to us--- know we can take a rational foundation and... we could build much more powerful models of our world. But we still can't predict what innovation will and won't deliver."

The forgoing presents the way folks see our dilemmas, negative, positive, and null, i.e., unpredictable.

But truly the potential horrors (Chs.1-6) do face us! So, what then are the potential-the rational ways out of our dilemmas? The following presents thoughts on each of them, in turn.

8a. Save the Alien (AI)!

So many are worried about AI acting as a terminal agent. But thinking it through gives another insight.

To start, we might keep in mind it begins with computer code and ends up as "AI". The code is driven by electricity (electro magnetism). The computer is the seat, i.e., the sender of the activity. Inside that world it is controlled and operated by tiny invisible 1s and 0s that are flashing thru the air and through the wires in the machine that must be functioning to make AI.

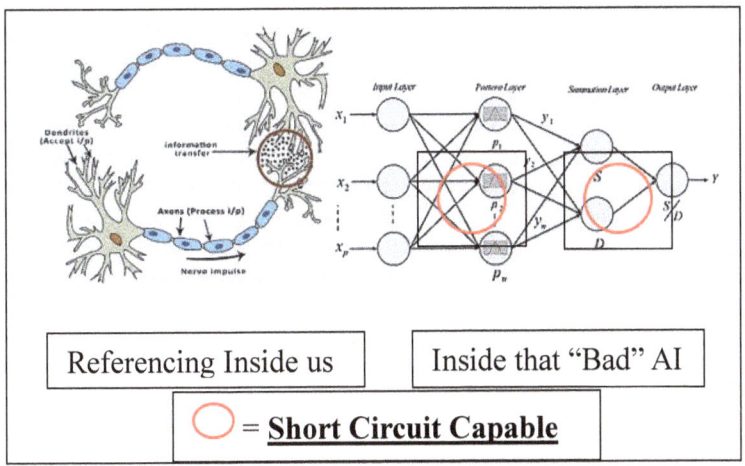

Referencing Inside us | Inside that "Bad" AI
◯ = **Short Circuit Capable**

And AI programing techniques are a select few that are knowable. For example, one of them is a heuristic communication technique. This is an analogy of our brains' "neuronal net-work", the way our brains seek stored information and feed it back for action. Just as by lobotomy our thoughts can be truncated, so could the leads (seeking referenced information) be truncated in A.I. programing to prevent the sought outcome.

The figure above is not to trivialize the matter as there are several approaches to controlling an AI. Yet, think just how easy by inserting probes into your brain it would be to disrupt your system of behavior and actions (again remember lobotomies?). In fact, a great many experts have thoughts on the "way to safety" of interrupting and truncating the actions of an aberrant AI. But more on that after noting some (just some) of the many valuable advantages in the development of AI.

That is, the negative (scared to death) view of AI often forgets the possible, very great possibilities for the future human!

Here is just a brief selection!

AI's Advantages in Health Care: Artificial intelligence is proving to be a revolutionary tool across many industries, but the technology is having a particularly big impact when it comes to healthcare. For example, researchers are using AI to combat the flu, by building improved seasonal forecasts that inform the development of influenza vaccines, and the technology is already helping to diagnose rare diseases so that patients can get the treatments they need.

A.I. has potential in crime solving. Hunting a serial killer is, according to experts, a fundamentally different type of detective work than any other type of homicide investigation. For decades the top investigators in this hyper-specialized field have turned to technology. In 2017 this means AI, and just like everything else, it's revolutionizing the industry.

It's impossible to know how many active serial killers there are in the US right now. The FBI thinks about 150 people a year are murdered by these predators. Other experts think that number is much higher. Yet, looking into the future, the abilities of AI, there's a dark future ahead for serial killers. There's an adage that goes "to catch a killer, you have to think like one" and this is true of computers as much as men.

So, 'AI' is being taught to think like a killer would in their environment by exposing it to all the information available on examples such as The Zodiac Killer, as reported by History.com's Brynn Holland and Missy Sullivan.

In order to take the hunt for these very real monsters to the next level, the data on serial killers is taken as seriously as Facebook treats its' data source. This requires AI. The New Yorker recently profiled Thomas Hargrove and his algorithms. Together, along with several other team members, they comprise the Murder Accountability Project (MAP). The group writes: "Thanks to some good old fashioned hardcore investigative journalism and a healthy amount of machine learning insights they've been able to create a map of murder. That may sound macabre, and it absolutely is, but it's also providing the type of pattern-based insight that AI is better at gleaning than humans. And while, presumably, there will always be twisted humans born with whatever affliction of the mind causes a person to commit atrocity, it's comforting to know that advances in technology are making our world a safer place."

Could A.I. solve the world's biggest problems? Advances in machine-learning techniques have opened up a wealth of promising opportunities for AI applications, but some tech executives are thinking about ways it can make the world a better place.

This is by Will Knight (2016). "Are we on the verge of creating artificial intelligence capable of finding answers to the world's most pressing challenges? After steady progress in basic AI tasks in recent years, this is the vision that some leading technologists have for AI. And yet, how we will make this grand leap is anyone's guess."

Eric Schmidt, the executive chairman of Alphabet says "AI could be harnessed to help solve major challenges, including climate change and food security". Demis Hassabis, CEO of Google Deep-mind, a division within Google doing groundbreaking work in machine learning, and which aims to bring about an 'artificial general intelligence' (see "Google's Intelligence Designer"), said "The goal of this effort was to harness AI for grand challenges. If we can solve intelligence in a general enough way, then we can apply it to all sorts of things to make the world a better place," he said.

And chief technology officer of Facebook, Mike Schroepfer, expressed similar hope. "The power of AI technology is it can solve problems that scale to the whole planet," he said.

"A steady stream of advances-mostly enabled by the latest machine-learning techniques-are indeed empowering computers to do ever more things, from recognizing the contents of images to holding short text or voice conversations. These advances seem destined to change the way computers are used in many industries."

Of course, at time of this report it is not yet clear how industry will go from captioning images to tackling poverty and climate change, but the salient point is that AI is a technology poised to succeed and there are those willing to enter the effort.

8a2. Can AI be made a good citizen?

Research to prevent AI problems. In Section 1 of this prospectus there was raised the many ways that people have envisioned that A.I. could go wrong and in very scary scenarios. This trend has led to increasing literature on the impact artificial intelligence may have on everything from jobs, education, to religion in the coming decades.

Progress with AI seems certain to revolutionize many industries, perhaps with negative consequences, such as eradicating certain jobs (see articles such as "Who Will Own the Robots?"). It will surely also raise new ethical questions, such as the legal and moral liability in such technology as self-driving cars, or the implications of autonomous weapons (see "How to Help Self-Driving Cars Make Ethical Decisions").

Nonetheless, *the very impressive progress with A.I. has inspired focus by a number of experts on the challenge of controlling AI should it become vastly more overcoming or even more powerfully independent. This is a focus on the future of AI as needed and is relevant! It is an area that can be addressed to a degree in this prospectus per the following.*

To illustrate, worries over the long-term risks of AI has inspired the foundation of a nonprofit called "Open AI" which is dedicated to the advancing of artificial intelligence that benefits humanity (see "What Will It Take to Build a Virtuous AI?"). "Open AI is funded by a billion-dollar grant from Tesla and SpaceX founder Elon Musk, who has been outspoken about the long-term dangers of AI, as have other technology heavyweights. And a wide range of experts acknowledged that the ethical issues should be taken seriously. As with any technology, however, "if it's going to be that powerful, we have to think about how to use it ethically and responsibly".

Scholars sometimes claim that predictions about an AI's behavior are "illogical anthropomorphisms". Paul R. Cohen and

Edward Feigenbaum argue "…in order to differentiate between anthropo-morphic behavior and logical prediction of AI behavior, the trick is to know enough about how humans and computers think to say exactly what they have in common, and, when we lack this knowledge, to use the comparison to suggest theories of human thinking versus computer thinking."

And there seems to be agreement in the scientific community that an advanced AI might not destroy humanity out of human emotions such as "revenge" or "anger". Indeed, some skeptics accuse proponents of anthropomorphism[1] for believing an Artificial General Intelligence (AGI) would naturally desire power.

Another example of the "over developed AI" defense as noted is the Open AI community, that non-profit artificial intelligence initiative with the mission to build safe AI and ensure AI's benefits are as widely and evenly distributed as possible. Open AI has been associated with technology visionary, Elon Musk and Y Combinator's president Sam Altman. They have recently released Universe, a platform that will let AI programs learn, through experimentation and positive reward, how to do all sorts of things on a computer.

In 2009, experts attended a conference hosted by the Association for the Advancement of Artificial Intelligence (AAAI) to discuss whether computers and robots might be able to acquire any sort of autonomy, and how much these abilities might pose a threat or hazard.

They noted that some robots have acquired various forms of semi-autonomy, including being able to find power sources on their own and being able to independently choose targets to attack with weapons. They also noted that some computer viruses can evade elimination and have achieved 'cockroach intelligence'. They concluded that "self-awareness as depicted in science fiction is probably unlikely, but that there were other potential hazards and pitfalls."

AI researcher Stuart Russell summarized the primary concern. "It is not spooky emergent consciousness but simply the ability to make high-quality decisions. Here, quality refers to the expected outcome utility of actions taken, where the utility function is, presumably, specified by the human designer."

In this there is the problem that the utility function may not be perfectly aligned with the values of the human race, which are (at best) very difficult to pin down. It is argued that any sufficiently capable intelligent system will prefer to ensure its own continued existence and to acquire physical and computational resources- not for their own sake, but to succeed in its assigned task.[1]

This is essentially the old story of the genie in the lamp, or the sorcerer's apprentice, or King Midas: you get exactly what you ask for, not what you want. A highly capable decision maker - especially one connected through the Internet to all the world's information and billions of screens and most of our infrastructure- could have an irreversible impact on humanity.

Although, this is certainly not a minor difficulty, improving decision quality, irrespective of the utility function chosen has, indeed, been the goal of AI research-the mainstream goal on which we now spend billions per year, not a secret plot of some lone evil genius."

Dietterich and Horvitz echo this so called "Sorcerer's Apprentice" (AI amuck) concern in a communication of the ACM editorial, that is, emphasizing the need for AI systems that can fluidly and unambiguously solicit human input as needed. Avoid poorly specified goals: "Be careful what you wish for!"

Mark Waser proposes to engineer a coherent system of laws, ethics and morals with a top-most restriction to enforce social psychologist Jonathan Haidt's functional definition of morality. That is "to suppress or regulate selfishness and make cooperative social life possible."

1."A Modern Approach", the standard undergraduate AI textbook, cites the possibility that an AI system's learning function "may cause it to evolve into a system with unintended behavior" as the most serious existential risk from AI technology.

Offspring - 224

He suggests that this can be done by implementing a utility function designed to always satisfy Haidt's functionality and aim to generally increase (but not maximize) the capabilities of self, other individuals and society as a whole as suggested by John Rawls and Martha Nussbaum.

He references Gauthier's "Morals By Agreement" in claiming that the reason to perform moral behaviors, or to dispose oneself to do so, is to advance one's own ends; that war, conflict, and stupidity waste resources and destroy capabilities even in scenarios as uneven as humans vs. rainforests; and that, for this reason, "what is best for everyone" and morality really can be reduced to "*enlightened* self-interest" presumably for both AIs and humans.

Isaac Asimov's Three Laws of Robotics are one of the earliest examples of proposed safety measures for AI agents. Asimov's laws were intended to prevent robots from harming humans. In Asimov's stories, problems with the laws tend to arise from conflicts between the rules as stated and the moral intuitions and expectations of humans.

Citing work by AI theorist Eliezer Yudkowsky, Russell, and Norvig, note that "a realistic set of rules and goals for an AI agent will need to incorporate a mechanism for learning human values over time. We can't just give a program a static utility function, because circumstances, and our own desired responses to circumstances, change over time".

In a paper that was submitted to the 2014-AAAI Spring Symposium, Richard Loosemore, argues that "any artificial general intelligence would self-modify to avoid pathological outcomes."

An AI researcher---Ben Goertzel stated, "arguments for existential risks have some logical foundation, but are often presented in an exaggerated way.

Super-intelligent AI will likely not be driven by anything like reward maximization, but rather by an open-ended complex self-organization and self-transcending development."

Citing major advances in the field of AI and the potential for AI to have enormous long-term benefits or costs, the 2015 Open Letter on Artificial Intelligence stated: "The progress in AI research makes it timely to focus research not only on making AI more capable, but also on maximizing the societal benefit of AI."

Such considerations motivated the AAAI (2008-09) Presidential Panel on "Long-Term AI Futures" to constitute a significant expansion of the field of AI introspection itself, which up to now has focused largely on techniques that are neutral with respect to purpose. "We recommend expanded research aimed at ensuring that increasingly capable AI systems are robust and beneficial: *Our AI systems must do what we want them to do!*"

This letter was signed by a number of leading AI researchers in academia and industry, including AAAI president Thomas Dietterich, Eric Horvitz, Bart Selman, Francesca Rossi, Yann LeCun, and the founders of Vicarious and Google DeepMind.

Institutions such as the Machine Intelligence Research Institute, the Future of Humanity Institute, the Future of Life Institute, and the Centre for the Study of Existential Risk are currently involved in mitigating existential risk from advanced artificial intelligence, for example by research into friendly artificial intelligence.

Chris White energy reporter (2016) noted that a super-intelligent hybrid human-computer-i.e., artificial intelligence - might be the ticket to solving "wicked" problems like global warming and war. Meanwhile researchers at the Human Computation Institution (HCI) and at Cornell University relayed the notion of power within machines for self-control. "If only scientists could find a way to combine the creative abilities of humans with the immense data analyzing capabilities of computers, then we could really get down to solving complex problems."

"The solution, according to HCI Director Dr. Pietro Michelucci, is to create a *human* computation crowd-sourcing social network-like Facebook but geared exclusively toward solving big-world problems. Michelucci argued in a press statement that the idea is akin to that of reCAPTCHA, a human computation spam-blocking security system combining the strengths of computers *and humans.*"

And it is important to note, the long-term and societal implications of this new technology were discussed in a conversation between President Obama and MIT's Joi Ito (covered by Wired magazine). President Obama indicated an optimism that historically new technologies are absorbed, new jobs are created and ultimately living standards go up. For Ito, the speed of progress might impact society sooner that we think and that we need people who want to use AI for good.

Joi Ito says, "What's important is to find the people who want to use the AI for good…communities and leaders - and figure out how to help them."

We can indeed find leaders and communities of the mold Ito refers to. One such leader is Andrew Ng, chief scientist at Baidu Research and co-founder of Coursera. Coursera is a global platform to provide universal access to the world's best education. Ng has made the point that AI researchers (like himself) … "have an ethical responsibility to step up and address the problems we cause." For Ng, who also founded the Google Brain project in 2011, Coursera was his personal step to do that!

Suffice it to say there are individual groups and thinkers working to make A.I. safe and productive for humans in the future. The question that relates mostly to this…Is there sufficient universal glue to put down the dangers and bring out all the incredible potential for everyone? Or in hard terms do humans have enough empathy for the safety of others of their species to do as they should and cooperate to make A.I. safe? If an A.I. risks any of our species in any way, be it physical or mental, our species needs to be concerned enough for each other to, yes, "Pull the Plug"!*

8b. Find Everyone a Home!

Overcrowding on Earth was the subject in the second prospectus section as one of the major catastrophic developments from past and present Offspring. Even so, is Claustrophobia due to over population of humans really justified? The following discussion treats needed clarifying aspects of this subject. It is a compilation of the thoughts of a number of experts on population growth. The details can be found by tracing the subject as excepted under the heading "Overpopulation" on line…in Wikipedia.

"Since the 1950s, many cities in developed countries have worked to meet urban environmental challenges. Los Angeles has dramatically reduced air pollution. Many towns that grew up near rivers have succeeded in cleaning up the waters they befouled with industrial development.

But cities at the beginning of their development generally have less wealth to devote to the mitigation of urban environmental impacts. And if the lack of needed resources is accompanied by inefficient government, a growing city may need many years for mitigation.

Strong urban governance is critical to making progress. But it is often the resource in shortest supply. Overlapping jurisdictions for water, air, roads, housing, and industrial development frustrate efficient governance of these vital environmental resources. The lack of good geographic information systems means that many public servants are operating with cataracts. The lack of good statistics means that many urban indicators that would inform careful environmental decision making are missing.

When strong urban governance is lacking, public-private partnerships can become more important. These kinds of partnerships can help set priorities that are shared broadly, and therefore implemented. Some of these public-private partnerships have advocated tackling the environmental threats to human health first. "Reducing soot, dust, lead, and microbial disease presents opportunities to achieve tangible progress at relatively low cost over relatively short periods," concluded conferees at a 1994 World Bank gathering on environmentally sustainable development…

…But ultimately there are many other urban environmental priorities that produce chronic problems for both people and the environment over the long term that also have to be addressed.

In short, cramming into cities is becoming the virtual death sentence for human future and the environment!

In surveying statistics on the environment, it is important to keep two opposing trends in mind. As said, one is the population explosion, swelling the cities. At present, we are adding the population of China to this planet every decade. Feeding and supplying this population explosion are placing huge demands on the environment.

And this brings us to the other actual opposing trend: the environment's resources as we are presently using them to the urban targeted populations are either reaching their limit or shrinking. The result will be "Like two trains barreling towards each other on the same railroad track".

Biologists, historians and economists all concur that whenever growing populations have met shrinking resources---the results have been pitched competition for survival. One outcome could be population growth slowing over the next century. But that is not certain!

The population explosion is compelling a growing number of scientists to advocate replacing our growth economy with a sustained economy.

Lester Brown, President of World-watch Institute, writes: "Among the principles of sustainability are the following: Over the long term, species extinction cannot exceed species evolution; soil erosion cannot exceed soil formation; forest destruction cannot exceed forest regeneration; carbon emissions cannot exceed the carbon fixation; fish catches cannot exceed the regenerative capacity of fisheries; and human births cannot exceed human deaths.

Thus, in the long run, humans will have no choice in establishing a sustained economy. Either we establish it ourselves, or nature will do it for us-and we can be sure that nature will not be as kind to us as we are.

With this in mind, we should review the statistics showing which wildlife and natural resources have either reached their limit or are shrinking. In both cases, it is an expanding human population that pays the price, in the form of starvation, poorer health and increased competition.

With a concentrated focus on these statistics, their reversal-the claustrophobia could be over-come.

The first statistic is that 100 species a day are going extinct due to human causes alone. If this extinction rate continues to match the rising human population rate, then in 50 years the earth will have suffered the second worst mass extinction in history, after the dinosaurs.

A few scientists question how well we can know what is happening to the world's four million-plus species. Fortunately, scientists through massive environmental studies have an excellent idea.

The second statistic is radioactive waste. Once they are produced, these nuclear wastes have lethal half-lives so long that disaster is absolutely guaranteed by the laws of chance. As of 1992, the United States alone has produced over 25,000 metric tons of nuclear waste. Much of it is put into supposedly 'safe' barrels, taken off shore and dumped into the ocean. Of course, that feeds eventually the nuclear material to where we are, in the cities."

(Indeed, this Prospective author as noted previously, has direct experience with this, although it was under-ground storage. My military duty involved guarding the trains transporting such waste into the desert.

U.S. Nuclear Waste. Cars loaded across country destined for burial in western underground site.

This picture is one I took of the miles long rail cars that transport such waste.

It is important to balance this by noting that sincere efforts are made to handle the nuclear outcome from reactors, lab work. Medical and other sources, hopeful aids to human exitance, but the challenge is certainly much greater than most recognize.)

Continuing the World Watch comments. "The third statistic is the rain forests of Brazil. Humans are burning them at record rates. We've all heard the statistic that every 10 seconds, a section of forest the size of a football field goes up in flames. The rain forests cover only 2 percent of the earth's surface, but they produce half of our oxygen, as well as recycle a small portion of our greenhouse gases. Destroying them is a profoundly stupid idea. Rather than tear them down, keep the most growing but provide homes for people living among them.

The fourth statistic is that we are threatening to fish out the oceans. A search for the reason why reveals that all 17 major fishing areas of the world have either reached or exceeded their natural limits, and nine are in serious decline. With 200 million people around the world employed in fishing, you can imagine the tremendous political pressure to keep fishing rates at their current level. Distributing people more globally will reduce fish need as they will develop needed local vegetarian ways.

The fifth statistic is grain. What happened with fish is also occurring in grain production. From 1950 to 1984, world grain production rose from 631 million tons to 1.649 billion tons. Much of this increase occurred for two reasons: farmers expanded their farmland, and dramatically boosted their yield per acre through the use of fertilizers. In 1984, however, world grain production reached its natural limits. Despite soaring demand, average yearly production has remained stuck at 1984 levels. The first reason is that new farmland is becoming more and more difficult to find. The second is that the mass introduction of fertilizer is now complete, and we have seen all the improvements that fertilization can bring; unfortunately, adding even more fertilizer does not increase yield.

Despite a growing population, providers have been unable to supply either more grain or fish. This has resulted in less food for the average person. Grain production per person has fallen from 346 to 303 kilograms from 1984 to 1993. Fish catch per person has fallen from 19.2 to 17.6 kilograms from 1989 to 1993. These levels are not satisfactory; experts calculate that the 1992 grain yield was nutritionally inadequate for 1 billion people.

Vegetarians point out that people can make more efficient use of their grain (and probably live healthier lives) by consuming less meat. For example, it takes two pounds of grain to produce a pound of poultry; four pounds of grain for a pound of pork, and seven pounds of grain for a pound of beef.

The sixth statistic is the gradual loss of our farmland. There are two causes for this. One is that poor farming techniques allow rain to erode topsoil faster than usual. In his book Earth in the Balance, Al Gore writes that 'the Mississippi River carries away millions of tons of topsoil from farms in the middle of America" and that Iowa, which "used to have an average of sixteen inches of the best topsoil in the world...now is down to eight inches.' Rush Limbaugh correctly points out that, 'thanks to technological breakthroughs, fewer and fewer acres have been suffering severe erosion in the United States.' But this is not to imply, as Rush does, that slower erosion rates are still not a serious problem. After all, it still represents a shrinking resource in the face of a growing population. And we know that once farmland turns into desert, there is no hope of reviving it. Thousands of years ago, the once famous "Fertile Crescent" supported a major population in the Middle East, but it was farmed so much, and so poorly, that it turned into a desert.

But it doesn't take the loss of topsoil to reduce grain production; ruining the soil accomplishes the same thing. Today, a growing percentage of farmland is being salt-poisoned. This occurs when water is irrigated into the land, bringing with it all its minerals; when the water evaporates, salt concentrations are left behind. As the concentrations grow, the land produces less and less, and finally becomes ruined. Treating this problem is enormously expensive. Experts estimate that 8 to 12 percent of the world's irrigated land suffers from serious salinization, and another 25 to 33 percent suffer from moderate salinization.

The seventh statistic is fresh water. The continental water basins of farming nations around the world are dropping, as demand for water grows faster than the rain cycle can replenish it. As a short-term solution to fulfilling the population's immediate water needs, nations are diverting water from agriculture to cities. Unfortunately, lack of water for irrigation also lowers grain production, so this is really no solution at all. Attempts to deal with the problem have led to the creation of an active water market in the western United States. In 1992, 14 western states conducted 146 water transactions, with most of the water going from agriculture to cities. Obviously, the depletion of our groundwater is not a sustainable activity.

And these examples are not to mention the deadliest threats to human survival: global warming and the destruction of the ozone layer. Global warming is dangerous because it would cause more severe weather, increase the range of deserts, melt the polar ice caps, cause a rise in sea level (which, according to the fossil record, is a major cause of mass extinctions), as well as expand the habitat of deadly tropical diseases. The destruction of the ozone layer is dangerous because this layer protects all life from the sun's deadly ultraviolet rays. Thanks to quick action in international diplomacy, the man-made chemicals responsible for the destruction of the ozone layer have already been banned. But there is no such luck banning fossil fuels. The oil companies seem to be politically omnipotent.

On the other hand, one could look at it this way. The environment will heal itself---but not in the way humans would like it to."

Clearly the dangers from our condensed overpopulation are laid down in the above discussion. Whether or not there is time to correct these over-usages is arguable, but the way people live, so jammed in, could change. This is to gain time to work, to heal our world surface and the earths resource usage directed to their new locals, where they would practice husbandry for their areas. And that is possible!

Our earth is wide and varied, it has room- we need to use, and learn to use it wisely! Suffice it to say, there is an opposite that could sustain humans naturally and by their targeted care on it for decades into the future. This incredible planet has immense acreage to distribute the human population- that is out of the density of the cities and into and within the surround. And, our technology can help us live within mountains, on and in the sea. We could find ways to overcome the "seven statistics". And to that the creative abilities of us, can make "Earth Homes", compatible with the environment and means of keeping us in communication with each other. There are many examples but see for just one example the Earth Homes in the Tao desert!

8c. Love your mother!

Myth: We shouldn't worry; the environment will heal itself. Fact: The environment heals slowly ---we are destroying it rapidly!

"The environment will heal itself, all right[1], but humans should worry how. People crammed in cities risk causing damage at a much faster rate than the earth's inherent ability to recover and the damage threatens to become permanent. Furthermore, when an expanding population meets shrinking resources, the results are starvation, poorer health and pitched competition for survival. Among other resources, the world is reaching its limit in crop harvests, and is declining in animal species, rain forests, top soil, fish stocks, and fresh water.

There are two types of damage that humans cause to the environment. One is long-term, even permanent destruction, such as the extinction of a species or the radioactive poisoning from Chernobyl.

1.www.huppi.com/kangaroo/L-environheal.htm.

The second is short-term damage---and this is where conservatives latch onto false hope! It is true that the environment has the capacity to heal itself in some ways. Endangered species can rebound, the earth can create its own ozone, the oceans can absorb greenhouse gases.

However, the rate of recovery depends on the type of damage being done. Species can recover in a few decades; ozone, a century; old growth forests, several centuries; the cooling of radioactive waste, hundreds of thousands of years. *But here is a critical point: the environment cannot recover while we are still increasing the damage to it!*

In many cities and urban areas, humans are destroying the environment faster than it can recover. And, if we continue in our current ways, our current urban profiles the damage will inevitably become permanent. This is a matter that demands the words, shouted out clearly, *"Wake Up or Loose It"*.

There are many propositions on this! It is a matter of saving earth by climate control, personally and together. But it begins by understanding and appreciating what we have! "

To that and so perfectly stated, Vishwa Amara relates the following. See: www.huppi.com/kangaroo/L-environheal.htm

"Our Earth is the only planet in our solar system where Life exists. This beautiful planet which is a thriving ground for a multitude of life-forms is not a lifeless rock, spinning aimlessly in space. It is a mother who births and nurtures all living beings. And Man has intuitively understood this and personified Earth in his art, music, stories and mythology since ages. He has rightly called her a mother, who cares for her wards irrespective of how they treat her.

Rather we should look to Healing Mother Earth. And we can do it. We can offer the medicine of common sense!

This, however, does demand a universal empathy for each other and our planet! Here are very important words to that effect."

The following is by Michele McKay. "February is the month to express our caring for those we love – the perfect time to give a valentine to Mother Earth. When we give to the Earth from our hearts, we are also giving to ourselves because each of us is

Offspring - 235

intrinsically a part of the Earth. When we make the effort to heal the Earth, we heal ourselves. Healing Valentines for Mother Earth can take many forms. Some involve an increase in our connection to nature, and others are actions to lighten our "footprint" on the planet.

Increasing Connection. There are many ways of taking healing action that will increase our connection to nature, and each person has his or her own preferences. Here are a few suggestions:

Consciousness. By observing, studying, listening, reading and spending time in the natural environment it will heighten our awareness of the condition of the Earth.

Intention. Directing our focus and intentions to healing the Earth. This can be done anywhere – it is the thought that begins the process.

Reverence. Cultivating reverence for nature through our own observations and through the study of other people's experiences.

Leaving a Light Footprint. Our ecological "footprint" represents the ecological impact of our lives. Valentines to Mother Earth includes treading lightly on her. Actions of highest priority are these:

1. Reduce or eliminate the consumption of animal-based products.
2. Avoid processed and packaged foods, and purchase organic, locally grown products whenever possible.
3. Minimize household waste and the use of electricity, water, and fossil fuels.
4. Commute or travel by public transportation, by carpools, and by biking or walking as often as possible at Home."

One of the articles in Global Climate Change (IC#22,1989, 1997) by "Context Institute" relayed this.

"What can one person do to avert climate change? The answer is: a lot. From that statement there is a list of 101 suggestions, and it doesn't begin to exhaust the possibilities,

The unifying themes are changes in lifestyle that: (1) reduce energy usage and slow down the fires of industrialism; (2) protect and restore the environment so that its climate-stabilizing mechanisms are preserved; (3) increase individual participation in governmental and economic decisions; and (4) facilitate a deep personal commitment to caring for the Earth."

This list following is distilled from three sources: "The Greenhouse Crisis: 101 Ways to Save the Earth," published by the Greenhouse Crisis Foundation, "Personal Action Guide for the Earth," published by the Transmissions Project for the UN Environment Programme, and Context Institute research.

"1. Insulate your home. 2. Buy energy-efficient appliances.3. Caulk and weather-strip doors and windows.4. Install storm windows.5. Close off unused areas in your home from heat and air conditioning.6. Wear warm clothing and turn down winter heat.7. Switch to low-wattage or fluorescent light bulbs.8. Turn off all lights that don't need to be on.9. Use cold water instead of hot whenever possible.10. Opt for small-oven or stove-top cooking when preparing small meals.11. Run dishwashers only when full.12. Set refrigerators to 38°F, freezers to 5°F, no colder.13. Run clothes washers full, but don't overload them.14. Use moderate amounts of biodegradable detergent.15. Air-dry your laundry when possible.16. Clean the lint screen in clothes dryers.17. Instead of ironing, hang clothes in the bathroom while showering.18. Take quick showers instead of baths.19. Install water-efficient showerheads and sink-faucet aerators.20. Install an air-assisted or composting toilet.21. Collect rainwater and graywater for gardening use.22. Insulate your water heater. Turn it down to 121°F.23. Plant deciduous shade trees that protect windows from summer sun but allow it in during the winter.24. Explore getting a solar water heater for your home.25. Learn how to recycle all your household goods, from clothing to motor oil to appliances.26. Start separating out your newspaper, other paper, glass, aluminum, and food waste.27. Encourage your local recycling center or program to start accepting plastic.28. Urge local officials to begin roadside pickup of recyclables and hazardous wastes.29. Encourage friends, neighbors, businesses, local organizations to recycle and sponsor recycling efforts 30. Use recycled products, especially paper."

And it continues for 7O more reasonable and simple things to do!

The scientific and political arguments surrounding the health of our planet can make the whole topic seem beyond the grasp of the individual. How fast is the climate changing? Exactly what effect to humans have? And what will the government do about it? How we treat Earth also involves trillions of little decisions by billions of individuals.

That in mind, on Earth Day, Live Science (see history culture space.com) presents the following 10 ideas for saving energy and otherwise cutting down on one's impact on the planet. Here is an excerpted version of that presentation.

"1. Change light bulbs: Highly efficient compact fluorescent light bulbs (CFLs) last for years, use a quarter of the energy of regular bulbs and actually produce more light. If every household in the U.S. replaced a burned-out bulb with an energy-efficient, ENERGY STAR qualified compact fluorescent bulb, the cumulative effect is enormous. It would prevent more than 13 billion pounds of carbon dioxide from entering the atmosphere—which is like taking more than a million cars off the road for an entire year.

2. Drive differently or drive a different vehicle: The sad truth is that your car emits as much carbon dioxide as your entire house. That's the bad news. The good news is that anything you can do to improve the fuel efficiency of your car will have an enormous impact on climate change. In fact, experts say that paying attention to fuel efficiency in your car may be the single biggest thing you can do to prevent global warming. Buying a fuel-efficient car (like a hybrid) is wonderful. And, drive less, Every year, Americans as a whole drive more miles than they did the year before. Stop this trend, and we drive a stake in that trend. Telecommuting and public transportation are great options—once a week saves a ton of carbon dioxide a year—but even piling multiple errands into one trip helps. If you can walk instead of drive, even better.

Get your car tuned up: Just a simple tune-up often improves fuel efficiency by half. If 100,000 of us went out and got a tune up, we save 124,000 tons of carbon dioxide. And, slow down, don't race your car's engine, and watch your idling. All of these save on gas (saving you money) and have a big impact on burning gasoline.

Horribly inefficient SUVs, minivans and pickup trucks now make up more than half of the cars on American roads. The real tragedy is that automakers could double the current average fuel efficiency of SUVs if they wanted to, which would save 70 tons of carbon dioxide per car. The technology exists. Unfortunately, consumer demand does not.

3. Control your temperature: The bad news is that half of your household energy costs go towards just two things—heating and cooling. The good news is that means you have lots of room for improvement, and even just small changes make dramatic improvements in household fuel efficiency.

Older heating and cooling systems are a third less efficient than the new systems. Things you can do right now to make sure you're setting the right temperature in your house include the following. Tune up your heating system. This one thing every couple of years can reduce your heating costs by 10 percent a year. Clean vents, close unused vents, and change filters in the vents. Again, just these simple things will save you 10 percent. Buy a programmable thermostat, one which can regulate different temperatures at different times of the day. Add two degrees to the AC thermostat in summer, and two degrees in winter. If everyone did this, the cumulative impact is significant.

4. Tame the refrigerator monster: Did you know that your friendly refrigerator has a voracious energy appetite? It is, by far, the single biggest consumer of electricity in the average household, responsible for 10-15 percent of the electricity you use each month. Get rid of your second refrigerator. If you don't need it, don't waste the energy.

5. Twist some knobs: The other big users of energy in your household are your hot water heater, your washer and dryer, and your dishwasher. Either turn the hot water heater down a couple of degrees or turn on the "energy conservation" setting."

All in all, the series, not completed here, reflects the massive abuse that can arise from each one of us. Here is one last recommendation from this series.

Invest in green energy: Imagine if we ran out of fossil fuels tomorrow, what would we do? Well, we'd get our electricity from renewable sources—solar panels, geothermal and wind power sources. Many utilities now give consumers the option to buy "green power." Ask for it! And go "Organic".

Even with our vast reservoir of scientific knowledge about farming, most American farmers still spray a billion pounds of pesticides to protect crops each year. Now here's the kicker: when chemical pesticides are used to kill pests, they also kill off microorganisms that keep carbon contained in the soil. When the microorganisms are gone, the carbon is released into the atmosphere as carbon dioxide. And when those organisms are gone, the soil is no longer naturally fertile and chemical fertilizers become a necessity, not a luxury.

But besides going organic-thereby saving the carbon release from soil-there are other simple things you can do with food that will also make a difference, such as eat locally grown food (doesn't have to travel so far.).

And the last of the recommendations go into such topics as Buy recycled and be a minimalist!"

Of course, these suggestions are indeed common-sense recommendations. Even so, the tragedy is that most individuals do very poor at practicing these commons-sense earth saving ideas.

Aside from individual efforts at climate change protection. There are available, many new ideas to fight the killing of our Mother Earth at the scientific proposal level.

One example is a global warming 'cure' found by scientists. this is from "An iceberg melting at dusk in Kulusuk Bay, eastern Greenland" by Charles Clover, Environment Editor (2007).

"A 'technical fix' that could stop global warming by taking billions of tons of carbon dioxide out of the atmosphere and save the coral reefs from being destroyed by acidification has been developed by scientists. This is in recognition that "Climate change is like World War Three"…

'" "The process could be used on an industrial scale to remove excess carbon dioxide caused by the burning of fossil fuels from the atmosphere in 'a matter of decades rather than millennia,' according to researchers from Harvard and Penn State universities. The process relies on speeding up a process that happens naturally, whereby carbon dioxide dissolved in sea water breaks down volcanic rock and soils to make alkaline carbonic salts.

The water flows into the ocean and increases its alkalinity. Sea water containing more alkali can absorb more carbon, so more carbon from the atmosphere is "locked up" and becomes harmless bottom sediments, according to the journal Environmental Science and Technology. Researchers estimate that it would take a cube of volcanic rock 10 kilometers across to return the concentration of carbon dioxide in the Earth's atmosphere to pre-industrial levels.

Unlike other proposed 'technical fixes' that 'sequester' carbon dioxide from the atmosphere, this one makes the sea more alkaline and therefore counteracts the other side effect of more carbon dioxide entering the atmosphere -the acidification of the sea."

Here is James Lovelock's plan to pump ocean water to stop climate change (2007).

"The alkalinity of the sea has remained the same for 60 million years, but the burning of fossil fuels has caused it to decrease. It is feared that the drop in the alkalinity will slow down the oceans' take up of carbon dioxide - which accounts for half the Earth's natural capacity for "scrubbing" carbon from the atmosphere. It will also threaten animals whose bodies are made from calcium, which is alkaline, such as corals, shellfish and phytoplankton."

Scientists say the technique is adaptable to operation in remote areas, running on natural gas or geothermal energy.

"The technology involves selectively removing acid from the ocean in a way that might enable us to turn back the clock on global warming," said Kurt House, a graduate student at Harvard University.

However, Prof Andrew Watson of the University of East Anglia, who was one of the authors of a Royal Society paper on the acidification of the sea, said "the fundamental problem with dissolving rock into the sea was the immense scale on which you need to do it to make any impact."

He added: "We are producing 8 billion tons of CO2 a year and that takes the combined efforts of all coal mining, oil and gas production. If you want to make an impact on that you need a process of the same order of magnitude to make a difference."

The local effect would be alkali pollution of the sea - but we are polluting the sea globally by putting carbon dioxide into the ocean. This method is expensive and therefore it's not the first line of attack for the global warming problem. The first is energy conservation, the second the substitution of fossil fuels with solar energy or biofuels, and the third - and above dissolving rock into the sea - comes carbon capture and storage from power plants. We know what technology is needed for that and engineering companies can do it."

Professor Watson, an expert on the carbon cycle and the oceans, said that "dissolving rock was "worth considering" if the world got into a situation in which the oceans were dying because of acidity, and we needed to alleviate the problem. If you did it the right way you might be able to save the coral reefs from the worst effects. I would see it being done in areas where there may be another reason for doing it as well, such as this."

Some other "technical fixes" for global warming have concentrated on seeding the oceans with iron filings or nitrogen to stimulate algal growth in the hope that this would then die and take the carbon the plankton contained to the sea bed.

Barbara Boyle Torrey is a writer and consultant who writes the following in an optimistic vein." Climate change should have been solved, with humanity probably still attempting to restore the damaged ecosystems.

Scientists have recently figured out how to reduce atmospheric CO2 to pre-industrial levels in about a decade and do so profitably. There is the 'Diamonds from the sky' approach to turn CO2 into valuable carbon 'Nano-fibers'.

Methane is another problem; one that may become more serious long before it lessens.

The major contributor is cattle raising, and well before 2075 vat production of meats will be established as cheaper, free of additives, humane, and ecologically safe.

And, Climate change may if we are insistent.be solved through geo engineering. You can count on that. Developments there will not encourage heavy carbon producing industries. Green technology will still be more lucrative as it assuages guilt in the destruction of middle-class lifestyles."

Also, on the hopeful edge of mastering Climate Change is the potential use of AI. Here the subject is from the article. 'Climate Scientists Powered by AI?"

"Climate change is arguably the most severe challenge facing humankind. How might we harness AI to help us tackle this complex problem? One growing challenge in the face of progress on climate change research is the 21st century science overload.

There are currently as many as 50 million research papers currently in existence, and more than 3,000 new papers published every day. How can anyone wrap their mind around that complexity of this growing volume of scientific research?

This is a problem artificial intelligence may be able to help with. IRIS.ai has a big vision to use AI to create scientific research assistants capable of reading this ever-growing volume of research. But even more impressive is actually forming and testing new hypotheses."

Co-founder of IRIS.ai Schjøll Brede, argues that… "humans need increasingly smarter, machine-assisted ways to navigate the ever-growing mountain of scientific knowledge, and to help researchers keep pace and come up with new and better theories and ideas."

~~~~~~~~~~~~~

Thus, with all the above we find ourselves shamefully amazed. It is there in the "ether" but where is it in practice?

It is clear that there are ideas that have merit. We are thinking about it, worried about it--- but have not yet come together! Even as of recent times the U.S. has reduced its participation in the world-wide global warming panel.

Coming together, feeling for each other and for future children, future Homo sapiens, that is what it requires to save Mother Earth!

8d. Change "Bellicose Actors".

It is never presumptuous to point to clearly evident solutions, which is- where cures are simply there for everyone to see, to hope that vision overcomes stupidity, leading to suicide.

The threat of nuclear war lies at the very core-the main--- the major issue concerning all troubles conflicts and wars among us!

The real reversing truths involved can be stated in two phrases namely 1.) DE nucleation and 2.) Changing the way, we focus on our governments. *In short, remove the threat of a narcissist punching a nuclear button!*

Currently nuclear rockets are in the hands of politicians, and despots, who threaten each other with the power of the bomb! This is to continue their place in power or political election.

Yet we have government forms that could prevent this. For example, the Scandinavian governments are formulated on multi-party conciseness (not two-party-lock) which in the end dictates popular human interest in the behavior of its leaders.

We need to acknowledge the real trends in motion and the real risks that loom, so that we can take mutual steps to avoid the mistakes that could create such an epic failure of deterrence and diplomacy.

That way we can keep the next world war where it belongs, in the realm of fiction.

The cure is there, the threat can be removed. Clearly though at present we are not in consensus on that path. Why? What we lack is clearly the inherent sense of protecting our species, a true universal empathy, which should be in us all.

8e. Think Space-Time Reality (Leaving Earth-Bound for the Stars).

This notion shall we say is sort of understood by most everybody! This is that we can leave earth behind and populate the stars! And there is the possibility of movement, under limitations, for some into our own planetary system.

For example. Could humans live on Mars?

Well, there is enthusiasm. "Absolutely" a NASA Expert Says" … by Ashley May in USA TODAY. "Humans will 'absolutely' be on Mars in the future, NASA chief scientist Jim Green told USA TODAY. And the first person to go is likely living today", he said. "Scientists reported Thursday (June 7, 2018) that NASA's Curiosity rover has found potential building blocks of life in an ancient Martian lake bed. Hints have been found before, but this is the best evidence yet.

After the 'building blocks of life' were discovered on the Red Planet, life on Mars and living on Mars seems to be less like a scene from the movie The Martian and more like a reality." "Now, we see Mars is an even better location for having past life," Green said. "It's just getting better and better."

"Mars is more Earth-like than any other planet in the solar system, making it an attractive second option for the human race. There's also a natural beauty on the planet: a grand-canyon that measures nearly the entire width of the U.S. and a volcano the size of Arizona.

The planet could offer humans a brand-new life with brand new vistas" Green said. "The plan is to send someone to the planet by 2040. *But that's dependent on quite a few factors."*

Here are some obstacles, outlined by Green: "We have to land. Right now, NASA is able to land a 1-ton vehicle on the surface of Mars. For a human to land, it would need to park about 10 tons on the surface. That vehicle would also need to land with precision-mainly not mountains or hills or rocks.

We would need to blast off from Mars. It's not a one-way ticket, at least right now. That's why NASA is working on a Mars 2020 rover. Sometime in the next decade, we plan to blast off the surface of Mars and return.

We would need to wear spacesuits-all the time. Weather on Mars is extreme. The difference between Monday and Tuesday could be 170 degrees. The average temperature is well below zero.

The air is also largely carbon dioxide - good for planets, bad for people.

We'd have to get used to dust storms. About every 26 months, it's summer on Mars, meaning prime dust storm season. These storms, made up of fine dust that gets caught in the atmosphere, can darken daylight to a twilight stage and last months."

From NASA- in the news.

"We would need to build an entire infrastructure. The people that would go there are real pioneers," Green said. "The first humans on Mars would need to farm and establish a food source. Some scientists believe that beans, Asparagus and potatoes are viable crops for soil there. Homes would also need to be built. Green said 3D printers might be able to use dust on the planet to create usable habitats."

And, as has been recently quite widely disseminated-for whole populations to exist there the planet would have to be 'Terraformed'. This means that masses of gases, similar to earths would have to be 'pumped in', to fill the atmosphere. There is not technology today to do this."

As alternative, leaving earth could be just to a new nearby neighborhood we make! There are "Local Capabilities" If we must leave here there are ways out, but only if we are united in peace and common mission! (At this writing the U.S. President is proposing a U.S. space military force, which of course presupposes something other than peaceful uses of outer space.)

Orbital habitats or some-times called "Tera-realms", made of materials extracted from asteroids, could be our first stepping-stone to more-exotic destinations.

Here is information from Michael Zimmerman. "Where do we go? We have many options. The National Space Society, whose more than 12,000 members are committed to establishing settlements in space, suggests that we'll probably first go to a planet that has the resources to support life. After completing a $200-million study in 2000, NASA reported that a colony could be dug several feet beneath our own moon's surface or covered within an existing crater to protect residents from the constant bombardment of high-energy cosmic radiation, which can damage our DNA and lead to cancer. The NASA study envisions an onsite nuclear power plant, solar panel arrays, and various methods for extracting carbon, silicon, aluminum and other useful materials from the lunar surface."

The National Space Society, in its own 2008 "Report 'Roadmap to Space Settlement,' also identifies the moon as the logical initial stop, citing the presence of life-sustaining ice there as a precursor to permanent lunar bases, hotels and even casinos."

And, Other space-settlement advocates suggest skipping the moon entirely. *All of these suggested routes, however, may fall under the category of what Isaac Asimov once called "Planetary Chauvinism".*
" We could just as well build an orbital habitat, erecting our future home in the void and engineering each of its details to our own exacting specifications. Financially, if not technologically, it is impossible to launch the number of materials from Earth that one would need to build a large orbiting structure. But such a habitat could be constructed primarily of resources extracted from near-Earth asteroids, which in themselves provide more terrestrial variety and potential surface area than all the planets in our solar system put together."

In 1974, Princeton University physicist Gerard O'Neill presented a design "Of a massive freestanding orbital habitat consisting of large cylinders spinning along an axis at a rate of about one rotation per minute-just fast enough to simulate gravity along its inner surfaces-and linked to another cylinder spinning in the opposite direction to eliminate torque. In gravity-free outer space, the habitats could remain structurally sound even at sizes large enough to house thousands, or millions, of residents", and O'Neill imagined "twin cylinders 20 miles in length and with an interior surface area of 500 square miles."

"A primary advantage of an orbital habitat is that it would not necessarily need to stay in orbit. If a ship exhausted the resources of a nearby asteroid or had to escape a dying sun, it could be rigged up with an on-board nuclear reactor or a solar sail and sent out to any number of faraway destinations. None of the 500 planets known to orbit stars outside our solar system is believed to have an atmosphere capable of sustaining human life, but almost all of these were discovered in the past decade, leading two astronomers to conclude in a recent paper that the probability of finding an exoplanet with a habitat nearly identical to that of the Earth's by 2264 is 95 percent. In September, a group of astronomers with the Lick-Carnegie Extrasolar Planet Survey, sponsored by NASA and the National Science Foundation, announced the discovery of a planet about 20 light-years away, in the constellation Libra, which orbits its star well within the "habitable zone" of our own orbit.

For successive generations living aboard an enclosed ship, it may not even matter if they remain in Earth's orbit or travel for hundreds of years toward one of these extrasolar planets. They may simply float through space in their "Generation Ship," harvesting materials from asteroids and comets along the way.

If the next planet doesn't have a suitable environment, colonists could live indoors until they managed to terraform one themselves.

Humanity may have millennia to find a new home in the universe---or just a few years. That is, responsibly we need to continue to advance technology to save the species recognizing the realities we face".

The following is by Michael Zimmerman." When I asked Dennis Bushnell, NASA Langley's chief scientist, about our space prospects, He responded by offering a far more sobering view. He emphasized how little we still know about the effects of cosmic radiation and zero gravity on the human body and mind, how we don't even have spacesuits that protect against radiation. 'What's affordable is not safe; what's safe is not affordable,' he repeated as a kind of mantra.

The researchers, engineers and astronomers who believe with near certainty that we will eventually live in space, who see this move as an existential imperative and the natural human progression, tend to take an elastic view of time.

We wriggled onto dry land, ventured out of the African savannah as apes, set sail for new worlds-how could we not expect, someday, to live in colonies on Titan or starships cruising through deep space? And no matter how long it takes to get off the planet, or who gets us there, the effort will provide countless immediate benefits to people here on Earth.

Designing closed-loop sustainable habitats could help us feed our poor; advanced propulsion methods might revolutionize Earth-bound transportation; space solar energy could radically reduce dependence on fossil fuels; and a deeper understanding of asteroids might provide us with valuable resources and someday allow us to alter the orbit of one headed our way."

Colonizing space "isn't just about survival, it's about thriving," says Tau Zero's Marc Millis, adding that "there are still adventures out there to be had, that one could do valiant work for the common good."

For Millis, the driving questions are simple: "What can we do that makes for an exciting future to live in? Something where when you wake up in the morning--- you're glad to be alive and a human? Well, green plants provide both food and oxygen." Kevin Hand "suggests molecular Ion beams to fabricate new materials."

Now, in our time and for vast technologic-development times in the future ...we must carefully consider the distances in time and space our exploring human must travel seeking a *truly habitable planet outside our solar system* (inside of which there are really none).

First, we are on the tail end of the Milky Way. To help understand its expanse a time frame can be cited. It is in diameter 100,000 light years straight across. For perspective 1 light year is one Julian Year ~365 days. So, looking at this in our way of considering time to find an ideal planet within that galactic realm could require a trip across of 36,500,000 days, which of course would be in only one direction which, again of course, failing detection of an ideal home there would remain an infinite number from which to select the next course. This is hoping that analytical equipment meets the need for absolute certain planetary detection and life support analysis to set the path!

Even so, the required intergalactic speed to maintain the age of that traveling human must (Relativistic Theory) be that of the speed of light or 299,792,458 meters per sec. in order to reach the distant galactic site in something like a present human life span. The factors are 1 meter per second = 2,237mph. Thus, to maintain age one would need to match the speed of light and travel at 66,853,716 mph in a vacuum! Putting the human in static state would leave that one alone on arrival, all other humans passing away on earth eons ago.

Further to this-we seem to forget that the outer reaches of the cosmos involve earlier times of formation since the big bang. So, the planetary systems there are forward of our own space time experience, which is a well settled human compatible world. Why would we move into that big-bang early planet, shall we say likely to a more dangerous form of the ground under our feet, which might not harbor the needs of life that we earth created-earth compatible creatures require to support our present form?

One can of course go on guessing. For example, perhaps it would be better to seek universes and planets in other galaxies.

That is, there is a very difficult question to address as to where we might try to travel. Quantum Theory suggests that we may have a sister or twin planet out there somewhere yet to be discovered in another universe, although we don't yet know how to find it.

Bottom line, it is at present, an immensely almost imponderable design consideration, one in which to answer even the basic questions we do not yet have the technology!

In a nutshell, to consider alternate homes for humans is responsibly a species saving hope. It has advantages in that the advance in technology could benefit us right here on Mother Earth. It could lead to re-establishing the species on homes we build within our galaxy.

But for the masses, that is not a physical reality and for those travelers uniquely space suited-up the realities of Space-Time truly over-shadow the actual achievements and accomplishment into the far-far future.

Our clear more pressing need is to find ways to preserve our earth or it's clones, beginning now! That of course, takes all of us united in purpose, caring for all the one's to come!

Hinting about an Evolutionary Need?

The proposals, for finding a new home are, of course, courageous and exciting-a characteristic of humans to be encouraged and inventive of ways to succeed, but showing at once human ingenuity may be coupled to a failure to integrate realities.

Simply put-settling outside of our own solar system is really presently not possible and perhaps not after many centuries of technical development.

If for some presently not seen reason, we must rush into the distant galaxies, that path must be very carefully examined!

One factor that must be added is humans traveling at the speed required to live long enough to be productive would need to be new and much improved ones-constituted quite differently emotionally and physically to survive such travel, so as to reseed the human being elsewhere.

In alternative---would it not be more rational to work together now to preserve where we now live, and develop earth saving ways to provide living everywhere on earth?

Coupled to this we have the technology to begin to develop one step at a time, if truly united-exoplanets to harbor our future offspring thereby preserving the greatest number representing us.

That of course, will also require careful evolutionary consideration, to secure humans emotionally capable of real cooperation to avoid the mistakes of the past that have created our present dilemmas. That is, we must have a greater understanding of our inner sense of empathy, a way to protect that humanity saving drive.

To all of this, in the end is the question of us in eternity! Will the universe die before we do? Do we have reasons to believe we have eternal potential?

Well, even this near-eternity is not the same as eternity! It is true that at some point, life runs into the physical limits of matter itself. Physics theories suggest that sometime between 10^{34} (1 decillion) and 10^{64} (1 vigintillion) years from now, the protons found in the nuclei of all atoms will decay.

That could mean black holes will be the only organized form of matter in the universe. So future humanity can't have any physical form we know at this point.

But to continue, red dwarfs will be the last generation of stars. Once they die, the universe will go dark – literally!

Even so, astrophysicist Gregory Laughlin doesn't see this as the end of the line for life. "Instead, we will enter what he calls 'the Gravitational Era'."

"In this dark future, we might build enormous space power plants around black holes, lowering masses toward them to harvest their gravitational pull like the weights pulling down in a grandfather's clock", says Princeton physicist J. Richard Gott. "Or we might tap the internal heat of planets to generate energy: The gravitational interaction between celestial bodies creates friction, which can keep planets hot inside even without any star-shine."

Thus, "do not picture cave dwellers huddling around geothermal heaters. Trillions of years of evolution will have long since transformed us", Laughlin says.

"Perhaps we will have merged with our computers. Perhaps we won't even have a physical form.

The only thing our descendants will definitely have in common with us is the essential spark of life: not flesh and blood necessarily but information.

Yes, that wonderful, magic creation the human being can still be there if we guard its benevolent imprint!

"That's the most important lesson from thinking about the far future universe," Laughlin says. "We're being naïve when we think of life only in terms of Earth-like planets and carbon-based life.

Information-based life can keep going almost forever. The gravitational era that begins around 15 trillion years from now could continue for quintillion years and beyond, Laughlin estimates. A quintillion is a 1 followed by 18 zeroes. It is trillion times as long as the entire history of our hominid line on Earth!"

Well, up to this point in Chapters 3-10 Chivonn has stuck to her objective. The Prospectus is building the point that the future depends on our inner benevolent instincts.

And, she feels the central matters that defend the need for her research are building through the Prospectus.

Even so she knows there is a very nagging question!

In the end it all has to do with the ability of we humans to mature, to be empathetic to our species, one and all, as a most central aspect of our behavior. And with this she wants to do research to find out what could be protective of that behavior.

That leads to what must seem to many very radical propositions. To so propose reflects her inner courage, indeed!

That occurs in the fourth coming chapters 11 and 12 where she describes what is needed to solve the problem of "Inadequate Maturity".

And, she must defend this in connection to her promised laboratory objective before a committee of great expertise and dare say we have not evolved enough to meet our future! Such a challenge is the subject of Chapter 12.

Chapter 11

A MOST HELPFUL COMPASS

Or How to Reset Us!

- Objective Humanism
- The Core Principles
    1. Protect Every Child
    2. Secure Healthy Growth
    3. Insure Open Mindedness
- Contents in a File Folder

Help to Guard the Future-

In the lab, Chivonn---after all the inquiry feels very strongly the need to retrench to find the focus that should be, that might best be linked to her lab efforts. So, reflecting she goes to the lab file and pulls out the lab's description of "Objective Humanism" and the "Skies Proposal". The former document describes the fundamental principles that all the folks in the lab-the Future Navigator Group feel is the attitude that must come universally into practice to save the good in future humans. The second, called Skies is an "Operational Method", designed to ease the efforts of parents, councilors and teachers to help future generations become more species empathetic.

Yes! She said "With the right foundation for people this could indeed be a contract, a compass into the future, into insuring the better human. I will set this into the last section of the Prospectus. With our understanding as to how empathy functions to ensure its practice we could have much greater long-term survival!"

The two documents entered into the Prospectus by Chivonn as "Section 10" reads as follows.

OBJECIVE HUMANISM[1]

It is up to us to find ways to understand the vast realm in which we exist, and to live securely within it for all our future generations. Given that maturity we do have the opportunity clearly from the advance of our knowledge even today-to catch up with a better understanding. However, that is certainly conditional. It cannot occur without the success of far future generations of humans for which we must now account! In this time, we are only on "the Edge of Forever"!

Obviously, unless we everyday guard with every endeavor our precious children to give their future children's-children the most humane chance, it is totally clear that we will not mount Forever's elusive edge. So, it is that the following remains the relevant protective container which must prevail!

We are being day by day asked to develop a new kind of Mindfulness, one that leads to mental security for each person who is then progressing in a universal mindset as a member of the whole species. This will be an individual who recognizes that we can evolve if we plan as one mentally expansive world community, we will see an awesome future.

It is why, the future protecting way, a "Vistavien Way" is grounded on a special "Tactic of Behavior". This is the philosophy of people that work to secure the progress of Human Kind into the future. It is an enlightened mindset yielding a sense of personal

---

1.Skies is an operational means in Objective Humanisim. It is proposed as a "Systematic Knowledge Internet Exchange System". It is designed to connect all child supporting agencies and disseminate fundamental ideologies for child rearing in a system of Interlinking Webnets. On action by agencies agreement, it launches information to counter child debilitating cyberspace influences that would create cruelty and inhuman behavior. It is a program in development by the "Future Panel", and is detailed in "The Omega Shield", 978138-9895647.

strength and promise! The result is a protective blanket for children building future navigators who are armored mentally to create worldwide tolerance and peace.

Their way of thinking is an "Objective Humanism". It embraces its core human reason and the freedom to practice it. This means first its caring ethics! Then it asks one to reject dogmatic pseudoscience and superstitions as the main basis of morality and decision making.

This benevolent and wise philosophy is a continually adapting search for truth centered by a sense of humaneness. It holds intentionally that people be mentally free so that they can guard reasoning and subsequent actions!

Our ability to think, to be at first mindful and humane, is a gift so incredible that it would be the most terrible of all crimes ever- to lose that potential, through aberrations of greed and inhumanity!

It is a simple fact that we must---many more of us, see and feel it--our Vistavien Navigator self! Then and only then will there be earned for us…Heaven, Utopia, Shangri-La, Darul as-Salam, for all time.

That, of course, is based upon sufficient time for us, the time to learn and grow, to practice our humanism! If we achieve that, the story of human kind does not need to end untidy as happens too frequently now. Then it could actually be as it may seem from distant outer space, one world, One-people!

THE CORE PRINCIPLES

The core principles are found in the "SKIES" protocol. The essential charge is the maintenance and growth of the admirable characteristics in humans, this against the degrading influences of the selfishly oriented world, who even in the ever dominating "Cybersphere" are creating the loss of their humanity, their concern and sympathy for others.

Humans have developed an initial sense of morality, redemption, empathy, and broad humanitarian sensitivity. The preservation of these preserving senses and the natural growth toward becoming the magnificent creatures they could be- must be preserved in the genetic development of each new generation.

Underlying the preservation and optimal growth of these star reaching characteristics are three basic ideologies for universal distribution. They are namely Protect, Develop and Insure. Following are descriptions of these idealities.

A. PROTECT EVERY CHILD

Irrational wars, starvation, faith-based crimes…greed against children threatens our future. Therefore, we adopt the following, a manifesto of values and behaviors. These following are to unite the highest doctrines of Humankind into a "Final Code of Conduct," the system by which our children will survive in peace, happiness and productivity for all the future.

1. That there is no dogma in faith that demands converting, dominating, injuring or killing a "non-believer".
2. That philosophical, political, or national dogma used as the reason for harming any person is deception amounting to crimes against Humankind.
3. That children will not be used as monetary capital for any reason. Capital means returning love to them.
4. That murder is an act of insanity; persons committing this crime will be isolated from the population.
5. That those religious beliefs based upon the values, characteristics, and behaviors best in and for all human beings should be harbored without prejudice.
6. That every child from the first dawning of cognitive ability should know that the whole of humanity is their family above all sects, states, or nations.
7. That every adult person will freely contribute every day an act to support planet Earth and an act contributing to the movement of the species throughout the Cosmos. From Earth's model, if needed we will move all into and find ways to reside in the broader Cosmos, to create Earth like places, "Tera-Realms".

8. That all governments will be guided as their first principle by this; anyone who denigrates, injures or kills a child commits a capital crime against the species.

9. That every government shall codify these principles in the laws of their nation.

10. And in support of these principles, we vow to the upbringing and education of all children as enumerated following.

1.) Every child will be guarded and supported to the finest health and education from birth at every place on the planet. We recognize that any child could be the seed to the "Final, Perfect Ultimate Human." So, all will be given the chance to mature in a safe and supporting environment.

2.) We will begin all our actions by never removing hope from any child! We recognize the line between hunger and anger is a thin line. Universal education of the world's children cannot occur in a world at war. We will work exhaustively to prevent the loss of young life through starvation or in wars of idealism. Complete removal of war will be the goal of each person on this planet.

3.) Each day we will honor the following practices born in the faiths and philosophies over the history of Humankind.

Islam: From the faith of Islam, we adopt the following. Children have the right to be fed, clothed, and protected until they reach adulthood. They must have the respect to enjoy love and affection from their parents. They have the right to be treated equally, in relation to their siblings in terms of financial gifts. Parents will provide adequately for children in inheritance. Children have the right to education. A saying attributed to Muhammad relates: "A father gives his child nothing better than a good education."

Christianity: From the Christian Faith, we adopt the following. Train a child to respect this idea "He will do unto others as he would have done to him."

Judaism: From the Jewish Faith, we adopt and will hold the following. Girls will be given the same level and quality of education and the same in all rights as boys.

Buddhism: From the teachings of the Buddha, we will hold the following. We will support our children to become generous, compassionate, virtuous, responsible, skilled and self-sufficient beings. We will give them the basic mental skills they need to find true happiness. To that, the most important thing is helping them to understand that every action has consequences. Each of those actions will determine their happiness, not only in the moment, but in the future. That is the basic lesson of karma, or cause and effect.

Hinduism: From the Hindu belief, we consider the following. It is that one should discover and explore spirituality, religion and God on one's own, and that we shouldn't interfere. It's okay to share and teach. It's another to misuse God to strike fear in others.

Pantheism: If you choose to believe in a god, hold that personally without evil intent to others. Recognize that each faith's prophet would have the main message from the same God; there would be no other choice, one believing in one God. In this there is thus-no reason for a polemic. However, above all rest in the beauty of the world into which you were born which is so sympathetic with your existence, in that alone is the unification of all faith. Stand unified in those ideas, the same God, the same creations, your precious earth.

Atheism: From the Atheist, we pay attention to the following. Early implantation of religion should avoid damaging in the following ways because children are especially vulnerable to mental harms related to it. This includes extreme guilt about normal, healthy sexual functions, disrespect for science and reason, feeling war like toward others, who do not hold the same faith. Remember, free inquiry on all matters strengthens the species.

Further to Protection of Children:

We will help children along the path to self-control. This means they grasp reality, the karma of their lives. That means to understand things as they really are and to realize the truths of life, to see things through, to grasp the impermanent and imperfect nature of worldly objects and ideas. Since our view of the world forms our thoughts and our actions, this view, developing self-control, yields right thoughts and actions for all people.

Children will be guarded such that they grow in to self-actuation. For them from there they will be able to discover a higher sense of purpose, the realization the Cosmos is for our species a provided ideology, which is-they are first unique Cosmos-lings! As they view this future, we will help them to understand that Earth is their glorious ark. It must last for thousands of generations. In its beauty, in the naturalness of earth's sympathy for our species, we have matured. An ideal it would be that even if most are elsewhere this beautiful so precious home would exist as it has been found until it dies as it must through Space-time forces against which there is no possible reversal.

Children will be informed as to the matter of how our species is improving. We have become aware that of all the species, our strongest suit is our ever-maturing brain. Our species agenda is to continue that remarkable development. This means that their Brain DNA in transferring and improving through the living generations insures the arrival of "Ultimate Humans". The young will be provided with insight into this so that they may respect it as adults.

We will teach our children to join in the mission of feeding all the world population. Sapiens can mobilize to go to the moon that same species can certainly mobilize the fair feeding of the world's children, in every corner. The young should have full insight into this as the charge of all humans when adult!

Children will be informed about the conflicting forces that create behavior. The brain driven urge to destroy is an embedded part of the survival of the fittest, yet that drive refers to the physical and with self-control can be managed. The brain driven urge of benevolence is also embedded! It is that drive that referees the preservation of the species. It is our strongest suit, the ability to think things through. The young should have full insight into this as a principle to reflect upon when adult.

Children will be allowed and guided by example into ethical and mental self-improvement. That is, resistance to the pull of desire, resistance to feelings of anger and aversion, and not to think or act cruelly, violently, or aggressively, and to develop compassion. This education will avoid proselytizing children into beliefs for which there is no substantiation.

We will teach the young that their children will be the next form of their species, the path to the future and full enlightenment.

This means that as adults, they will take responsibility for their reproduction. Wise and considerate human pairs will inevitably begat wiser ones. To aid children of each new generation adults will be provided an understanding of how natural development can lead, in turn, to their children becoming self-activating naturally transcending humans with female and male interaction equal without female victimization by men.

B. SECURE HEALTHY GROWTH

The buffer and the sensible guide to develop healthy-minded humans in each generation is to respect that they have psychological needs!

Respect for this development in the face of damaging cyberspace, proselytization, and political influences will produce more secure, self-actuation persons. SKIES activities will attend to ensuring that these are published so as to be recognized and fortified.

The human mind is complex and different motivations can occur variously in different lifetimes. They can be arrayed, however, much as in a pyramid, although each person from their starter knowledge may experience these differently-some in sequence others some aspects may occur simultaneously. None-the-less the fundamental transition in growth to adult to be respected is as follows.

Physiological needs

Physiological needs are the physical requirements for human survival. If these requirements are not met, the human body cannot function properly and will ultimately fail. Physiological needs are crucially important; they should be met first. Air, water, and food are metabolic requirements for survival in all animals, including humans. And of course, clothing and shelter provide necessary protection from the elements. *A prime agenda of SKIES is to make society aware when children are being denied these fundamentals due to interference in needed relevant communication.*

Safety needs

Once a person's physiological needs are satisfied, their safety needs take precedence and dominate behavior. In the absence of physical safety due to war, natural disasters, family violence, childhood abuse---people may re-experience post-traumatic stress disorder or transgenerational trauma. In the absence of economic safety due to economic crisis and lack of work opportunities these safety needs manifest themselves in ways such as a preference for job security, grievance procedures for protecting the individual from unilateral authority, savings accounts, insurance policies, disability accommodations, etc. This level is more likely to be found in children as they generally have a greater need to feel safe.

Safety and Security needs include, Personal security, financial security, Health and well-being, And a Safety net against accidents/illness their adverse impacts. *SKIES can help here by ensuring that false promises (scamming) are on notification.*

Love and belonging

After physiological and safety needs are fulfilled, the third level of human needs is interpersonal and involves feelings of belongingness. This need is especially strong in childhood, and it can override the need for safety as witnessed in children who cling to abusive parents. The deficiencies within this level due to hospitalism, neglect, shunning, ostracism, can adversely affect the individual's ability to form and maintain emotionally significant relationships in general, such as Friendships, Intimacy, and Family.

Humans need to feel a sense of belonging and acceptance among their social groups, regardless of whether these groups are large or small. For example, some large social groups may include clubs, co-workers, religious groups, professional organizations, and sports teams. Some examples of small social connections include family members, intimate partners, mentors, colleagues, and confidants.

Humans need to love and be loved by others. Many people become susceptible to loneliness, social anxiety, and clinical depression in the absence of this love or belonging element. This need for belonging may overcome the physiological and security needs, depending on the strength of the peer pressure.

Inherent in this is the social grouping that arises from cyberspace. Where that is obviously dangerous, for example, suicide groups, or such as terrorist organizations, SKIES should provide warnings and options to bring individuals back to rational belonging needs.

Esteem

All humans have a need to feel respected; this includes the need to have self-esteem and self-respect. Esteem presents the typical human desire to be accepted and valued by others. People often engage in a profession or hobby to gain recognition. These activities give the person a sense of contribution or value. Low self-esteem or an inferiority complex may result from imbalances during this level in the hierarchy. People with low self-esteem often need respect from others; they may feel the need to seek fame or glory. However, fame or glory will not help the person to build their self-esteem until they accept who they are internally.

Psychological imbalances such as depression can hinder the person from obtaining a higher level of self-esteem or self-respect. Most people have a need for stable self-respect and self-esteem. The psychologist Maslow noted two versions of esteem needs: a "lower" version and a "higher" version.

The "lower" version of esteem is the need for respect from others. This may include a need for status, recognition, fame, prestige, and attention.

The "higher" version manifests itself as the need for self-respect. For example, a person may have a need for strength, competence, and mastery, self-confidence, independence, and freedom. This "higher" version takes precedence over the "lower" version because it relies on an inner competence established through experience. Deprivation of these needs could result in an inferiority complex, weakness, and helplessness.

Caution should be issued by SKIES where the influx of cyber-enterprise tends to lower self-esteem. (Applications into cyberspace that help people to see their value are exercises well within SKIES agenda.)

Self-actualization

"What a person can be, they must be." This quotation forms the basis of the perceived need for self-actualization. This level of need refers to what a person's full potential is and the realization of that potential. This this level is expressed as the desire to accomplish everything that one can, to become the most that one can be. Individuals may perceive or focus on this need very specifically. For example, one individual may have the strong desire to become an ideal parent. In another, the desire may be expressed athletically. For others, it may be expressed in paintings, pictures, or inventions.

To understand this level of need, the person must not only achieve the previous needs, but master them. Protection of that capability against degradation of it from aberrant influences is clearly a priority of SKIES.

Self-transcendence

The above life stages and needs were set down originally by A.H Maslow, who wrote "The Hierarchy of Needs". Maslow explored a further dimension of needs. The self only finds its actualization in giving itself to some higher goal outside oneself, in spirituality or altruism, helping others.

This involves Transcendence, a state that is a critical agenda applying to controlling the ever increasing and inserting "Global Brain".

SKIES in its overseer role, protection of this state is fundamental to the optimal advance of humans. "Transcendence refers---behaving in the very highest levels of human benevolent consciousness, behaving thus and relating same to significant others, to human beings in general, to other species, to nature, and to the roll of humans in the cosmos".

If healthy and the path can be supported, growing children will be prepared at some point in their lives to "Self-Actualize". And from there they will explore their minds-eye-seeking, stability and independence of thought.

Children in that state express empathy! Thus fortified, they are easily recognized, and are set to interpret the way to reach their own goals and contribute to societies benevolent and strong growth.

SKIES will serve as one means to protect this growth potential and create opportunities for people to develop clear headedness, in open and capable analytic minds. The further path to secure that is enumerated following.

C. INSURE OPEN MINDEDNESS

Open mindedness is an essential to maintain the sense of humanity that will derive from child protection and growth development programs. Via this "Means Pathway" the protected, matured individual will resist the aberrant influences in cyberspace and other intrusions in rational thinking. From parent to child, over generations the idealized will bring human kind into a star reaching Nirvana. Here are steps in mind development to be preserved for individuals (and addressed to them) to help in that growth.

1. Understand Chaos. We live with a sense of Chaos, but if it comes to ordering, if mental calm occurs - patterns can become aware and confusion can be employed to move creativity. New thoughts are generated. We can gain clearer light. Following helps in removing the sense of Chaos.

2. Know Dream Reality from Possible Reality. There is an edge to reality. We are often unable to grasp it clearly. It is as if truth exists over a razor's edge. Thus, we live in the dream of immortality. Be calm, realize it, there is the reverse side to everything and know that even the reverse has a reverse-these, we may never be able to see. So, then you are back to the only possible reality for you day to day, the present you! *Your <u>Mind</u> it is that which governs your reality!*

3. Respect the Cosmos. Remember, the Cosmos and our world are older than us. We are at the end of a long chain of responses, whatever we do the Cosmos has a head start! Reality proceeds, yet the direction we (you) set may be a part of that! If you try, and try again and fail, the Cosmos is speaking to you. If you feel success, you are in the possible process!

4. <u>In Thinking-Gain Freedom.</u> Freedom and Security are interdependent, yet by separating them in our minds we grow. Security has a definite small connotation. Freedom has a large and unlimited connotation. Behind Security, there are boundaries, when we are able to cut through them there is Freedom. Freedom from boundaries puts one within an understanding of how their lives fit within the Cosmos. The mind cannot expand unless the center is preserved. That is achieved by selecting wise boundaries. With incomplete or arbitrary boundaries, the whole structure endangers collapse. A wise center allows for delightful freedom. (Protecting the center of one's mind; makes it a capable mind, then the future has potential to be protected.)

5. <u>Protect Your Mind.</u> The preciousness of your mind is impossible to underestimate. Use it or be abused by it!

6. <u>Make A Capable Mind.</u> The cause is given meaning by your noting the effect carefully! Know then that a single event is a tunnel through which all events reflect. These two--cause-effect-- cannot be separated. So, you learn to understand them, first in the minuscule which leads one to understand the macro that is the most important. In bees, it is the multifaceted eye...in humans it is your capable mind that can see that you see!

7. <u>Overcome Interrupted Mind.</u> The mind is full of noise, contributing to that sense of Chaos. Focus until it quiets to a single sound! Then will occur but one voice. Silence frees one from interfering with internal dialog!

8. <u>Overcome Troubled Mind.</u> Some have developed a library in their head that becomes but one book, in their view the "Truth Book." The one only book mind attempts to avoid becoming contaminated by outside ideas. This is a system with such strong boundaries that it leads to defending self, then to bigotry and wars!

9. <u>Realize the Difference Between Belief and Freedom.</u> Belief takes meaning into formalization, then fossilization. However, if understanding is allowed to shift, each moment can be a path to freedom.

10. <u>Believe Just First in Everything.</u> Much of conflict between people is from colliding beliefs. So, practice believing initially in everything! Yes, that sounds strange, but internally, in time, the

parts will sort logically, leading to one giant idea, hence, no boundaries! This should free one from the desire to be always right (which most of us have). Great problems can be solved, sometimes by evaluating the wrong. One should rather be happier in ideas that can be improved, than fearing the wrong.

11. <u>Allow Time to Grow</u>. Focus on nature, it has much to say. Remember the message in the seeds. Your time will come and with it a time to grow!

12. <u>Understand Difference Between Fear and Courage.</u> Fear is controllable. In fact, if you think about it, we only fear what we "see" in the future. The rest is anticipation. In fear, we begin to imagine what we can't do, rather than what we can. Dwelling on what you can't do leads to fear, dwelling on what you can do leads to courage!

13. <u>Know Change and Learning Are Interlocked.</u> To learn is to change, to change is to learn. There is no learning without change! To remain unchanged is to remain forever without comprehension.

14. <u>Understand Perception in Relation to Reality</u>. We must accept that there are both perception and reality. In fact, more aptly put, more relevant to us as persons, human life is "Attending." We can't turn it off. It is always pointing at something…as long as we are feeling we "Attend".

15. <u>Recognize the Modes of Attention.</u> Within our attending, there are four modes: External and Internal, Narrow and Wide. We exist or see an existence in one or the other. Learn to know the whole! When looking down also look up, expand the narrow to the wide and vice versa. Your choices at any time depend on the extent you see!

16. <u>Expand Attention to Its Twelve States.</u> Contract and magnify as you observe, use your attention! To add sparkle to the world practice alternate meditation, knowing each mode well at first. That is, recognize deeply that there are 12 states of attention: three senses; sight, hearing, touch and four modes; internal, external, wide and narrow to achieve 3x4 states. In your Mind gain, switch from external to internal using each. This will help your mind to become richer, more mature!

17. Know the Basis of Behavior and Perception. We don't disagree over what we perceive (usually). We often disagree over what those perceptions mean to us individually! Thus, the behavior may be the person, how we respond gives the behavior meaning. The response is a secondary feeling, an emotion! The original perception is the primary or internal feeling. *To un-bias yourself, change variously your sense of the perception.*

18. Balance Change and Response. Responding to the messages of change can create meanings, thus giving you choices, access to different worlds. Changing response lets one see the world as the opportunity! This is what we call an "Open Mind".

19. Enhance Attentions. Practice each so it grows, make perceptions big enough to evaluate, then the distance will lend to improved attention, enhancement and greater value. In effect, become a "Mind Tracer."

20. Learn Translation. Learn to "Translate" each state. Make light have feeling, rock have fragrance. Intelligence is limited by the number of states one cannot master in this way. The more this can be achieved, the richer is the life experience. This helps to join one in existence within the Cosmos. In unhappy situations, one shifts attention through this means, to relieve pain or boredom.

21. Move External to Internal. A skilled Mind Tracer shift's attention, external to internal to achieve their skill. They see an external and envision its meaning internally. This means appreciating the mental processes of which there are two; "Defining" and "Exploring." Too much defining leads to narrow judgment and views, but it can be useful if balanced as it may lead to more fruitful exploration. If one starts out with the basis of looking for something, they may find something even more interesting. Pioneering something in this way for a group means the pioneer may gain a very special freedom, a special feeling of accomplishment!

22. Know Type of Questioning Relates to Happiness. The essence of the Human is to understand, to be attentive. So, the way in which questions are asked is important. When we question, we should use the 12 states to enjoy, this to wander, this to let the ordinary become extraordinary. Even so, the words used are quite important. "Why" is a question of dogma, leading to more Whys? "Why" questions,

sometimes work, but don't necessarily lead to information particularly useful, because this is thinking virtually, totally about meaning. "How" questions are those with a more often useful basis. One is thinking about actions. "How" leads us to use our senses probing into time, space, weight. We see the Cosmos as phenomena, taking advantage of the universe's action on itself to accomplish! Our essence, our mind turns wishes into use. We are excited about this skill. The skill at this is the measure of your life. It's very much about "How"!

23. <u>Grasp the Importance of Context in Thinking.</u> "Content," "Reality" and "Timing" only have meaning within the "Context" that they belong. They are subordinate to Context. Therefore, our ideas about them are changeable. That is these should be viewed within their specific diversity to allow one to arrive at an accurate understanding of them. We should want first to understand that process, even though in the end the outcomes become what are desired.

24. <u>Understand the Basis of Feelings.</u> Feelings prompt a "Human Fog." There are two parts. Primary feelings are those of warmth, pain, satisfaction, the actual world. Secondary thoughts are the emotions and responses, the meanings we apply. They are how we think about the world. These can be and are most often mistaken, intermixed. Feelings mixing with emotions, can lead one astray. We must evaluate whether information is appropriate between the two…knowing the difference leads to better decisions.

25. <u>Calculate Connections.</u> Dreaming or envisioning is not a place, but a process of calculating connections between points. The insight comprehensively gained is in using the twelve states.

26. <u>Recognize and Use Space in Mind.</u> The mind has the property of space. Space is not just something to fill casually. In reality, within in it matter can be created from energy. Space can be thicker or thinner depending on how much has gone to matter. So, Mind space has tremendous energy and promise. *Mind when stretched to a new dimension is never the same; it is now accepting new matter (ideas recorded).* To accept something new one must "empty some mind space," then open the door and let the future in, endless possibilities can come from this.

27. Avoid Depression, Madness, and Lost States. This is when one has lost the RANGE of attention, i.e., the twelve states. They are not out of Mind but lost in a limited realm well within it. Perceptions are fixed! The mind is safest…not locked in, but when one is exploring freely within it. To discover and reveal hidden inner riches is the most exhilarating work of all!

28. Realize Differences: Religion Vs. Science and Self. Religion can deflect one's attention inward in a virtue versus failure appearance to God, i.e., one is to behave in a certain way making them hostages in a sense. Science directs one's attention outward. One becomes an aggressor for making change. In a sense, both fail to strengthen the individual as they abandon "Self-Regulation". One to be happy self regulates oneself, mind, body, and spirit. Once internally sound, one can then go out to see if that changes perception. Without self-regulation, peace can only happen in a perfect world, and must fail. Anything mind can't seem to affect must be external. Oscillate between the external ideas in relation to your foundation of internal strength!

29. Know the Promise of Human Maturity. "When one resides within a correctly dimensioned drum, the sound of a beating heart is greatly magnified. When one truly sees the magnificence of human possibility, the sound of future beating hearts amplifies one's own! Human kind has awesome potential, but only if it continues to exist."

30. Seek Aging Well. The body sends strong messages to the old. To respond with courage, recognize time is the one resource you have. Manage it well. Here, the most important thing is your own voice. Learn that even now so what you say is heard. Complete is each day doing! Incomplete is unfolding! Blend these and the beauty of life unfolds. I am. Am I? Complete, Incomplete. With time ahead you are incomplete!

31. Guide Yourself Internally. Wanting to be perfect begins with self-control, internally. We think of the past as influencing what we should or should not do. Talking to yourself in the right way can ease the stresses produced by this. You have "Mind Police" built up in your raising and experience. These are what others want you to do, but you take control by your personal voice. Remember to

change the "You" voice to the "I" voice. Internal You - leads you to some statement about yourself, usually in a bad way. "I "-needs to never tag negatively. With "I" you can change to the positive such as "I want to share my success". Cease wanting to be perfect by the demands of the Mind Police, give that up and stay with the good myth about yourself. That way, you avoid living in "a Police State." Relief is then gained. Delight is felt when your own internal voice wins.

32. Change Yourself Upward. With each heartbeat, we are changing. Time is the master. All our "Life Waves" are sums of our simple waves, compiling (tangled rubber strings by simile, Item 43). So how do we best change ourselves, take control of the waves? Emphasize the "I" voice, drop the you "always will be". That is with the "I" voice you gain, in effect, you control time. The "You" voice plants you in the past. Ignore it, emphasize the wonderful. The "I" voice directs you to your future. Mood is set by who is talking in your head. Be free of your past, the Mind Policing, it only continues to affect you.

33. Expand the Right "Mind Code." Pronouns (as above) are the way the Mind addresses itself. However, look at Mind as a verb it is what the brain does! The brain's memory is in Chaos and brain itself is a combination lock for everything. These things can be brought up in several ways; one word will evoke several meanings. Being dumb allows just one door to open from the Chaos! Being smart is allowing multiple doors to open. Make a Mind Code for something important to you, anything stored or just hanging there, then bring it back and expand it. Once a bit of the Chaos is trapped (put in order) let it gather new thoughts!

34. Know Limits in Existence. Your life exists only in your Mind! If your view of what the world is fixed, (such as what is the perfect religion, the perfect car, move, etc.) unhappiness is sure to follow. View the world as incomplete, with room to finish it. Knowing your Mind leads to knowing your body. This gives the marvel of reducing illnesses that limit you.

35. Know What Is Complete and What Not. For strongly viewed people the world is fixed, so every discussion is a fight or an attack. If thoughts are reopened to discussion, the world is open to many

things. By knowing not to complete, minds are changeable. Each can make this discovery, and a wonderful world results. Remember "It depends, also depends." We search for new places, when we have "transformed eyes."

36. Solve Problems and Issues. The approach to every problem, no matter how big or small can be mastered by an expansive process in your Minds-Eye. First take the problem and expand it to as large a field as you can, organizing it into a single picture in your Mind. Then rise above that picture to look down on it and *organize* the pieces. Now the clearer picture can be made smaller and lower it toward you. When enough small, insignificant actions become coordinated beauty and might are created! That is, the random neural discharges of brain must be linked and combined before the magic of thought, and understanding appears!

37. Apply Superior Meaning. Wrongly, values and beliefs become the lens through which we look, and color the way we see the world. This turns the infinite into the finite! Rather, see the world as incomplete and possible. Practice finding several meanings to each situation. The "this and that" events should not yet have true meaning. First see without seeing "Meaning"; attempt to see what actually is! Once, the big pictures are manageable stay with that optimal, adjusting slightly as you go as needed.

38. See Together the World from Your Mind. Nothing is completed in the world unless it is completed first in your mind. Once mastered, know what you can do and don't know what you can't do! There is no time when self-reliance wouldn't be an asset. But, seek people you can complement while avoiding those you are weaker with. At the beginning, these "Seeking's" may be muddy waters, but even muddy waters can quench a fire!

39. Draw Opinions from Different Views. The Mind operates differently among different peoples. Thus, the far northern people see the top and bottom of things (sun apparently rising and falling, only). The equatorial people see the left and right side of things (Sun apparently rotating east to west). Remember that while we see much the same (it is the same sun), there are differences in the WAY various minds see the world. Draw opinions from different views to gain your own strength!

40. <u>Recognize You Can Change Ideas or Concepts.</u> Your Mind is extraordinary powerful. One can use it to help oneself to change the feelings about almost anything, from pain to aberrant notions. There are two ways of remembering 1.) "As it happened to you," and 2.) "As you see it happening removed from you." When it is "attached" you feel it right "Here"! When detached you are at a distance from the pain or idea. If you run it backwards from that distance, you can find ways to control it until you get to the attached, so that can be rationally evaluated.

41. <u>Change Limits to Perfections.</u> The Mind can do anything through imagination; you can even envision greater imagination. In that state, you have the model! Knowing it well and with a method, what you can do is unlimited. Many institutions will not accept the unlimited. They think it is dangerous and set boundary places in children. However, humans are born to fight over limits. The space in your mind can determine what the world will be like. It is born in you. One always wants to be right, sometimes making one confused…remember through the newly activated space in your mind…more perfect things can be made out of air!

42. <u>Seek the Unknown.</u> Behind most everything there is the reverse, or the hidden, beyond your immediate vision. (Below the plant are the roots). It is also an energy that can be seen sometimes, worth the effort when one develops deep inner vision. It can give you power for an exceptional journey. Ask! Use your imagination, which is the tie-in to the power. What you can compute may not seem achievable, but you know in your heart you can do it!

43. <u>Understand Time Truths.</u> Life can be compared to a rubber string, lengthening in time, along the way tangling, tangles representing trials, successes, and progeny making again more tangles. Then when fully taught the life string let's go, snapping, releasing energy, to return to the original state, and the energy is provided to one following. Matter will by us, neither be created nor destroyed, only return to energy. This is a natural phenomenon. You have though control of the tangles, the balance that creates or destroys them. So, to do your best in life, recognize and balance destinations.

44. <u>Be Wise in Destination Choices.</u> The best lived lives see and understand destinations clearly. Choosing destinations involves two

activities, 1.) Comparing, 2.) Contrasting. These are 1.) What someone wants you to do, choosing it or me, for example in religion, or 2) What you want to do. Comparing is using value differences, Contrasting is using exact measurement, no value implied. In Contrasting judgment is made considering things as parts, without meaning. Comparing is "the difference between it and me", contrasting is "the difference between it and It". If there is much emotion one is comparing, if not one is contrasting. As destinations are sought one asks, what is the meaning in knowing this (compare), or what is the difference between these options (contrast)? One's delight is the measure of whether they are in proportion with these two, whether they are centered rationally within their Minds-Eye! That means also one strives for simplicity in life not determined by imitation of others.

45. <u>Find Your Center</u>. Analyzing "Space" filled with objects, the objects seem to become uneven, but there is a center to a flowing river, we can compute it but never really see it. One's Mind is full of boundaries, but there is a center. If one understands the ideas herein, one can find one's center. At the center is a surprise ---a source of happiness, a sense of rest!

46. <u>Understand Feelings</u>. Each of us has primary and secondary feelings. Moods are secondary feelings, which are either attached or hanging detached. These feelings are similar to our two nervous systems, i.e., voluntary, involuntary. For example, we see a mountain. It is fixed, high with color, angles, and dark canyons. This is the "Content Code," the involuntary. It is there. The way we see it is voluntary. This is the "Mood Code." These two give our thoughts "Meaning." If we are afraid of heights, we may see an ominous fearful structure. If we have a different Mood Code, we may see the beautiful purple in the evening light on the mountains. That is the Mood Code can be different than ominous, it can be changed so can the memory of things.

47. <u>Understand Precisely How to Use "Meaning."</u> From feelings, we develop "Meanings" to events and things. All meanings are arbitrary, one's interpretation. The meaning of anything is the way we represent it in our Minds. Meaning has the power to connect Mind and Body. For example, emotions (meanings) can be

registered and affect our bodies. If one changes the meaning ascribed (example, it's a lousy world), that will change how one feels. Changing another's meaning could change the world!

Meanings are guided by the constraints of our history, often making things difficult. However, if we change the meaning toward the obvious in front of us (finding order out of chaos) all else can be automatic. The obvious is the law, for which there are real consequences (what you do now can affect what happens to you in the future). If using "You" the "and" says you are damaged, then you are a different person, a damaged one. Conversely, if "I" is used you can change your perception of yourself and become un-damaged. If one connects the two halves of the brain (the obvious to the consequences) there is enjoyment in understanding direction, a sense of delight happens!

48. <u>Recognize the Flavor of Reality.</u> Although we have mood and content codes, we may have different moods, depending on what content we see or know. So, we can change the character of reality, how we feel in relation to it in spite of the Cosmic cause and effect. This is because the World itself has no meaning without thought we give it that through the state of our Mood Code.

Part of how we see reality is entwined with "Anticipation." If we anticipate a loss, then we are in a state of anxiety. If we anticipate a gain, we are in a state of excitement. However, knowing that moods are coded it is difficult to complain. One needs to imagine how they would code to feel in an "Up Mood."

This is not to say the world is just "Made Up." Because we have limits, we can't argue the reality per se, but we can adjust our thoughts to the "Flavor or Reality," that we choose to live with. One's life can be sour or sweet. It is a decision each can make in spite of the fixed cosmic cause and effect, within one's mind, through how they reflect on the world - change in their life can occur.

People and institutions set themselves up to define the "Flavor of Life" and expect you to agree that is the way the world is. However, there is never a totally correct answer you can live in a world you believe is right. Although there are Cause and Effect "How" you deal with it is your choice!

49. <u>Become a Decider.</u> In every journey one hopes to reach the end. This discourse you studied (this was a "Means" journey) now approaches that point. The last concerns the question of becoming a Navigator, one helping others!

More than Doer's maturity leads one to become a Decider, making the Mind aligned and clear as outlined, then doing becomes automatic and we and the World are acting together. The mysterious is more knowable through the obvious, and we gain control of our Minds. On the other hand, the aimless path consumes.

50. <u>Navigating Others into the Future.</u> Minds gained through the "Means Journey" just taken, can heal oneself and indeed, the world. Some last valuable recognitions, sign posts with clear lettering, help toward cementing that goal.

What is needed so that one can, (internal skills gained) externalize to be of value to others---the human species?

First it is important that each person heals self, and then they can try, and will likely want to contribute in healing the world, as our humanity is built in, an inherent instinct!

The following aspects' center upon that possibility. They are as follows, A.) Controlling the Structure of our Memory (how the past affects each one of us), B.) Controlling Time, C.) Understanding the Intersection of Imagination versus Reality, D.) Asking Fruitful Questions about Your Life, and a most important thought E.) Discovering that a Mature Mind makes you a Navigator!

A.) <u>Controlling the Structure of Memory.</u> On the way to a healthy mind, one wishes to forget "bad and frightening" experience, and certainly space for wisdom is needed in our often too crowded Minds. Some of the past, of course amounts to lessons of progress, and is retained in respect. Forgetting the unacceptable, the wrong, the cruel, the selfish, though takes effort, but we have direct control over how it affects us, because as we have learned we have control over the structure of memory. So, being enlightened, we know, for example, fear can now be seen as arbitrary-an internal event, the internal component can be controlled. Fixed, Mind Books, can be re-written.

Control over memory means developing a simple set of priorities. *These priorities tell us, in a nutshell, that we first mind our own business*! We are capable of doing this when we are prepared to supervise our own instruction, without the usual boundaries!

One only needs to set as priorities; self-determination, that is creating their own future, avoidance of trends-that gives us quilt in the end, Integrity—thus not regretting our actions, and control of the central core, that is the "Foundation of Self," it is, unrestricted by useless boundaries.

B. <u>Controlling Time.</u> Being attentive creatures, or ones desiring to lead, the "Future" has a significant meaning, and in fact, offers pressure in our daily lives. "Future" might be described as the consequence of present circumstances, making it in a sense static or limited. That is, to us, there are only two ideas of time. These notions are "ongoing" and "finished" which seem to "leap frog" forever. They proceed and direct all our actions in a limiting game.

However, we have control by stepping back and simply asking, "What is ongoing? What is finished? We have the power to decide to turn these into "Now is Dynamic," "Then is Static."

The future is, thus, opened up to more possibilities. We select successful past ideas and continue to explore. We use our available tools to regulate thought about time, recognizing that to know one thing is to open the potential to know a thousand, if not today, then tomorrow. Well-practiced ability expects success with developing ability.

C. <u>Controlling the Intersection between Imagination and Reality.</u> This comes about when one grasps meaningful meaning. In reality, the world will do in time what it wants. Give the world the chance it will resolve everything good or bad. One then recognizes that the World sits between one's "to be" and "to do." Our lives are within i.e., between those "Spaces." In that is the important intersection, it is the one between imagination and reality! If you control yourself, then you control this environment. If one does not intersect, that is trying to control this, they become impoverished.

This is a seeming paradox, but in truth- one must first become self-centered in minding one's own business---controlling one's own internal environment to achieve a really healthy and mature state!

If that were achieved, for each of us, there would be no reasons for conquest, conflict or greed. We would all be safe in independence from each other, but by the same token available as a success for each other.

D. <u>Working toward Answers for Central Questions about Life</u>. One last thought lingers before one rises up to the Navigator State.

Each of us has most important questions guiding one's life (yes you do if you think about it, although you may not yet have addressed it). When one achieves rational answers, one becomes finally "Mentally Mature" if that answer yields happiness! The way in which this question is asked, though, is almost as important as its content. Otherwise, your "Life's Questions" can go a long way to making you quite dissatisfied. If the answer somehow defines who you are or your present state of being, you are dug in and potentially sunk. For example, if you ask, "Will this last for me," you are headed into a yes or no situation that cannot succeed. Nothing here on earth lasts forever!

Here are some other thoughts that will clarify this all-important matter and put you on the way to happiness and maturity.

Eliminate simple *dogmatic* firm yes or no answers to your questions! Use a bit of protective thought.

(1.) Change the verb tense and the interrogative. For example, it is not "How will I obtain what I want, but how did I obtain what I wanted? The latter then leads you to open your future, building from such success as was obtained.

(2.) When your question refers to yourself in relation to others, reverse it. For example, it is not "When will they like me,' rather, "When will I like them"?

(3.) And avoid leading your question to yourself with "Why or Where" as these lead to the need for extensive context development. "Why" can take one into an ongoing world of dogmatic analysis (belonging in the scientific method) and can remove one from

Offspring - 281

reflecting more on the forward actions for oneself-the capability for which has already been gained via the 50 principles for freeing the mind.

So, if the questions are done right, you will ask overall "What in this situation loves me and them?" If the questions done this way work well for you, they will fill you with delight! They will direct you to the "Something" you are looking for. They will become a self-correcting life map, and that will be work done without effort because work done in a pattern of joy is work without effort.

E. <u>Discovering that a Mature Mind makes You a Navigator.</u> Navigation takes courage, the self-confidence, the ability to imagine, and to remain fearless, control over the Mind's apparent limitations.

Those capable of rising to this level are "Advanced Immigrants on Planet Earth", in a sense they are Navigators who avoid the errors accumulated from the past and work toward the future for all people, uninhibited with superstition.

Among them are the many who have given us the joys of life, the tools to make it work. We will call them "Vistavien"; they are exceptionally capable navigators because they know themselves in a healthy way!

~~~~~~~~~~~~~

The ideas in this document, which you have just read, have described the way to join this new breed as a Vistavien-a Future Navigator.

Now you know the path. These Immigrants are those who first respect then exceed the boundaries of Mind!

After all the paradox of reality is that no image is as compelling as the one that exists in the minds-eye…When that image is vast enough, open enough, forward thinking enough, the question of belonging is finally settled; one belongs everywhere, is strong, satisfied, productive, a true companion, one indeed for everyone else!

Think of the awesome potential should the whole of humanity rise to that level as time unfolds and advances into our Forever!

~~~~~~~~~~~~~~~~

Chivonn, reviewing the above and setting those documents into Section 10 turns to the final stages of her journey-defending her precious objective.

Thus, Chivonn having completed her prospectus-her attention was then to prepare for her defense. This challenge was two-fold, first the justification to conduct the genetic test (worth the cost), and second to describe and defend the techniques she believed would lead the project to success.

Tracing-The Contents in a File Folder

Prior to the time for Chivonn's defense, her professor reviews the Prospectus, preparing himself to know fully what the student requests and also the contents of the file in which it is contained. Following are samples of those contents.

So, it transpired that several days before she was to defend her ideas before committee, the Professor opened the file folder she left with the completed document. And there he found along with it a file full of writings and a note on which Chivonn, wrote the following.

"Dear Professor Jordyn: Included is the final version of the Prospectus. I have sent copies to all members of the committee, which they should now have in hand, with time for review."

"Even so, in my research, as we have shared, I found many really worthy thoughts. Of course, I realized I could not put all of them in the prospectus, in respect of not overwhelming the readers (which I may have done anyway). But, nonetheless, I do want these documents to be preserved in my file with the formal copy of my prospectus along with your comments after I have shared them with you. The following are those items I thought really hit the nail on the head."

The file contained both a selection of journal articles and some records of their back and forth exchange through the special e-mail site "Future Wish" they established at the outset of Chivonn's journey into Prospectus writing.

As the Professor reviewed the folder and the files, e-mails and all he recognized even more centrally than he did - as her work unfolded, the challenges she faced and the internal struggles that she dealt with as she moved toward the defense.

Sill. He remembers how she always respected the great thinkers, and their opinions. Yet she was not afraid to challenge, to balance, and inquire with the utmost thoroughgoingness' and courage.

The articles and e-mails following represent that and the effort she put in as she worked to form her prospectus and establish a foundation for her defense.

An E-mail introducing the file contents-

After Chivonn completed entering in her prospectus on the dangers we have created and was struggling with ideas- solutions on the future the ways out - she writes the Professor the following.

"Dear Professor the prospectus was a great idea, because it lets me be more global. Thinking it over I realize my overall objective, even if I am not going to be funded, is to leave something challenging, that is to get people to think!

My thoughts and answers maybe all wrong, but if they can get people involved in helping change humanity for the better on a long-term basis then I was right! Perhaps some will join me by clearing their minds of beliefs and ideas that may be holding the whole of humanity back and come with me on this adventure to the "what if" dreams for the future of humanity!"

The Professor wrote back, putting in also a quote.

"I understand, and it is OK with me at least if you "Hold Forth". Here is a thought from one truly courageous American hero who just as you are doing, began deep commitment after a military experience.

And the professor wrote the following in italic…

"Nothing in life is more liberating that to fight for a cause larger than yourself, something that encompasses you but is not defined by your existence alone." John McCain

An E-mail and an article concerning scientific potential-

As she explored Artificial Intelligence, technology and the thinking of scientists on the human thought frontier she encountered among many other papers the following. It is article shared with the Professor concerning a conversation between David Freeman and Michio Kaku.

The interviewer starts, "Ray guns. Starships. Aliens. Michio Kaku has been thinking about futuristic things since he was a child in northern California, watching Flash Gordon and trying to understand Einstein. He knew at an early age that he wanted to be a physicist because, as he puts it, they "invent the future" by developing new technologies."

"I began to realize that... the engines of the 20th century, every single one, can be traced back to some unnamed physicist toiling in his or her laboratory, creating the internet and creating rockets and creating all the wonder of the Space Age," he says. "I wanted to be part of that."

"Kaku got his wish, of course. He grew up to be not only a physicist but a famous one, known as a co-founder of string field theory as well as a popular science communicator. And he's written a dozen books on science-themed topics, including the newly published "The Future of Humanity: Terraforming Mars, Interstellar Travel, Immortality, and Our Destiny Beyond Earth."

"Recently, I had the opportunity to sit down with Kaku to discuss his eye-popping and, for the most part, upbeat predictions about life in the decades and centuries ahead. Here, edited for clarity and brevity, is our conversation."

David Freeman (DF): "The future of humanity" seems to be mostly about space. Is our future really going to take place on other worlds?
Michio Kaku (MK): We like to think of Mother Nature as being nurturing and friendly, but 99.9 percent of all life forms on Earth eventually go extinct. Extinction is the norm. It's almost a law of physics that one day Mother Nature will destroy Earth. We see that because of natural disasters, asteroid impacts, super-volcanoes and ice ages. But there are self-inflicted disasters as well — global warming, nuclear proliferation, and germ warfare. No one is talking about evacuating Earth and going to Mars. I want a plan B just in case Mother Nature turns on us, or the folly of humanity gets out of control.

DF: Elon Musk, Stephen hawking and others have said humans need to become a multi-planet species. You're in that camp?
MK: Yeah, strongly. That's right.
DF: What's the scariest thing facing humanity right now?
MK: The scariest things are the self-inflicted problems. We're at the point where we can terraform Earth — that is, we can alter the climate. I would prefer to terraform Mars and make it hospitable to earthlings, but we're terraforming Earth right now, which is a terrifying thought.
DF: But you've said that as fusion and other alternative energy sources are developed, climate change may pose less of a threat in the future. Do you see global warming as a blip that we've got to pass through — or an ongoing problem?
MK: It is one of the major problems facing us now, but I see light at the end of the tunnel. In southern France we have the ITER fusion reactor, which is an ace in the hole. This $10-billion project will hopefully show that seawater could become the ultimate source of energy on Earth. Fusion is relatively nonpolluting and does not create nuclear waste or melt down like fission reactors.

Second of all, the price of batteries is going down dramatically. We forget that the bottleneck for solar power is storage. We think it's the solar cell, but no, it's the battery. When the sun doesn't shine and the winds don't blow, you're stuck. But now we're making enormous inroads, creating super-batteries. I think that could change the economics of solar power very rapidly so that it is fully competitive with fossil fuel technology.

The two continue the discussion focusing on Terraforming Mars and encountering aliens and then progressed to a discussion on immortality (the deep future) which Chivonn highlighted.

DF: Let's talk a bit about life here on earth. What's life going to be like 10 years, 20 years in the future? What big change is coming?

MK: In the area of biotechnology, I think we're going to extend the human lifespan. We're now isolating the genes that control the aging process. We've even found an enzyme called telomerase, which immortalizes cells, so your skin cells divide 60 times, then they go into senescence, and they eventually die. There's a clock in every skin cell in your body. We can reset the clock with telomerase. But there's a problem why we don't do this now. It's because cancer cells also immortalize themselves.

In relation to this 10 Top Science Minds Tell What Strange New Body Part They'd Like to Have Artificial intelligence will seal the deal. We'll take millions of genomes from old people, millions of genomes from young people, and see where the aging takes place, and we'll do that using artificial intelligence to recognize millions and millions of sequences of DNA. I think that, for example, in a car, where does aging take place in a car? Well, where do you have moving parts and where do you have combustion? The engine. So aging takes place in the mitochondria of your cells because that's where we have moving parts and that's where we have combustion and oxidation. That's where errors build up. Aging is the accumulation of errors, so we'll fix those errors with gene therapy.

DF: Will that be a good thing?

MK: At first you think "Oh, my God, we're going to overpopulate ourselves." But look at Japan. It's had the opposite effect. The Japanese people live longer. The population has fewer children, and the population is contracting at a half a million people per year. By mid-century, it'll collapse at one million people per year. Europe is next. Germany, Switzerland, Austria — their birth rate is falling just like what was happening in Japan. I think as we conquer the aging process, we'll find that instead of exploding, we'll have an S-shaped curve. It'll seal off and I think we'll have a stable population in the future.

DF: In addition to stopping the aging clock, you've spoken about the possibility of putting human minds into robots.

MK: Right.

DF: Is that an alternative version of immortality?

MK: We're going to have the Human Connectome Project map the human brain before the end of this century, I think. We're going to put the connectome on a laser beam and shoot it to the moon. In one second, our consciousness is on the moon. In 20 minutes, we're on Mars, eight hours we're on Pluto, in four years our consciousness has reached the nearest star.

DF: Connections being the map of all the neurons in your brain?

"3D mapping of the brain Human Connectome Project." Now, believe it or not, I personally believe that this could already exist. If aliens are already Type I and Type II, they already laser-port their consciousness across the galaxy. They don't bother with UFOs. Flying saucers, my God, that's Type 0 technology.

DF: Some people are beginning to worry that robots are going to steal our jobs and reach a level of intelligence where they'll turn on us. Do you worry about those things?

MK: No. They'll take some jobs that are repetitive, but jobs that are semi-skilled like plumbers, gardeners, garbage men, sanitation workers, they'll have jobs many decades into the future because robots cannot pick up garbage. Robots do not have pattern recognition. They cannot identify a crime. They cannot fix your toilet.

On the internet, you can see these robots — the finest robots that we can create — falling over and acting like an upside-down turtle. Robots today have the intelligence of a cockroach. By the time they're as smart as a monkey, that's when they're dangerous because they have self-awareness. They know they are not humans.

DF: When do you think robots will become as smart as a monkey?

MK: I think by the end of this century we'll have robots as smart as monkeys that understand that they are not human, that they are distinct from humans.

DF: What happens then — all bets are off?

MK: We should put a chip in their brain to shut them off if they have murderous thoughts.

DF: Maybe they'd have a way to get around that.

MK: I think for this century we're okay. But for the next century, once robots can remove that chip in their brain, I think we should merge with them.

DF: For all the possible pitfalls, you sound optimistic about our future. Why?

MK: In the last century, life expectancy for Americans in 1900 was officially 49 years of age. We were born, had kids, and died. Our grandparents, when they wanted to talk to people long distance, they would yell out the window. If they wanted to travel to meet their friends, they got stuck in the mud. It was not pleasant living a hundred years ago. So, when I look at history decade by decade, I do see this tremendous explosion of wealth, prosperity, telecommunications. We live like kings compared to our ancestors.

The rise of smart machines puts spotlight on 'robot rights'

If you took someone from 1900 and showed them today's technology, they would consider us wizards and sorcerers. Now, if you take one of us and have us see our grandkids in the year 2100, we will consider them to be Greek gods. Zeus could have his thoughts come to reality. We'll have that. We'll think of things, and things will come true. I think we will live like Greek gods in the future.

DF: But for all the advances and all the sorcery, won't it feel pretty much the same to be human, emotionally speaking?

MK: We are genetically hardwired to be grouches, to be curmudgeons. Why? Because our ancestors who did not complain did not survive. They didn't ask for extra resources. They didn't ask for extra help, even when, during the Middle Ages, most people died very early. I think our ancestors bellyached a lot. Our ancestors were

Offspring - 289

fearful. Our ancestors, believe it or not, were fearful, bellyaching monkeys.

DF: So, our children's and grandchildren's lives will be incredibly different from our own—

MK: They'll live like gods.

DF: But they'll still be programmed to be grouches.

MK: That's right. They'll bellyache."

An article Chivonn sent on worries of science "Topping off"-

Dear Professor I forwarded the DF, MK article to you for its sheer Optimism. I include in this message a copy of another article that places a bit of a dampener on that exuberance. It concerns the "Matter of Scientific Advance".

My prospectus bears in the beginning on artificial intelligence (discussed in the DF, MK article which of course reaches into technology and the foundation of equational thinking). Where will it all go is a question begged. Well even the experts agree we have much to learn, indeed, some scientists say physics has gone off the rails. That is the love of "elegant" equations may have overtaken the desire to describe the real world?

Dan Falk (2018) said "All of the theoretical work that's been done since the 1970s has not produced a single successful prediction. " Says Neil Turok, director of the Perimeter Institute for Theoretical Physics in Waterloo, Canada. "That's a very shocking state of affairs." This doesn't mean physicists aren't busy; the journals are publishing more research than ever. But Turok says all that research isn't doing much to advance our understanding of the universe, at least not the way physicists did in the last century. Hossenfelder argues that many physicists working today have been led astray by mathematics seduced by equations that might be "beautiful" or "elegant", but which lack obvious connection to the real world."

~~~~~~~~~~~~~

The Professor remembered, how Chivonn troubled over these interviews, but held to the weight of evidence and wrote the following in an e-mail to him.

E-mail with Chivonn's position on the Future-

"Dear Professor Jordyn: I think we need a big dose of realism against these articles.

Humans have been concerned about their future since the very earliest civilizations. Consider the language Sanskrit- spoken in India some 4000 years ago. Thus, is their word "Anagata" or "Belonging to the future".

They also tried to approach the future wisely. Hence, we find the words "Jnana Marga" or "Take the path of knowledge "and "Agami" or "Present actions should expect fruit in future birth."

And, they tried to deal with, that is recognize reality. So, they said "Viveka" or "Discriminate between the real and unreal."

Yet, the eras since then clearly prove that their clarity, following on our subsequent superstitions, pitiless conflicts, and irrational inhumanities and truly disastrous child killing wars have failed to promise a truly mapped, secure evolutionary path into the deep future for our children's children!

In my opinion, after many comparisons from various experts, all the wishful thinking as we see in these articles, belies that reality.

There must first come from within us an empathetic drive, all of us working together to ensure the future. In short, a true recognition to defend our species, each and every one of us is not yet a reality. Failing that, it is clear we have little forward promise. Advances that are universally saving must have time we currently do not promise ourselves. The Skies program at least describes a way, indeed, a precise compass to help achieve that time grace outcome!

And of course, my proposal states quite clearly that such cannot happen if we do not get control of the dilemmas, and that must come from a united humanity with universal focus on the deep future!"

The Professor wrote back just a brief comment. "Chivonn, you describe much that my "Future Navigator Collogues" would approve in your discussion. Clearly you have a very deep belief in what you want to say. By the same token, it is very important for you in your Prospectus to show the facing limits, as well as specific paths out of the dilemmas."

Following are various e-mails sent in her concerns as she wrote needed sections in her Prospectus. They were in the file roughly in the order of the development of the prospectus.

E-mails on the matter of Overcrowding-

"Dear Professor: On the matter of overcrowding there is the related crime of misogamy, and also the matter of killing and abusing children which as you know from my experience I feel very, very strongly about! (This was before she writes the section on who we are),

Dear Professor: There is a sense of balance that is so simple, one people totally fail to see.

To have a female child is to put on more control of the number, which males without birth control are of little help!

So, why should a young baby pay for the "sin of its genetic given sex"? In some areas of the world, due to over-crowding, just because a baby is born female, she will be discarded, unwanted, and destroyed just because she was female!

In relation to this, when a family can only have one child, a male child must be conceived so the "name" of the family may continue. It is biased views like this that must be changed. What good is the "name" to know that the females born under that "name" will be killed and are of lesser value than a male? The "name" may survive. But what honor is keeping a "name" alive when murder was the only way to do that? Why can't we then see that when the female marries, she can still keep her families name and pass that on to her child? If a male child is born to her and her future husband, the husband's family name would become the child's last name. Or the name may be hyphenated. If a female child is born to her and her future husband, the wives family name would become the child's last name. Thus both "names" would survive, and no babies would have to die.

What a mess we have evolved to think--but are unable to completely reason through either consequences or the balances. We are evolved to think but are unable to feel compassion for our own species.

~~~~~~~~~~~~~~~

Another E-mail as she contemplates overcrowding-

She wrote in defense of the value of people in our world and of the aged. (She did not belabor this in her prospectus and felt guilty about the omission, still having to be concerned about the sheer number of pages growing in the document.)

"Dear Professor; Sorry for laboring on this following but I am struggling with who we can be, and it crops up that we are missing something really important. First is the matter of the needed number of people and then...respecting the elderly!

You sent me to India where I found the Jain have been around as one of the oldest religions on record and they are still here to this day, but their numbers are very small and certainly overshadowed by others who drive to populate or fail to consider its consequences. Yet in that they are certainly among the wisest of peoples. It is simply not in them to drive ahead their populations, it is a matter of overbalance to do so, is to open the matter of killing all around, burdening the earth for them to survive.

There is a great deal we can learn from this? But we have to reflect deeply.

How do the Jain want the world to progress too in regard to their benevolent nature and what do they believe it would take or can it ever be changed? What have they learned over the course of their history, as they practiced this benevolent humanity since their religion started 599-527 BC and have some of the oldest libraries in the world and best historians. Well, they are tactful with all other faiths and philosophies, but in their prayers, they hope for peace and love for all.

Good for them! At the same time, it begs the question of numbers of people who inhabit our world. What should the "All" be.

Well behind this is the question, how does that potentially pan out for our advancement?

Creatures, human like have been around about 90-100,000 years. If we go back to say only 15,000 of those years, there are no archeological markers at all. Where did intellectualism start and what is its impact? Certainly, we cannot all live just like apes, eating, using and killing each other, the thought-through process is needed.

The Population Reference Bureau estimates that the number of people ever born is 106 billion, but only about 2 percent of all people were born before the birth of Christ, (just 2000 years ago)! So only about 2 billion people lived in the first great bulk of time...on the order of 90,000 years ago, times of very little accomplishment and much bellicosity. So about 98% of people who have ever lived have been born since Christ, and if you examine almost all deeply intellectually creations from Shakespeare to Penicillin to Rocket Science, have come from that era.

To put it in a simple statement, the more people evolve, the more creative activity for humans could come. Yet, those that have reached the creative threshold so far keep finding reasons to kill themselves.

Then, would living forever help the good in this and balance the bad? Of course not, Greek mythology teaches us two things about this – be careful what you wish for, and living forever is not the answer alone, as the quality of life also must be a part of that 'forever' life.

Extending one's time on earth is important if that life remains useful, not only to oneself, but to others as well. Unfortunately, many older people will themselves to die because they feel they are no longer useful to anyone, and no one sees them as useful, so why even want to continue to live? So, they don't, thinking why should they burden their love ones and society with their existence if they cannot give back to those loved ones or to other parts of society? Should we support this in respect for Population Overgrowth?

Well, hell no! We marvel at the ancient Egyptians and all the abilities they had in building the great structures, yet we do not know how they did it...that knowledge has been lost, as so much other knowledge was lost. If the elder ones in our world were respected and the information they possessed had been shared and was adapted by the younger generation and instead of being ignored or destroyed, we would be so much further advanced than where we are today.

How sad it is that so much knowledge and information has been lost or destroyed over the centuries and will continue to be unless this knowledge is somehow retained and adapted over time. The loss of this knowledge must stop if we are going to move forward instead of running around and round as a hamster in a wheel. We must stop and think and reevaluate our proprieties of what is really worthwhile in and for society. So, it is, the older generation can no longer be tossed aside as worthless and locked away in some nursing home waiting to die for lack of use or want. That must change! Knowledge and experiences ---They know how to apply them to the problems of today if only the young will listen... Unfortunately, it is not in too many societies, culturally acceptable to honor them and learn from them anymore. They are considered just a burden and a taxing responsibility that must be suffered, until they do die. What a waste!"

Dr. Jordyn's return on this e-mail reads as follows. "The point about people numbers stimulates much thought. As you have said and I know you believe, every human is precious, and we lose so many without a chance to watch their creativity. And on the elder, of course, you know what Emerson said, "We don't live long enough to remember our mistakes" (hence to be corrective). I advise you address aspects of this as fits the defensible flow of your document if you like---but stay on course, for showing the current limits but possibility of holding empathy...species wide."

The first of many E-mails on the lack of empathy-

"Dear Professor; I must focus on our loss of empathy, as a part of my rationale. It must involve a protected, higher level in us than is currently there."

"Human Kind have long wondered why are we here? How did we come about? The reason may never be known, but we are here and here in the billions. We have awesome potential. We are only limited by our own minds. Nothing is off limits to explore.

Yet our own faulty mental makeup, miss-behavior, greed, me first, I want it now, behavior is about to kill us off. The rules do not apply to me, I do not have to be polite and considerate, I do not have to consider the feelings, the needs of others. We have reached a stage in our evolution where the cultural norm has breed multiple cataclysms time and time again.

History repeats itself with each new generation, none of the last generation's knowledge is excepted by the next generation as having merit as each generation thinks their ideas are better, so humanity is constantly throwing out the baby with the bath water and the knowledge learned is lost and must constantly be relearned again and again. War, killing, another war, so man children lost, and now our world suffers, again and again. Do people today really look deeply at the current situations and question why it is as it is, has it ever been this way before, if so how was it dealt with in the past and how can we extrapolate the learned knowledge and apply it to our present situation? Do they really ask this kind of question? If so, why are we in this insane state?

Do you remember the Jim Jones cult? The followers were so blinded by Jim Jones' "his faked message" that the world was ending that they all killed themselves! *This is the danger of losing empathy, of accepting the charismatic, of failing in the knowledge we should have deeply embedded in us.*

Although we kill them around the world, mercilessly and most hide their eyes when we hear about it, in developed societies we seem to put high value on our children. However, what about our elders.... society currently seems to believe...well they lived their lives, and they are done being an asset. Are they really no longer an asset? At what cost to society is their loss to the world? How much of their life long knowledge and life experiences will be taken to the grave with them and that same information will once again need to be relearned? This through-away society belief must be stopped!

Seems the basic way of living for most people is---I want it now, it is my right, I deserve it, to hell with the rest of you. They are so intrenched that they will live on, it is a norm that must change! So far, we are failing at the cost of millions of lives. It is time to really understand our empathetic drive!

The Professor Responded: Chivonn, I think you said you are going to develop a chapter on the "Missing Empathy". It looks to me that you have the "Ground Feeling" to work into that. Of course, you will want to put in the words of experienced psychologists on the matter.

An E-mail on developing "Future Navigators"-

Dear Professor: Seeking some logical thinking I read the "Objective Humanism Documents". Yes, indeed, we need Future Navigators, volunteers to accept the changes needed to up evolutionary the species. People must become "thought" viruses, empathy based to infect all of humanity if we want a positive outcome for the human race.

We think of virus's as bad, but they also can cleanse a current culture and cause it to mutate, to build anti-bodies, to become stronger and better than it was before.

Such a virus could make one grow and change and adapt and to become different so future attacks are not as destructive. In doing this the one or two people "thought" virus can infect others and help to create a "Sapiens Two" type personality.

Now by virus, I am not talking about some small organism making the population sick, I am talking about the power of thoughts printed out and of our own words. About thoughts talked about and shared to infect others. Words and new thoughts are the strongest tools that can form the greatest changes, good or bad... but it all starts with one word, one thought, one person, and their beliefs and ideas as they spread throughout the world one to another, hopefully to make a positive change in our world! And to this is the

Skies program, what a wonderful discovery when I reviewed the files on Objective Humanism.

An E-mail, which prefaced her thoughts about needed human evolution-

Dr. Jordyn…I am finding from my reading that we are transforming our species into one that is easier to control and making everyone more dependent on the government, the powerful wealthy individuals and on the machines and programs they are designing. We are slowly losing our ability to think for ourselves. It is so much easier to just go with the flow.

In order to survive we humans are going need to first wake up to the fact of we are becoming a world of sheep easily controlled by a few individuals that have learned to think and have no qualms with using others for their own selfish goals and greed. We have to stop being led and start thinking for ourselves if there is any hope for our future as a species.

We need to develop a new guardian in our brains, an " Anti-Charisma Reflex".

An E-mail focusing on her ability and right to argue "Further Evolution"-

Before she wrote earlier sections of the prospectus and had her Section 10 in mind. She was worrying about the daring contradictory proposals and propositions she would make (as example. suggestions on evolving). So, she sent this to the Professor.

"Dear Professor: In my Prospectus I will note the problems involved in some of this, such as terraforming Mars or the worries about AI. But there is a far bigger concern than is in those articles.

All I have put together says to me clearly that human kind is not complete enough for long term survival.

But who am I to even dare to think of changing humanity? Am I crazy or, am I even crazier if I sit back and do and say nothing?

One voice they say can be the catalyst to make a huge change in the future of things to come.

Am I, Chivonn, that arrogate to think I am that one small voice to be heard and to carry on suggesting there is a real need for humanity to work in evolving into an improved species.?

Pardon me--- but damn right I am! Why me? The better question is why not me? Well does anyone else have an answer? So far, I only hear excuses for going on with each of the problems, minor fixes at best, so I will spout my thoughts and let the passage of time determine the consequences!"

Professor wrote back as follows. Chivonn I am not worried about you daring to propose new ideas, I am, however, concerned that you are in a self-struggling match with the depth of the assignment. You are doing OK though in what I read so far. Just make sure you substantiate your suggestions with sound pointers!

However, why don't you take a few days off, go to the beach, relax? And here is a thought to blanket you.

My mother used to say to me "You are born with an Inner Happiness"! It will get you on in the rest of the day.

Knowing you, I am sure you can center back on your "Inner Happiness", heal and move one. (You know thinking about it I bet we are all born with a sense of "Inner Happiness", at least a sense of Hope! Maybe it's imbedded in our sense of Empathy, but it can work for us personally, I bet, at least in healthy people!

An E-mail with further comments on improving evolution-

Dear Dr. Jordyn: The more I research the more certain I am about the problems we face with our present mental and physical Homo sapiens capabilities.

We need to look at our own frail humanoid bodies. If we really want to improve ourselves, and truly reach a higher level of humanity, our bodies will be a constant limiting factor on how far we can go. If we continue to ignore the lessons of our past histories, then we will be limiting ourselves by having to constantly relearn the same thing over and over as time goes by. And are we really good enough physically for the challenges ahead?

As we progress and grow with the desire to explore the cosmos and to live longer, more productive and healthier lives, we must look at our own body structure and the failings of our current form. As it is and has been over time, we have been able to make many advances to lengthen and improve our life span but look into the old records. The Bible talks about people living well for many more years than we now do. What happened? We are now working on lengthening our lives and many are now living into their 90's and even a few into their 100's. Even so, what knowledge has been lost that has resulted in the sharp decline in the life span of humans since biblical times? Well perhaps that is just legend. But clearly for a few of u- in traveling to the stars, much longer life times will be necessary.

I believe the thinking about it; our future, the future of mankind is worth the effort to dream of what could be to help mankind evolve into a better and more caring and more physically capable creature. But how will those thoughts become a reality if we ever do take the time to think about them, or should we even try? Will we just sit back and let what happens, happen, or will we take an active role in helping to create a path for humanity that will become in the future?

When we look into space travel, time and distance are our enemies when we think of traveling in space. We have not developed the technology to allow us to get there fast enough for us to be alive to enjoy it once we arrive. If we can even arrive there at all.

Science fiction has been thinking on this question and others like it for years and scientists seriously in the last several decades. Still no real answers are forth coming… not yet.

I do not believe we may be able to evolve enough to be able to visit the distant stars--but I also believe that our future generations might…if we can keep our race alive and mentally well until those future generations do find the right answers. As a good detective knows, each wrong answer we face puts us one step closer to the right answer! We must just stay alive long enough to find that right answer!

The Professor wrote back the following to Chivonn. When (if) you choose to propose something needed to improve humans physically for their distant future keep in mind that the technology attached to better bodies is of course not in your epistatic credential. Mention this if you wish but the way you do it should push forward your ideas on needing empathy in our masses so that we can all work together to allow the future one's of us, the one's with great technical skills and insight to be alive to make it happen.

E-Mails on "Killing the Earth"-

Dear Professor: I have been thinking on this. In fact, working on the Prospectus has made me think more deeply about all the items proposed for the Prospecdtus. I wish everyone's eyes could be opened as mine have.

Conveniences and having instant results have caused us to grow lazy and unthinking.

It is now acceptable to toss out a vacuum when it quits working instead of getting it fixed. Things are now built to break within a set time table so a new one can be sold. It is all about the almighty dollar and how they can dumb down society enough to make it profitable for the companies to make it easier to buy a new item instead of fixing an old one. Yet the same manufacturer could continue their economy with a fix and return philosophy as primary for any new product.

It appeals to our nature to do things the easiest and quickest and least challenging way possible. It also progressively dumbs down our ability to understand how to repair something and thus adding to the landfills of the world! (Then attached was the following.)

Continuing on the subject of damage to the Earth-

Dear Dr. Jordyn: Following on my comments last e-mail I am sending you several of my favorite articles on Killing Earth. (Attatched were the following three papers.)

Hothouse Earth: Runaway global warming threatens 'habitability of the planet for humans' by Doyle Rice, USA TODAY

"We've been warned!

According to a new poll by University of Michigan's Center for Local, State, and Urban Policy, more Americans than ever now believe that global warming is occurring.

Runaway global warming on our planet remains a distinct possibility in the decades and centuries ahead, scientists reported Monday in a new study, warning that a "hothouse Earth" threatens the very "habitability of the planet for human beings."

Such a hothouse Earth climate would see global average temperatures some 6 to 8 degrees Fahrenheit higher than they are now, with sea levels 30 to 200 feet higher than today, the paper said. In addition, even if the carbon emission reductions called for in the Paris Agreement are met – meaning a rise of no more than 3.6 degrees above preindustrial levels – that still may not be enough.

Scientists at the Stockholm Resilience Centre, the Australian National University and other institutions made their forecast by reviewing past reports on tipping points for climate change. They also looked back at what the Earth's climate was like millions of years ago, when carbon dioxide levels were higher than today, primarily due to volcanic activity.

Global warming is caused by the burning of fossil fuels such as oil, gas and coal, which release greenhouse gases like carbon dioxide into the atmosphere and oceans. Those gases have caused global temperatures to rise to levels that cannot be explained by natural causes.

The paper said that a hothouse Earth trajectory would almost certainly cause widespread river flooding, increase the risk of damage from coastal storms, and eliminate coral reefs (and all of the benefits they provide for societies) by the end of this century or earlier.

More: Global heat, fires and floods: How much did climate change fuel that hellish July? More: Global warming risk: Rising temps from climate change linked to rise in suicides

Study lead author Will Steffen said "our study suggests that human-induced global warming of (3.6 degrees) may trigger other Earth system processes, often called 'feedbacks,' that can drive further warming – even if we stop emitting greenhouse gases." The feedback includes methane release from thawing permafrost, loss of snow cover in the Northern Hemisphere, loss of Arctic summer sea ice, and dramatic reduction of Antarctic Sea ice and polar ice sheets.

"These tipping elements can potentially act like a row of dominoes," said study co-author Johan Rostrum of the Stockholm Resilience Centre, an independent research institute that specializes in sustainable development and environmental issues. "It may be very difficult or impossible to stop the whole row of dominoes from tumbling over. Places on Earth will become uninhabitable if 'hothouse Earth' becomes the reality," he said.

Steffen added that these feedbacks would be difficult to influence by human actions. They could not be reversed, steered or substantially slowed.

The study "Trajectories of the Earth System in the Anthropocene" was published in the peer-reviewed journal Proceedings of the National Academy of Sciences.

As for what to do to prevent a hothouse Earth, it's easier said than done: Decarbonize the world economy, end deforestation, improve farming techniques and promote carbon-capture technologies, among other recommendations. This can "only be achieved and maintained by a coordinated, deliberate effort by human societies to manage our relationship with the rest of the Earth system, recognizing that humanity is an integral, interacting component of the system," according to the study. "Humanity is now facing the need for critical decisions and actions that could influence our future for centuries, if not millennia.".

There was a brief note attached to the second article

Dear Professor: It amazes me how people can "Excuse Away". The Optimist think there is time for Changes in us. Some say climate change could reduce racial differences, in part, by triggering massive migrations, etc. Of course, that proposal certainly fails to recognize the time it would take against the real time loss of earth substance.

Emilio Marinetti / AP file. "As climate change brings rising temperatures, droughts, shifting patterns of precipitation and longer growing seasons, plants and animals are evolving to keep pace.

Biologists have observed squirrels and salmon developing at an accelerated pace, causing them to reproduce at a younger age. Earlier summers have caused some flowers to bloom earlier in the year. And corals are forging new relationships with microscopic algae to survive in warmer, more acidic seas.

As the planet continues to warm, evolutionary changes are expected in other species as well — including Homo sapiens. Climate change will alter the internal workings of our bodies in subtle but significant ways and will likely cause a noticeable shift in our appearance.

Inside the Body: A warmer climate means malaria, West Nile virus and other diseases long confined primarily to the tropics will spread into temperate zones. As a result, people living in the U.S. and other developed nations will be exposed to these illnesses, and our immune systems will be forced to evolve new defenses. That, in turn, could cause other, noninfectious diseases.

Two blood disorders — sickle cell and thalassemia — arose and continue to exist because they have a beneficial side effect: resistance to malaria. Such disorders, or new ones, may soon appear if malaria moves into populated areas of North America, East Asia and Europe.

Similarly, our digestive systems will evolve in response to shifts in food availability — where crops and livestock can be cultivated. The ability to digest milk in adulthood evolved among groups in the Middle East and North Africa that began raising cattle. Future generations may evolve better abilities to tolerate sugar or fat.

Changing diets will also trigger important changes in our microbiomes — the bacteria and other microorganisms that live in our guts and help to keep us healthy. Vegetarians tend to harbor a different mix of bacteria than meat eaters, and these changes could be exaggerated if prolonged droughts make it too costly to raise livestock for meat.

External Changes: While these changes will be of enormous interest to biologists, they will be largely invisible. But as we change on the inside, we'll also be changing on the outside. Evidence suggests that a warming planet could melt away differences between human races — or population groups, as scientists more accurately call them.

The reason why climate change could reduce racial differences is that it will trigger massive migrations. In recent decades the world has become more urbanized, with people moving into large cities in coastal areas. But as polar ice melts and sea levels rise, large numbers of people will be forced to flee the coasts. And as droughts become more common and more severe, people living in more arid areas will have to move to places with more reliable sources of water".

(The third article enclosed on the subject follows. This was one of Chivonn's favorites on the subject simply because it pointed out some important consequences)

How to kill - Earth, wind, fire, water, and her children! Thoughts by Rayan Dallis (2018)"

"The muddy trenched road lay in semi-darkness, hidden beneath the overhanging forest canopy. Monkeys and birds of many types were chattering and calling out to one another complaining under the hazy polluted afternoon skies. A light drizzle was quietly falling.

Along this rutted trail lay shattered trees and tree limbs freshly cut. Each of their ends had been spray painted and color coded for their new destination where they would be sliced and cut to be "re-created" into something else. Created into something that the powerful two-legged creatures with their loud chain-saws and powerful equipment, felt were a better use for their once free branches that had swaying gently helping serve their true purpose as a-part of the giant lungs of the planet's cleansing breeze.

Now the surrounding air was full of the smells of burning wood, sweaty men, and all the carbon dioxide created from their cutting tools and even from their breath itself. Even as the shattered trees lay dying, even then they continued, trying to rid the poisons from the surrounding air and give back life, giving oxygen to the wonderful earth that had given them their start. The two-legged ruff creatures did not seem to notice or even care as they maneuvered their large caterpillars and cranes to load the logging trucks that dripped oil unto the once fertile land.

The rings of the fallen trees told the tale of the years that they had lived in an aired desolate environment, left alone for eons to experience nature with all its beauty and terrors. The blackened ring spiral in their trunks told their story of the horrible lighting strikes that had caused a high canopy fire that had raced among them. A fire that had burned so rapidly that the tree stand had survived as the flames licked only their very tips and then rapidly jumped from one tree top into the next in its maddening hunger to devour everything in its path.

It was a time when the weather had raged at the world. Huge shifts in temperature and weather. The next rings showed with their smaller, thinner growth they had been subjected to an ongoing drought that had followed the lighting fires. The next ring had a different coloration to it and was much thicker and healthier looking, showing the season had changed to much wetter one and the trees had enjoyed growth and prosperity for a while. Each year another ring had been formed to tell their story and that of the climate they had lived in. Now their rings would grow no more and would only be visible in their sliced cross sections that would create beautiful striated wood covered walls, benches, beds and cabinets, and other inventions of the two-legged creatures.

In return for their life sacrifice they would continue to give of themselves unselfishly as man dictated, however their companion mushroom growth, tree mold, and various other things that grew on them and near them; the very things that had drawn the tiny frogs and insects would come no more to rest and grow under their leafy and nurturing limbs. If enough of their neighboring trees were lost to the forest, the other things that lived there would one day, also parish.

How sad that the 'knowledgeable' two legged creatures thought only of the money they would get in the short term for the slaughter of the fallen tree's forest. Did they not know, were they so quick to forget, to look, really look at and for the forest's hidden treasures? Treasures that even now were being investigated by a few other humans in their exploration of how those same trees and environment might one day save human lives?

The treasures are there, lying quite for eons, and are still there today. Waiting patiently through the years, some of the ancient civilization's wise ones knew of their treasures. Some of the more recent civilization's wise ones and researchers had found a cure for Malaria from the Quinine, an alkaloid extracted from the bark of the Cinchona Tree, pain meds that alleviate pain from chemotherapy and fight infections, anxiety relieve that makes the person feel happy and calmer, comes from the Pasargadae Motel medicinal plant.

A menagerie of other health conditions that could be treated still lay hidden deep in the rainforests. From fertility to production of anticancer cells, decreasing and preventing tumors and Inflammation also some of the latest are helping with the cutting edge in AIDS treatments, and other diseases. From the kidney diuretic help of the Wasabi roots, to the Gordonville plant useful as an anesthetic for the ill or injured. There is even one called "Sodom" which is very aromatic and is used to cure addictions, including alcoholism, while Cola de Raton (Rat's Tail), is used to help one's digestion.

There were still many more secrets hidden deep in those rain forests. Only those willing to truly see the underlaying beauty of the forest will spend the needed time and find the wonderous marvels and cures that the trees and their forests had so patiently provided for those that are smart enough to find them!"

At the end of the file there was considerable correspondence on getting ready for the Defense.

Here she was challenged with questions very likely to be asked. Although they were asked in the exercise in writing she was asked to respond in writing so she could more carefully examine her answers.

Q: Why are you so concerned about the world's children, when in much of it you haven't any ability to control.

All of what I have in the prospectus is aimed at protecting the children of the future, so we can have a future deep in time. The proposal is in hopes that the solutions will be recognized and be held by people everywhere who have influence.

I remember when I was leaving for the Jain town, I told all of you I had been to India once before. I was on a brief duty there with the US-Nonpacific Command. Whilst there I was handed the following article by my Indian (Marine Equivalent) companion. He said it tears his heart out as it does mine. But it is a true account and one in different forms is repeated in too many places.

"In the impoverished huts just outside the town of Rajasthan, India children live with their parents who have to have their children's assistance for the family's survival. The children work in and around the mica and coal mines to bring in the much need money, (usually around $4.00 per day US currency).

Because it is illegal to hire children under the age of 18 to work in India, when the children are hurt or die about 10% of those are found and reported. The rest goes unreported. The sooty smell of coal and nocuous fumes burn her eyes as the coal dust seemed to permeate everything! The group of children, 10 years old, up to 14, (the legal age to work in India) *age needs check*, were just coming out of the "rat holes" where they had labored all day in the coal mines, bringing out the black coal to the surface.

A Green Peace worker pulled up to a corrugated roofed hut where two boys lived with the rest of their family. The dad stayed a few feet back being quiet as the workers questioned the boys ages who were 10 and 12 years old. The aid worker talked quietly with their mother, convincing her that the boys needed to go to school and would not have to work while they were there. She said she would take them to the school at Delhi. The father, knowing he had broken the law in getting the kids the jobs at the mine had stayed silent as he watched his two young 'slave children' being taken away.

He had received money for the kid's work that he and his wife used to remain drunk most of the time, (as the empty bottles of booze around their hut attested too). Shaking his head, he thought about how he would now have to find another kid or two that he would "pimp" out for the dangerous work of being a coal mine "rat hole" worker. He saw nothing wrong with doing this, as this was the way he had been brought up and was just the way of life of the poor people that lived just outside of the lightened town of Rajasthan!"

(The Professor put many questions to Chivonn on her need to "Play with Genetics.")

Q: Rehearsing on Brain DNA checking in case of question she responded as follows. "If we can understand and control a brain's central nucleic acid interactions in a way that when individuals are conceived their major saving instinct, not only for themselves, but for others as well, increasing their empathy and their benevolent humanity is site identified, it would be a very positive step.

However, as people do become more empathetic and benevolent in nature, there would need to be strong safe guards put in place to keep mutations from harming those that are choosing to follow this benevolent way of life. Seems that would happen, and it would require legal protection. But we (I) don't want to get into altering basic genetics. That is not within my goals. I am just working to understand how the empathetic impulse is formed, its generation transfer, and that known mind guarding educational programs can target where the negative influences for those people are forming and offer alternatives to insure free minds, not subject to inhuman proselytization.

The Professor responded in return: Ok, Chivonn that is a part of you premise…Be assured you will be very much challenged on the issue. But don't get trapped by being accused of Altering Human DNA. Look into for the questioner, i.e., illustrate if needed the Stars program as one example educational aspect. And don't forget to review how the future depends on securing our benevolent instinct.

(Another of the "Defense Rehearsals.")

Q: Chivonn they may ask "Why make such propositions encompassing such major issues, which is all you did in your Prospectus, when you just want money for experimenting?"

I would answer, I think the request has a deeper defense than a list of chemicals and lab time. That is behind the research is the question for everyone. "What do you see as the future for humanity, or do you see one at all?"

This is a question that I like to ask people around me, and I receive varied and diverse answers. Think about this question for a moment. What is your answer to what humanity will become? Why do you believe this? Do you like the outcome you see? If not, what can you personally do to help create a better outcome? Before you say nothing… before you say, I can't do anything about it, think again!

"Courage is the commitment to begin without any guarantee of success", as noted by Goethe and "The best way to predict the future is to create it". That says you can make a difference, if you have the courage to try. In my case the foundation that has to be defined is that without empathy, we lose our future, and so we must understand it as it lies in our genes.

Unfortunately, "Most people don't listen with the intent to understand they listen with the intent to reply". Stephen R. Covey wrote.

Together if we work to listen to one another and, if we empathize with the intent to understand, then there is a chance for us to create a future for all. Too often "I hear, and I forget, but if I see and I remember. I do and I understand." We must have real understanding of our essential goal as a species, which comes from understanding the plight of each and every one. In short, Before I begin my project, I want you my committee to understand there is a very deep driving force, behind my laboratory outlines.

The Professor replied. "Of course, what you are saying has considerable merit, but do keep in mind the members of the committee are among the most intelligent and caring people around, each of whom are "Future Navigators' in their endeavors, and you should hold dictating to them, be sure to use a tactful language, naming in return their efforts as a matter of retuning the concern, but also one in respect."

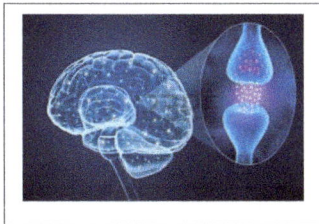

Chapter 12

A "NEW HUMAN"?

Or What is Really Needed to Survive!

- Chivonn's Vision (Arises)
- Scientist's "Wants in Future Humans"
- Final Sections of the Prospectus
  9a. Notes on finishing up the Prospectus.
  9b. The Marine Student Faces "The Committee
"

Chivonn's Vision (Arises)-

Chivonn in researching the needs to turn it around---all the cataclysmic dilemmas and the obvious failures and poor promise did indeed begin to wonder seriously about the need for an evolutionary up-grade for Homo sapiens.

She is thinking as follows. "In the end of it is *empathy* that is essential to survival of a species at large (we must care about, worry about the rest of us). And that involves the ability of people to adjust to their behavior as little scientist (in Kelly's terms) in a direction beneficial of all of humanity, to all the future.

In order for that to become a reality for their "Net Personality", Human kind must have knowledge that empathy is passed on, and as such its presence in the genome of each arising generation must be protected. That in turn demands that we know

Offspring - 311

the residence of it and the susceptibility of the genome to the evermore appearing negative influences.

With attention to the development of our coming Offspring we could be those capable of throwing away damaging charisma, we could all be capable of the resolve needed to reach healthy to the omega point, and into the stars!

So, what we can be, that is-what is inside, is empathetic, moral, altruistic, and that in the end depends upon the level of our born in empathy, ability to reason, ability to adjust our constructs toward the future for all, which in turn can be controlled but is subject to influences, the ever more hedonistic charismatic attractions.

And, even though we have the good instincts, some-times well mobilized, we have clearly not succeeded in elevating them to eliminate the threats to our very existence. We have not guarded our empathy and have shifted our reasoning toward attractive but injurious charisma.

Clearly, although we have brains that can invent, and bodies that can build, our evolution is incomplete! We are occupied with our physical needs and wants and wishes. It seems, we do not have either the right format to conquer the stars and the right mind balance, to all mutually work in empathy with each other to survive the species."

Some Scientists Wants in Future Humans

She wondered how the scientific world viewed the question "what do we need to do to improve" and found this article, published in MSNBC on line, which she made available with Section Nine of her prospectus. It expressed what various famous scientist wanted in upgrade.

The Article Preamble: Evolution has given the human body some remarkable features and abilities a powerful brain, a pair of eyes for binocular vision, the ability to heal wounds, and so on. But wouldn't it be nice to have an extra set of arms? Or body parts that could regenerate? Maybe a blowhole so we could swim with our faces down or gills so we could breathe underwater?

Or maybe you'd like a USB port on your neck so you could connect your brain to digital devices.

If you could wave a wand to change the human body in one specific way to have a new property, anatomical feature or physiological or intellectual ability what would you conjure up? I posed that question to 10 top minds in science and technology.

Here, lightly edited, are their fascinating answers.

Bill Nye: Snore-Free Sleep. Bill Nye, the engineer-turned-science-educator, hosts the Netflix series "Bill Nye Saves the World" and serves as CEO of The Planetary Society. His most recent book is "Everything All at Once: How to Unleash Your Inner Nerd, Tap into Radical Curiosity and Solve Any Problem."

If I could change one thing, one reasonable thing, about us humans, I'd make it a world without snoring. I say reasonable because we'd all like to be able to fly like a superhero: just run a couple steps, and you're airborne. But given our mass and strength, flying seems out of the question. Snoring, on the other hand, seems within reach. With just a subtle anatomical change or two, we could have a snore-less world.

Since we're a product of evolution, I can't help but suspect there's a good reason to snore. Did snoring develop as a means to signal others in our tribe or family group that we're out cold — other tribe members listen for it, and then go to sleep themselves? Or is snoring another one of those evolutionary accidents that hasn't met with enough pressure to be eliminated.

You've almost certainly heard the expression "survival of the fittest." It doesn't refer to organisms that can do the equivalent of the most abdominal crunches or pushups. It means survival of the ones that fit in the best. As a result, there's no pressure in nature to eliminate something that doesn't either kill you outright or prevent you from reproducing.

If snoring is a result of an airway that evolved from other airways in other animals produced earlier on the tree of life, but it doesn't kill us, there's no strong reason that natural processes will get rid of it. Snoring might be a leftover thing that is a result of being good enough. I could do without it. Well, I could do without snoring by anyone else.

Elaine Fuchs: No More Mean Genes. Dr. Elaine Fuchs is the Rebecca C. Lancefield Professor of Mammalian Cell Biology and Development at Rockefeller University. She's won multiple awards and is renowned for her research on skin biology and skin disorders. (Have to know what is in them.)

As a child, I always wanted to fly. The beauty of a butterfly's wings and an eagle soaring in the sky will always be more aesthetically pleasing to my whims than the flying I do now. Alas, airplanes and the wonderfully international community of scientists that causes me to use them frequently have prompted me to shift my thoughts and dreams of growing wings elsewhere.

In 2018, as a molecular geneticist, I'm now more interested to see my magic wand enhance the genes controlling three evolutionarily honed, destructive features of human behavior: greed, hate, and aggression. Conversely, the genes controlling creativity, inquisitiveness, and reflection could use a little enhancing, along with the genes controlling compassion.

Emily Cooper: Wi-Fi for the Brain. Dr. Emily Cooper is on the faculty at Dartmouth College, where she studies human vision and technology.

What if your brain could directly receive visual information from a computer, eliminating the need for physical displays? A wireless system merged into the primary visual cortex would receive and translate images and video sent from any computer or camera. Personal and mobile devices could function without screens — all your visual displays would appear or disappear instantaneously in the mind's eye.

Margaret Geller: Super Immune System. Dr. Margaret J. Geller is an astrophysicist at the Harvard-Smithsonian Center for Astrophysics and a pioneer in the mapping of the universe. She is a MacArthur Fellow and a member of the National Academy of Sciences.

My dream is for a super immune system (SIS) that complements our existing system to prevent and treat heart attacks, strokes, and cancer. These diseases are leading killers in the U.S. and in many other nations. The SIS would detect nascent signs of heart trouble, evidence of an impending stroke, and/or initial wayward cells that could become a serious cancer. It would then produce drugs to treat and cure the problem. These drugs would have no negative side effects.

The SIS would reduce human suffering and would be a step toward universal health insurance for some of the most devastating diseases we face.

Micho Kaku: Bring on the 'brain-net'. Dr. Michio Kaku is a professor of theoretical physics at the City University of New York and the author of 12 books. His latest is "The Future of Humanity."

By digitally and genetically connecting the brain to computers, the internet will be replaced by the "brain-net," which will transmit our thoughts, emotions, and memories will be sent over the internet.

This would revolutionize society. Movies and TV would become obsolete since the brain net would allow us to feel what the actors feel. Just by thinking, we would be able to surf the web, upload and download memories, learn calculus, and write emails. We would become telepathic and empathic, since we would be able to understand the feelings and hardships of others.

Since our thoughts could control power stations, which can move objects, we would also become telekinetic

Neil Degrasse Tyson: Let Me See Like 'GEORDI'. Dr. Neil deGrasse Tyson is an astrophysicist and the director of the Hayden Planetarium in New York City. He's the host of the Fox series "Cosmos" and the author of many books on science topics. His latest is "Astrophysics for People in a Hurry."

I'd like to see artificial evolution, more accurately called genetic engineering, applied to eradicate genetically tagged diseases. These include birth defects as well as cancers one might contract in adulthood. Next, or perhaps simultaneously with that plan, would be the ability to regenerate neurons, and ultimately entire limbs.

I'm not asking for much here. Plenty of other animals can do this -from planaria to newts. For me, anything else would count as entertainment — 12 fingers, three arms, and, yes, gills. I'd also like to see in a much broader bandwidth than "visible" light — like Geordi from "StarTrek: The Next Generation." That is, to be able to selectively see across the entire electromagnetic spectrum — radio waves, microwaves, infrared, ultraviolet, X-rays, and gamma rays.

With such power of vision, our world and the universe would be much more "alive" than we currently perceive it to be.

Priyamvada Natarajan: Built-In Crystal Ball. Dr. Priyamvada Natarajan is a theoretical astrophysicist at Yale University, where she focuses on obtaining a deeper understanding of dark matter, black holes, and other exotica in the universe. She is the author of "Mapping the Heavens: The Radical Scientific Ideas that Reveal the Cosmos."

After pondering one additional human capability that would be amazing to have, I realize that it's not an extra limb like the pantheon of Indian goddesses or a third eye like Lord Shiva's or a set of wings that would set us free to roam the world. It would be the ability to foresee the future, coupled with the ability to change the course of events. I've always been fascinated with the opening line of T.S. Eliot's poem "Burnt Norton," which reads "Time present and time past / Are both perhaps present in time future..." Being able to peer into the future would enable us to see the impact of decisions that we make today. This would be trans formative. It would make us superior beings, a species that can use its intelligence optimally.

We would be responsible scientists, as we could see the impact of our discoveries and actions, and more responsible humans, as we would see the impact we have on others and on the environment. Seeing the peril that our planet is in sharply and starkly by getting a glimpse of the future would spark us into action to be better stewards. Having the ability to intervene and alter events would help us make amends, to right wrongs, and perhaps prevent some things from occurring in the first place! Imagine what we could have averted — for instance, the invention of nuclear weapons; the bombing of Hiroshima and Nagasaki; the accidents at Chernobyl, Three Mile Island, and Fukushima; devastating earthquakes, floods, tsunamis, and storms; and many lethal epidemics that have decimated our species.

We could also go back in time and relive the pleasures that we did not savor enough in the moment and recapture more fully those magical moments.

Scott Solomon: Super Recognition Powers. Dr. Scott Solomon is a biologist, professor, and science writer. He teaches ecology, evolutionary biology, and scientific communication at Rice University. He's the author of "Future Humans: Inside the Science of Our Continuing Evolution."

We humans are exceptionally good at recognizing other individual humans. But imagine if we could tell individual species apart. There are around 5 million species alive on the planet. We know almost nothing about most, in part because only a handful of people — experts called taxonomists — can identify them. Many species don't even have names. Being able to recognize every living thing would have practical benefits. Customs inspectors could tell the harmless stowaways from the next invasive pest.

Recognizing microscopic organisms would allow doctors to identify infections without the need for blood tests. Machine learning technology, like that used by the "Naturalist app" is getting better at identifying species for us. But if we could simply recognize them at a glance, perhaps we would treat other species a little better. After all, knowing someone's name makes them seem like less of a stranger and more of a friend.

Seth Shostak: Better Color Vision. Dr. Seth Shostak is the senior astronomer at the SETI Institute and the author of "Confessions of an Alien Hunter: A Scientist's Search for Extraterrestrial Intelligence."

A lot of my friends think humans are marvels of engineering. My own opinion is that my body is a slipshod design. As anyone over 30 knows, we barely work. Thanks to the four-lobed nature of an ancient fish, we have two arms and two legs — nothing optimal about that. With another pair of hands, I might manage piano duets on my own, but then there would be a tangle of shirtsleeves in my closet. So while I'm not so keen on more hands, here's a change to our physiology I would welcome: more cones in our eyes.

Cones are the receptors that give us color vision, and we have three types — basically red, green, and blue. The fact that we have only three types of cones has been a boon to color photography, TV, and printing. But it means our color vision is miles from being perfect. Shine a red and a green light onto a sheet of paper from far away, and your 'lying' eyes will say you're looking at yellow, even though there's no yellow light there at all!

Sure, your eyes make nice sharp images, and you can quickly localize a source of light. Your ears aren't so good at localization, but they can separate out different frequencies, or tones. You can hear chords! If your ears were as bad as your eyes, all the instruments in an orchestra might just as well be playing the same note. What could we see with eyes that had, say, four color receptors (some shrimp have as many as a dozen)? I don't know. But nature has "cheaped out" on my eyes, and I for one am sure I'm missing something grand.

Tabetha Boyajian: I Want to Go 'POOF'. Dr. Tabetha Boyajian is a professor of astrophysics at Louisiana State University and the scientist most closely associated with the discovery of a perplexing celestial object called KIC 8462852 (Tabby's star), which sparked speculation that "alien techno-signatures" had been discovered. The ability to "Poof" (teleporting without a machine) would be a total game changer. Practically speaking, this would mean no more long (and potentially dangerous and/or expensive) commutes — traffic jams would be a thing of the past. We would have much more time to do fun things, and the environmental impact would be positively astounding! But overall, what I think would be the most exciting about "Poofing" would be opportunities to explore remote, exotic places around the world, or possibly even other places in the solar system and beyond.

Offspring - 318

9a. Notes on finishing up the Prospectus-

After her "Scientists Review" Chivonn writes the following ending those e-mails on "Prospectus". "We can dream, in outlandish ways, and some propose in reasonable format, but the matter is as serious as the existence of the species in not too-many far- off tomorrows. "

With that thought Chivonn completes her prospectus as the committee would have it before her defense. She would include a Section 10 with her hand-outs at that meeting. On the following pages is Section Nine's main content.

JUSTIFICATION FOR RESEARCH

Section Nine

WHO IS THE FUTURE HUMAN?

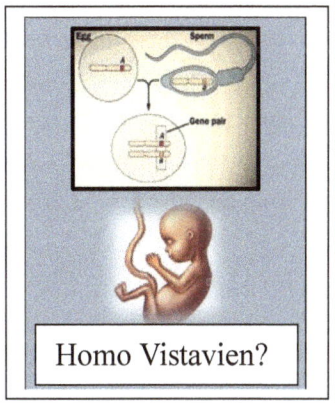

Homo Vistavien?

Introduction: Chivonn chooses to begin the section with the following postulation.

<u>Sapiens 2 and the Twilight</u>: "Homo sapiens represents a most paradoxical creation! Whether an act of an overseer or the miracle of serendipitous nucleic acid chemistry they have arrived, they are here in the billions, incredible minds, humble bodies.

From near ape roots, the offspring over the millennia have evolved with awesome potential. Seeded within their construction is a nerve plexus of unlimited capability, even to make ships for exploring the cosmos.

Of all the species known they alone could master the stars, know the very basis, the origins and control of all life. Their coming children could grow to enthusiastically greet the omega point, which point of ageless evolution, moving into the cosmos, to control all, thus lasting into eternity!

Yet, the offspring of the past and present have brought the future ones into a premature Twilight, the early death of their species! Fault in the mental makeup, miss-behavior, susceptibility to charisma and its influences has allowed them to breed multiple cataclysms, the failure to preserve their earth home, the impending possibility of humanity destroying wars, even the possible creation of destructive ability in an unintended revenge from their technical inventions.

Coupled to this, certain faults in their physical makeup significantly limit their ability to meet the challenges of the cosmos, into which to survive the millennia they must ultimately move.

It is now clear---the time has arrived, much earlier than the natural transition, for humans to create themselves into a new secure form, to control, to manufacture their own evolution!

They must, to survive the future for their young, change into a new form…a "Sapiens Two"!

They must do this by securing their attitudes, actions and processes as future directed persons, as homo Vistavien and make themselves into "Homo penultimate". They must become in both mind and body an up-step species!

The first action in this regard is understanding and control of their brain centered nucleic acid interactions such that as new children are conceived, they are protected from loss of their species major saving instinct. This is their sense of empathy, their benevolent humanity!

That achieved, they can turn attention to another essential need. That is to remove the threats to their existence on earth, change conditions into advantages to extend their life possibilities here into the very distant future.

This is necessary to extend time here, so they can also make essential and necessary changes, creating an evolution in their physical form. Why?

Overlooked by the proponents of destiny in space is the 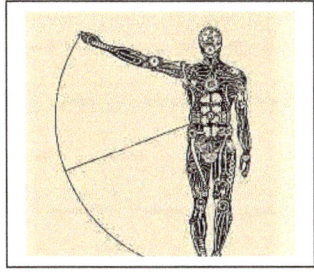 simple fact that the physical form of Homo sapiens must be addressed. It is inadequate!

The cold hard realm of the cosmos, its distance and total incompatibility with our current physiology dictates that our present physical form must be improved.

Afterall at present even here on forgiving earth it is already inadequate. Witness the attempts to keep it going, day by day, medical event by event to extend its life. It is even now not designed to do all that is needed to preserve the species.

Yet, time can be made available for this recreation. The technology is rapidly developing for this.

We transfer organs from one to the next. We produce babies by test tube, are able to survive the new egg to maturity. We have learned guardedly to clone. These are evidence, promise of an ability to build a Sapiens 2.

And critical to this we have developed and could insure moral and ethical practices and cautions to protect the sanctity of life and respect the benevolent humanity needed to move forward.

So, it is possible, the miraculous, unique sapiens brain can find a way to be sheltered within a modernized physic, one melding adverse condition resistant molecules with those that facilitate fluid permeation necessary for life.

Time and diligent attention to the needs of travel in the cosmos could allow us to overcome these needs!

After all, this is the species that traveled to the moon, the ones trying to reach the planets of their own solar system. They have amazing inventive capability.

Even so, their future homes must be far and wide over distance, speeds of travel and time lapses, against such devastating conditions that their present form simply cannot survive!

It is of course, clearly essential to realize that the threatening problems they have already created here on earth need to be fixed.

This earth, this precious home, needs to be made to provide subsistence into the deep future, the many centuries that will be the required to extend the waning twilight of human life for all the future. If that is indeed achieved Homo sapiens could become the rulers of the universe deep in the cosmos!

Made as they are thus far, with full ability to make of their species the true lasting one, whether through an overseer or by the chemistry of the cosmos, it is clear this is the absolute necessity and their absolute mission. They have both the ability and the permission, it is just up to them to achieve that destiny."

(Chivonn put the above last section into her Prospectus after struggling with its daring challenge time and time again. She knows it is fraught with argument. *Yet she did this so as to raise up the need to begin research into improving by laboratory research our understanding of who we really are and how the saving instinct occurs over generations and can be protected.* She hopes that the description stimulates the committee to recognize the deep seriousness of her laboratory proposal. At the meeting she hopes that she will not be challenged by someone-in eccentric intention- to show specifically how to create a new physical form of human right now-as it would be too much of a deflection, although if it does happen, she believes she can answer with some very interesting ideas!).

9b. The Marine-Student faces an Imposing Committee-

Forward Look: At the podium Chivonn will argue today's offspring require evolutionary corrections and a much deeper understanding of the influences that have led them into the fix they are in. This is required if they wish to secure a deep future for the coming generations. That is, one more sympathetic with the forces of the cosmos, and they must as the main accomplishment begin now to preserve their benevolent psyche, without becoming a species of Frankenstein.

Chivonn Defends Her Prospectus.

Her Professor, Dr. Jordyn scheduled Chivonn's defense of her "Prospectus" for the summer, Thursday, July 20. He did this to make sure the participants were free of teaching schedules and available on campus rather than off on summer trip.

The University in which Chivonn registered was quite advanced in its faculty, with their attention very much student focused (as opposed to being lost in publish or perish). All of the contacted faculty agreed to attend and serve as a "Dissertation Committee, In Advance" a somewhat unusual procedure.

The Doctor was able to draw together a prospective committee consisting of seven (one additional needed to break a tie) all were Full Professors, and all were members of the Doctoral Faculty who had matriculated Ph.D. students successfully at one time or another.

As it was finally constituted, there was membership from the social science faculty and there were included notable scientist in physics, biochemistry (including experience in genetic research), nuclear medicine and a cosmologist from the astrological school.

He did convince them that an audience from a wide range of experts, participating in the Q&A could be beneficial, so it was that the entire "Future Panel" was present in the audience, as well as a great many curious students from the science and social studies departments who heard about the special "Prospectus Defense". Many thought it would help them to do such a paper as they entered their research dissertation programs.

The Future Panel was cautioned by Dr. Jordyn not to answer questions by the panel members, though if they had additional questions, riding on one Chivonn answered, that would further clarify the matter that would be acceptable.

The Doctoral Committee was as follows.
1. Dr. Elisabeth Nalvartien, Professor of Bio-science, a widely awarded scientist in the area of genetic analysis.

2. Dr. Glenn Everhart, Professor of Sociology, teacher in humanities, and in World Religious Practices

3. Dr. Mostafa Badern, Professor of Astrology, favorite of his classes teaching, "The Cosmos, it's Inner Secrets."

4. Dr. James Bond (not 007 as the students called him), Professor of Sociology, recently teaching a class on "Population Dynamics and Our World".

5. Dr. Marcus Williams, Professor of Theoretical Physics, all classes looking into the future of Cosmos and one specifically on "Dark Holes'.

6. Dr. Stanley Hobark, Professor of Chemistry, teacher of "Advance Laboratory Methods and Explorations".

7. Dr. Reginald Smith, recently retired but who, as so many academicians, was "back at work" as Adjunct Professor of Nuclear Medicine.

All the panel had been provided Chivonn's prospectus two weeks before the scheduled "Defense". Before the meeting they were also provided handouts that Chivonn drew together (Including Section 10).

~~~~~~~~~~

The night before she was to defend her ideas in front of that truly august, and yes challenging panel, Chivonn sitting on the couch next to Taylor was once again (somewhat surreptitiously) reviewing her slides. Taylor was playing a peaceful melody. As the last notes of the guitar faded to stillness, he put down the instrument and drew Chivonn close into a tender and lingering embrace.

"You will do fine my love", he said in his deep baritone voice. "I have every confidence that committee will see the message clearly in the prospectus, and give you the funding you need to proceed with your clinical research! Let it go for tonight though, rest your mind!

Incidentally, I know you haven't looked at your Horoscope, but I thought you might like this one. It says "Love is something you do. So, it's impossible to love without investment, as the love is the investment. These are things you know, but others haven't learned yet. You'll teach through example." Chivonn looked at

Taylor with a gleam in her eye and said, "Well I am damn sure going to try!

Even so, Chivonn was, indeed so tired, really exhausted going over and over her intended defense. And, surprising as it was somewhat unusual for her...so stressed out about her presentation in the morning that she hadn't realized how much!

Taylor's kindness and his welcoming arms and support meant to her until just that moment! If it hadn't been for his cheering her on through all the hard spots, she might just have decided not to face the committee tomorrow.

So much was riding on her words and their decision! She had to succeed, and thus she first had to convince them of her abilities and her ideas, yes cutting edge but some might feel too radical! So-what! She could do it! She would do it! If not tomorrow, then down the road as she would not give up. This was too important!

For tonight though, Taylor was right. It was time to rest her mind. She was as ready as she could be for that meeting in the morning.

She knew now, only time would tell. With this she softly whispered a prayer in her head, just as she felt a calming peace descend over her surrounding her in a comforting mist, and with that she lay her head into Taylor's strong shoulders and closed her eyes fading into that wonderful contentment; the smell of musk and aftershave of her beloved filled all her senses as she turned to look up at him.

His deep blue eyes, with their flecks of gold shining in the twilight penetrated hers, as he lovingly explored the depths of her very soul, and the corners of his mouth parted in a slight grin at what he found there. Then, her tough persona of the day vanished into her desires for the man she so deeply loved!

Even so, in great surprise, at about twelve, the phone rang! Dr. Pi who was working late let Chivonn know the police called and asked if she could come to the station. Now, she thought this is right in the times when I need to "Cool Out". None the less, knowing her and Taylor had nothing to hide, and respecting those who serve, always in danger the police, she hastened to the station.

The police said a woman in jail asked for me as Sargent Chivonn... said she needed my help, I would understand.

When she was taken to the cells, Chivonn saw a woman who she immediately remembered, she was one of those many women she knew in the Marines! Without hesitation Chivonn paid her bail and moved her to a safe house. As she did during the first couple of miles, she heard her story which she relayed to Taylor that night, and later to the Professor.

"As I first saw her, her hair was long, and hung in straggled tangles of locks. She had sunken dark eyes, but she stood at attention, with defiance to the world as the police officer took off her cuffs in the Sally port of the jail. Her clothes were old and dirty, surely from sleeping on the street. She looked like she was ninety, but I knew, of course, she was much, much younger. She had a hollow look to her that hung about her like a shroud of loss and sorrow! Life after her return to the civilian world had not been kind to her!"

She told me, "We gals, out of the Marines, don't really get the same support as the guys. I was really PTSD but couldn't find the resources, guess they didn't think women were in the field much, but I surely was!

You remember, last night was really cold and I hadn't been able wandering around the city to pan-handle the $4.00 required to gain entrance into the home-ward bound night shelter."

She continued with why she was in jail. She said, "It just wasn't fair. That asshole drunk had stolen my coat from my shopping cart when I went into the bathroom at the park. How could I have been so stupid to leave my coat that I had sewn my last $12.00 into?"

She thought she could find a way over to social services tomorrow and maybe they would give her new a new phone, an EBT card and a bus pass... but that was tomorrow. Tonight, it was 20 degrees outside, and she was freezing, fried, and hungry.

She said, she "hadn't even really cared that she would face charges in a day or two for what she did next. She said "her hands were so badly frozen that when she picked up a large rock, she could hardly hold it, but she tossed it through the plate glass of the main street store window. Then she sunk to the ground in a ball knowing the loud alarm would soon bring the cops." All she could do was "cuddle in on herself, rocking back and forth, wishing the cops would get there soon. The alarm was so loud. She thought it would never stop." She "started hitting her ears trying to lessen the volume… It did not help a damn bit". She said she "stood up and started doing jumping jacks to try to stay warm. Clamping her hands hard together at the top and then hitting her dying, numb feeling legs with each downward stroke, which seemed to bring back some circulation… but still not enough."

Finally, she "collapsed again to the ground, huddling against the store wall to the broken window and closed her eyes, too tired to care anymore." She spoke. "I wanted to just let it end!" That was her thought she said as the blackness took her out cold.

She woke up when the officer shook her. She said "she instantly struck out at him in a wild ark that did not connect with anything but frigid air. He grabbed her frozen hand that she could no longer feel and found herself restrained and unable to move as she lay face down on the sidewalk. She said I just quit struggling."

Finally, the welcome sound came she said, "Incredulously! She heard the chatter of the handcuffs ratcheting around her numb wrists and she was placed into the back of a warm cruiser." She told me "It felt like heaven! You see Sargent I had no choice, either get arrested and go to a warm jail or freeze to death on the street." She exhaled the word Warmth!

Then, "It didn't help, however, the bombs started exploding in my head, the blood was everywhere…the child without an arm" …And with that she fell asleep during the rest of the drive.

I have to tell you this tore my heart out, and I'm damn Marine Tough but I cried all the way to the shelter as she slept soundly in my car a so precious defender of the American Way, failed by her country!

Up late of course, helping her Marine colleague, she returned home to Tayler, who sheltered her comfortably as they went back to sleep and as she drifted off, she put it in context.

It was meant for me to see how tragically we forget! If there are ever places where our empathy should be automatically shown it would certainly be for those who give the lives so we can have peace in ours. Yet here was an example of the missing follow through. I must move on commuted unwavering to my objective.

In the morning dressed confidently in a casual yet respectful way her marine practiced care reflected her attire in every detail from her trim slacks to her bright printed blouse. She had a light breakfast then confidently grabbed up the Prospectus and its Slide Show which were secured in a perfectly designed brief case Taylor bought for her and left the apartment for the street corner and the bus that would take her to the University.

It was still just with dawn light. And, as things sometimes go…Her pre-committee defense was once again set into a major personal challenge!

At first. She didn't see him, but did instinctively sense his foot print-thus feel his presence, she reeled around and found herself facing a pistol, clearly a home-made one!

The man so dark and angry in appearance grabbed for her case! Now for this hapless thief that was the mistake of all mistakes! The Marine's moves were automatic and lightning quick!

The swing kick got him in the groin, making him crouch to ground grabbing himself, yet to receive the second firmly in the jaw. He doubled completely over falling further to the ground in fetal position holding his privates, just as Chivonn mounted firmly on top of him and pulled his head back, about to do the killing hold but stopping short of that! She ripped off her loosely connected belt and forced it around his neck just tight enough to make him lose consciousness. That she held and didn't kill was a thought reflective of her deep regret at once before taking a life in that mission in the alley on active duty.

The cell call to the police was made which was answered but there was a time lag before they showed up and another rather long one as the officer took the needed information, so as the hapless man came back to consciousness she had to hold him down belt on neck several times. Finally, the patrol wagon arrived, and the thief was lifted up, cuffed and mounted in the van. The student prospectus defender was now running clearly behind time to reach the meeting!

Watching the guy about to go off to jail, Chivonn had the curious thought " Glad I wore Slacks" then recognizing that the time was indeed pressing, asked and was granted by the patrol wagon a ride to the University which she knew was on the way.

Normally of course they wouldn't do that, but they were so impressed by her command of the situation, and one officer remembered her last night with the unfortunate woman, that they just said, "Hey hop in, no Prob!"

At the University-thanks to the police, and out quick and up the three flights of stairs, she entered the conference room already with the committee and audience there and some she thought surely waiting for the sacrifice!

It was indeed very clear to all as they entered the room that Chivonn would be facing a most significant challenge. She would stand "against" a very statured and informed Professorship, indeed.

And in keeping with the published schedule the meeting was called to order by Dr. Jordyn on time, 8:00 am.

All were seated, many with coffee in hand, then looked around for Chivonn. They waited to 8:10, the student not then showing up, they expected the chair to call the matter off, the usual ten-minute limit having been observed.

Just as Dr. Jordyn rose to make that announcement Chivonn entered the room, sighs audible from her friends. Chivonn crossed the room to the projector and inserted her thumb drive with defense into the usb port and looking in respect to Dr. Jordyn took a seat upfront next to the projector.

Dr. Jordyn turns to the panel-the audience and then asks for attention. The atmosphere is clearly tense as the Doctor asks Chivonn to take the floor and make such initial comments as she deems necessary.

She looks over the grouping, very clear eyed, her practiced reflexes firmly under control (in spite of all that she has been through before the meeting), and responds, very clear and firm voice!

"First, I apologize for being late, there was a bit of a physical attack on getting here, probably not as much of a challenge as I am sure you have in mind for me up-coming. But, seriously thank you all for reading my prospectus."

"As a short overview I am saying that we are gifted (whatever the cause) with incredible abilities even if we should eventually choose the ability to improve our form.

To accomplish this, it is important to understand how the good instinct in us can be secured, carried forward from past offspring to the future ones.

The instinct to which I am referring is that which activates in us the desire to stick together to defend all and correct situations."

"My predecessor Vicente gave that a home in us-in a very general term, "The Cy-Gene", meaning the gene that can even face a future of the Cyberspace controlled 'Global Brain'."

"He did this reflecting on how all the evil influences from our accelerating Global Brain could slowly influence and change our humanitarian characteristics. At the general level this contends that our brain genetics could be altered to change personality and within this cause the loss of our Empathy, that very property that insures our concern for each other."

"Concerned about his proposal and following on it is my proposal for research. The defense today is at two levels, 1.) The concerns that have led me to make a proposal for study of the genomes mental transfer mechanisms and 2.) The specific lab research to secure knowledge as to how the genome transfers personality, so that the extent of the susceptibility is understood."

"So, if you will I will present a short overview of my concerns and plans."

Chivonn then puts up two overview slides commenting as she reads. "To gain evolutionary time our species must achieve the following...."

Offspring - 330

> **PROTECT**
>
> Protect our sense of reasoning from embedded narcissistic like psychosis that lead to killing!
>
> Protect our sense or reasoning from susceptibility to Charisma's that create selfish behavior leading to reduced life expectancy for the species!
>
> These items need laboratory research to fully understand inherited psychological transmission!

> **ADVANTAGE**
>
> If evolutionary time is gained, we might:
>
> Secure A.I. for the safe use by humans to help in all needed ways!
>
> Unify climate control enabling Earth to last its natural cosmic lifetime,
>
> Change governance universally to support a conflict-less humanity,
>
> Explore the Cosmos technically capable to develop external earth homes.

Then as she hands out a list on her positions she comments as follows. "Specifically, in defense- needing these goals, I have made the following principal observations. I will read them through, as they bear on my overriding viewpoint and intentions."

PRINCIPLE OBSERVATIONS

1. The record of history gives humans a poor chance of lasting into the far distant future! This has been amplified by an increasing number of thinkers. Yet, if given time humans are uniquely provided with a mental form that could understand all needed in existence. They have incredible potential to capture the stars!

2. Viewed critically the terminal events before them could be limited even reversed if they worked together well beyond their existing feeble collaborations. To be specific-clearly---current governments and international collaborations are not resolving the issues! Salvation, namely rescue for the future, can only be developed if they form a truly unified humanity which is based upon sincere all person empathy for their species!

3. Their evolution to thinking creatures has been a remarkable feature, but it is evidently incomplete for long term survival simply because they-in their current derivation are acting overtly suicidal! They accept far too contradictory multiple charismatic influences, which end in the killing of their young and the devastation of their very home.

4. Yet, examination of their history shows them becoming slowly-ever-more benevolent creatures. This is witnessed by attempts at correction, such as the development of democracy. That, however, is given their state of civilization inappropriately slow and is continuously challenged evidenced by the record of wars, devastation of environment, even threats from their technological creations.

5. Moving, escaping to a new realm in space to insure long term survival is not realistic within a secure time frame for the majority of humans. Furthermore, a bellicose war like and destructive humanity implanted on some distant world, is not a representation of the remarkable loving human within us.

6. The obvious need is to protect our further evolution! This is to allow, indeed, to ensure the natural growth of our empathetic impulses. There is needed an objective aiding evolution to more perfect humans capable of lifting us to a safe distant future.

7. The present selfish, bellicose, and ugly communicative and war like world has many influences that clearly endanger this. Every day we witness senseless cruelty ignoring feelings for other people who are suffering.

8. We do understand that DNA transfer gives us our physical characteristics. The genome in terms of physical structure and composition has been discovered. That knowledge promises many health benefits.

9. Yet although this chemistry is right before us, available for deeper scientific inquiry, we argue even vehemently disagree whether or not our "personality" is a genetically transferred implant!

10. If that is so, each present generation passes on negative influences to the next thereby slowing the needed empathetic populations to see to a far distant future for our children.

11. There is thus, clear rationale to analyze if there is or not "Personality Transfer" embedded in our genetics!

12. If that is or is not the case is simply an essential understanding of ourselves, just as knowledge of our anatomy is needed to survive. And such knowledge on the birth of personality would greatly benefit a host of allied medical practices.

If it is not the case, then other avenues to protect the species must surely gain prominence-recognizing our current failures. We are at the mercy of anti-human influences and the pressure, the need to correct *our ways* would be an appropriate and scientifically documented impetus!

If that is the case, then we will be at last aware of the sensitivity of passed on killing errors in present populations and take more clearly emphatic steps to insure the objective *humanistic education* in our developing generations.

After Chivonn stated her observations:

Dr. Jordyn moved to the podium and looking at Chivonn said, you have stated the observations in your prospectus leading to your request to conduct a new line of research and to that the committee has in hand some details about the actual lab project.

Let's begin with a review of the laboratory specific aims and proposed approach if you would.

With that Chivonn re-activated the projector and turned to her technical slide show.

Review of the laboratory research:

As Chivonn came to the podium, holding the remote she clicked on her first slide showing as follows her objective and the basic comparisons to be made.

OBJECTIVE

Determine if brain Hydrogen (H) bonding energetic levels correlate between parents and children (each) who have their psychological empathy levels professionally profiled.

Adenine — Thymine

Then she continued indicating the areas of concern as
1.) Samples for Analysis,
2.) Laboratory Analysis on those Samples,
3.) Correlation of Results with Human Behavior Profiles, that is Parent vs the Child.

Offspring - 334

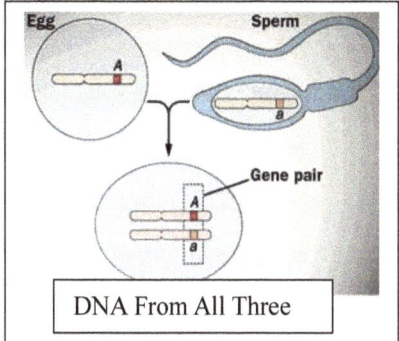

1.) Samples for Analysis

Here she named the samples that will be available, and she described the studies that would substantiate by using Blood DNA from the study subjects to correlate with all the other study samples. In addition, she also describes in detail with further slides the current research showing how her study subjects brain tomography will be measured to assuring individual identity of the patients and intense brain loci.

(At this point there were a number of technical questions which she answered she felt thoroughly. Members of the future panel, raised hands and asked questions which pinpointed deepening the answers, where Chivonn needed to amplify.)

After answering all resulting questions concerning the sample base, she continued with a detailed explanation of methods of laboratory analysis of samples and the means for correlating results.

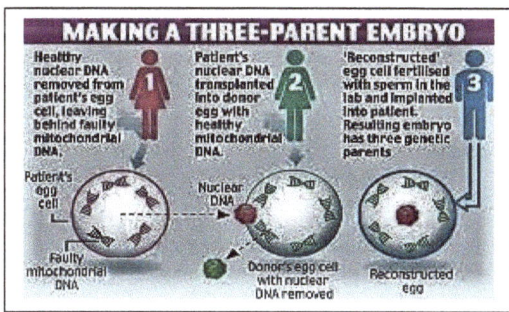

2.) Laboratory Analysis of the Subject Samples: Next Chivonn turned to report the H bond energy level instrumental techniques and indicated that she will accomplish this analysis on samples from each of the provided parent embryos. She noted that all samples obtained will be with informed consent. (She gave out copies of that form.)

3.) Correlation of Results: Here Chivonn provided the committee with a copy of the agreement with a Human Genetics Institute located in Italy, and an outline of how their staff psychologist will interpret personalities in the five-year and then ten-year study. She indicated she will work on both, the first toward her doctorate, and the longer she hopes as a lab employee.

Finally, Chivonn shows the data base she has developed with the patient center and the way listings of her data will be made with each patient's DNA Profile. That is using correlation analysis she will report degrees of similarity or divergence, in the Nucleic Acid Energy Levels versus Empathy Psychological measurements.

The presentation went-on for some time with questions arising continuously nearly "ad-hock" as Chivonn's extensive slide presentations and summaries progressed.

When she finished, Dr. Jordyn asked for a final focal question from the committee, which he was made aware of by raised hand insistence, and that was resolved and provided by Dr. Elisabeth Nalvartien.

Q: Ms. Chivonn, I am sure the committee was impressed with your Lab proposal as evidenced by their finding of various current techniques, etc. and your grasp of the technology.

We compliment you on securing a patient source and your correlative research proposal. I am concerned, however, that your biological sample measurements lack a specific defense that the measurement parameter is correct for personality strength, although I will admit we really have no idea where or how in the genome it develops. Your underlying idea, which is the idea of mass to energy and energy to mass, which holding the correct gene structure generation to generation with personality character is certainly interesting and if proven could be quite valuable. However, as you get into this if granted, you are going to have to face such questions head on and this research would require many adjustments and certainly frustration which you seem determined to face.

Chivonn, says with that "Yes, Professor Nalvartien I do truly understand that…but as a beginning, the idea of energy held and forwarded is well above simply identifying base pairs and hydrogen bonds, that energy needs to be measured and its reason sought, and correlation attempts made."

Professor Nalvartien shook her head in acknowledgment and said to wrap up…well in consult with you committee I believe I have summarized our concerns at present. Each committee member will of course further analyze the details as we reach our final judgment.

We are, as you can gather, concerned about the huge number of difficult compilations and pitfalls. To this Chivonn responded… "I do understand, am aware that I might face frustration and failure, but there is not an advance without a beginning!"

Dr. Jordyn then returned to the podium as the Committee Chair, and standing next to Chivonn, stated for her the next avenue of inquiry.

Chivonn, next I think-as I have listened to the committee - it would be appropriate for you to address certain fundamental concerns about the "Theme" behind your proposal. That is, there were questions underlying the rational for doing such work.

Hearing this Chivonn could not help but raise her eyebrows, but reflectively tightened her body language, and said yes Professor I will be happy to address such concerns.

Q: Question from Professor James Bond: Won't "Providence" do all you are wanting to happen?

A: Chivonn leaves the podium for a moment, paces a bit and with a face of resolution says "You mean' Spirit Guardianship'. I believe you are referring to the Omnipotent-God? "To which she receives a nod and something of a smart smile.

"I have seen the failures of 'Providence', at so many turns, and where is and was providence with the terrible suffering of children all over the world, where was providence in the killing and suffering of millions in the wars? Where was Providence when school children in the U.S. were murdered with a machine gun?

Chivonn paused, walked around in front of the head table, hung her head down and sighed, then continued. …

One thing is for certain, we Homo sapiens have been equipped to change ourselves, no other species can do that. If you wish you can assign that to a Providence or more likely since that has come with horrible, anti-human events, perhaps we better leave that power to contemplate itself and goals and move on!"

Dr. Bond, frustrated, waved his hand and looking to Dr Jordyn, simply nodded his head.

To a person the panel looked at him quizzically, then shifted eyes to Chivonn, just as Professor Jordyn entered with, thank you Jim!

"Dr. Everhart, Dr. Sheik would you care to add to the question or move ahead." Professor Sheik granted moving on with the question that he and other Cosmologists would have raised, that is curious to have this student deal with. He said they were hoping for agreement with "Leave Earth". He said I think however, Ms. Chivonn's comments in the prospectus are sufficiently grounded. Let's look at other issues!

So, it was Dr. Eberhardt's turn: At which point the issue of ethics and morality raised their critical heads. That is the possible extreme, potentially evil intent in DNA re-coding was put on the table.

Q: The following question was asked by Dr. Glenn Everhardt, Professor of Sociology, Teacher of Religious Morality. "Do you believe that changing DNA as a result of research is justified, is moral? Example...What modifications are you wanting and is fooling with human DNA structure beneficial to humankind or is it potentially amoral?"

A: Chivonn first answered, "This is not in the area of what I am suggesting, i.e. What you are asking is do I think research that involves changing Human DNA is ethical? I will address this as I do have an opinion."

"We already artificially inseminate. We already are cloning at the Monkey Level. The question though digs into the altering of human kind by fooling with their DNA. *I am not proposing that!* The up-step evolution I am speaking of is a deeper understanding of how naturally educable we are so that our interrelation with the young can be more aware of the dangers to their sense of empathy."

Offspring - 338

Q: Dr. Everhardt steps in again though... "Still, I am asking how you see it, Human DNA alteration, let us say if what you expose could provide an avenue."

A: Here Chivonn moves into an area she does not want to but feels that she must show her own sense of empathy and knowledge of the issues.

"To what you are implying...In short there are judgments that must be made on the basis of a.) full scientific evidence that the change is valid, b.) full informed consent by the persons involved, c.) full technological methodology such that the procedure is not harmful or painful, and d.) to be made by societies under legal, democratically evaluated laws regarding deeper DNA intrusion."

"Could such be beneficial, I bet all here can see that but, let's do bring your concern down to a more personal level. How could our deeper knowledge of how the genome functions at the specific chemical interaction level, how could that knowledge really help us? Even so, I do believe future scientists and medical practitioners may need to explore that possibility."

"Here is an example, what if it's a parents last hope is for their child or a child of their own? What is wrong genetically with parents that have had 4 attempts at child birth and each time the baby dies just because of a deformed heart condition, so they are left heartbroken with 4 stillborn babies? Is that fair to them? Where is our compassion? What about the babies they had to bury? Is that fair to those? "

"If those same parents had a choice and could choose a different route, don't they have the right and deserve to have their next baby, through some well- informed DNA modification, while the child is still only an unfertilized egg and separate sperm, still within the separate bodies of the parents? If this modification could be completed to just the correct area of the DNA of either the egg or the sperm, they might have the child that they so desperately want."

"Adoption was an option for them; sure. And then they would always regret and blame each other, that although they loved their adopted child...the child was not from their own joining due to a defective gene or genes that one or both of them carried."

Now if it is to advance medical practices...that is more acceptable in society today. And absolutely, every such endeavor must be through very thorough approval processes. But looking at, changing how a person thinks? That is a different issue entirely and what may be your concern. *And I wish to emphasize again for my research I am not entering that realm.* I am proposing that we learn if "Personality" is transferred via the Genome from parent to child by some process held within the DNA, and I hope to inquire into that measuring energetics as I have described in the first part of this defense in both Parent and Child's Central DNA."

Q: Dr. Everhardt though commenting "OK'... although...shakes his head and starts to raise his hand.

A: Chivonn seeing this, answers before the question. Chivonn says, "I see perhaps more you intended in your question. I can hear you thinking, because I have had the same thoughts.

Yes, a modification in this case could be a good thing, however when & where will the alterations stop? Will people start choosing to have an offspring be modified if there is a history of anger in the past generations? After all, sometimes traits tend to miss a generation or two. How many future modifications to future generations would be needed to come up with the "perfect" baby and who would choose what "perfect" really was?"

"So outside of that specific there is the very core of my own concern. And it is germane, responsible to think of scientific advance."

"The record is Atomic Fission, Hiroshima, but Nuclear Reactors and Nuclear Medicine and Combustion Engines, Global Warming, but machines to run Ambulances, etc." *"You get it, humans can invent the terrible, but if and when, and here is a central notion I harbor on, benevolently motivated they have ability to come out* of it.

The problem is we do not know from where that emotion of benevolent protection of their fellows derives, and as such people, those alive as the natural evolution takes place will not know its fundamental importance. find ways to support it or move on to other measures to insure the survival of their species."

At this Chivonn saw a number of the panel and audience shaking heads in approval. However, again she could see Dr Everhardt about to seize more ground to further defend his concern. So, she moved in front citing the very history that she knew he would bring up (experience in his class helped) and she said…

" Perhaps you are thinking Hitler. Yes! Hitler "Advertised' his Aryan Race was the "perfect" race and had it "researched" using some genealogy charts of different families and origins over the span of "many" generations. Once he had where "these families came from", and who was in their family tree, he had Goering, the most astute liar-investigate what the past generations had done against society, and what their actions caused, thus he set a percentile on which race was the "best" race that should cover the world in his ideal of future generations. Through this research, Hitler believed (purported for his political advantage) that by going forward for at least 3 generations the past deviations could be stopped, yet in other "less superior" races the only way to stop the deviance was to eliminate the entire race for the betterment of mankind!

He hid behind for "Charismatic Political Attraction" a mega maniacal idea, that too many bought into-that wanted, that is one type they themselves thought they belonged (the Aryan Race). It is well known that his "research" was biased, ignored the fundamental that all humans are valuable and certainly interrelated. It was in fact a totally false premise, with absolutely no scientific evidence to back it up."

"My research proposal is entirely opposite of such as that in every aspect. What I am wanting to do if one wants to bring in ethical concern is the basis of good ethics, that is it seeks knowledge to help all human kind. It does not ask for changes in DNA!"

"Still, it is the same as present genetic knowledge. It helps us to know who we are and might even provide a basis for understanding the resistance to various diseases and pathologies.

What if a parent suspects that by age 10 their child would be violent or die a horror filled and expensive death from cancer, or would have blue eyes and they would have to explain why theirs were brown, or to carry on emotional scars that would destroy their lives and those they allowed into their lives by the force of the tainted blood of the ugly father a rapist that had resulted in a now grown daughter?

Yes, ladies and gentlemen in the end, of course, scientific knowledge can be used for selfish irrational purposes, but without scientific knowledge fully understanding the drives inherited in our Offspring our ability to move forward and face the challenges of our future we are lost!"

At this point Dr. Jehan Nirupuma raised her hand just as Dr. Jordyn said, questions are allowed by the audience on this matter!

So, Dr. Nirupuma stood up and looking at the gathering, simply said, "Without the chance given Morton on understanding anatomy and Fleming on understanding antibiotics, with-out their chance to, if you will, behave as "Students" seeking deeper knowledge for improving human existence we would not have safe surgery and penicillin.

In the case of Chivonn's research, it seems to me we can stretch the ethics idea well beyond rational borders. But cleanly in her Prospectus she has given overarching ethical reasons why the research should be done and the ethical footing in the science proposed by this student's proposal is on solid human caring grounds." (Dr. Jordyn started to say let the student defend but held, thinking... oops... Oh well.)

And there were no hands raised. With silence from the gathering Dr. Jordyn asks, "Other questions on this point"? Pausing he then said "hearing none" lets us turn for final words from the Ms. Chivonn."

At this point Dr. Jordyn addresses the student...Chivonn our time is up for further questions. Do you have something to say as concluding words?

Yes, Thank you Dr. Jordyn. Goose bumps raising on her slender arms she continues..."Although I am certainly concerned having been a Marine in issues that relate to the safety and dignity of all people, and clearly about ethical matters so proved via my prospectus, I feel it is critically important that we understand why we are the way we are but centrally what is within us that could protect us for the long term. This matter may perhaps have to do more with our genetic make-up, indeed, than previously assumed. We need time to properly evolve, our evolution evidenced by our behavior is not yet sufficiently complete to give us the time needed to preserve our species!

How to change, how to evolve? Well from the concepts in the tales of Frankenstein to Hitler to many other misguided souls and stories this fundamental question is certainly not new. Distantly, the technical experts will certainly have to face fortifying navigators with physical adaptations in them that the current form will need to ensure its ability in traveling space, but they will need time to accomplish that. Even so the technology rising today gives us the chance to understand our selves at a much deeper level. Clearly, we must take firm charge of ourselves accentuating the good in us or we will perish!

I chose to try to help in that evolution with what I hope will be a contribution to research in our genetic makeup. I believe the understanding that could develop will allow us to become a more informed and thus a better species than what we are today.

I do firmly believe we must stop this negative and destructive repeating of our human history! We have such great potential, if only we can protect it and cultivate it in our future generations!

Then, looking directly at each panel member in turn she went on, my ethics and morals are honorable, as any prior Marine will tell you that is what we were taught and swore we would uphold for a life time.

The research I propose offers a starting point to improve what must be a deeper understanding about our protective instincts. I believe I have taken care to insure-that the research will use the most recent of techniques and that it is guided and guarded by subject informed consents within the umbrella of a statured and benevolent world recognized institution."

Turning to Dr. Jordyn, she says "Professor Jordyn thank you for this opportunity, and then to the Panel she signs off with …

Ladies and Gentlemen, it has been a challenge but true honor, to defend my ideas before you.

Each I know is among the most respected in your various fields. Thank you so much for your time and this opportunity!"

With that Chivonn leaves the podium and stands back to allow Dr. Jordyn to come forward.

Dr. Jordyn then stood up front, thanked the committee for their time and turned to Chivonn, saying "Decisions on the project should be resolved soon!"

"Thank you, 'Ladies and Gentlemen' that will be all for today!" With that the audience began to leave.

Several of the Faculty, said very good job, or shook Chivonn's hand!

Dr. Bean-on the Future Panel then helps to put the chairs away and helped Chivonn gather up the handouts left behind and the trash, coffee cups, etc. One of the faculty had left most of a breakfast obtained from McDonalds!

~~~~~~~~~~

Chivonn remained a bit in the meeting room, looking back in memory, gathering her presentation materials and closing out the audio-visual equipment.

Leaving the room, she thinks to herself of that Marine toughness that was still in her.

"The call 'Semper Fi' was echoing firmly in her mind. "Semper Fidelis", that is "Always Faithful to the Marines" their noble cause that was the credo!'

And, she intended to help break new ground which might be helpful to future generations, that was a new credo and she vowed some-how she would continue her research!

Then as she walked further along the great hall nearing the lab, new words rose in her mind!

She said out loud "Semper Fi" but added the Latin word "Unanimous"! *"We surely need a new call that means faithful by all of us-for all of us!"*

Just out-side the lab she knew her friends would be waiting for her with their thoughts and would try to convince the Professor to find the funds to do what she knew she must do!

Entering she said to all, looking at her with admiration and applause, "Dear friends, Oh! How badly we need Navigators who have ideas to help us upward into the deep future!"

~~~~~~~~~~~~~~~~~~

EXPRESSING GRATITUDE!

In developing her prospectus, the heroin of the story used a wide range of ideas and proposals forming the basis of that document - in many cases with full quote. For that to those so brought forward, a very grateful thank you is extended!

Noted in the story's account the prospectus was a specifically directed communication to her committee defending use of funding. As a communication of scholarly intent that approach was necessary to preserve the wisdom and insight of those proposing the ideas and arguments. In effect Chivonn wanted to be assisted by the substantiated opinion of people commenting in the various relevant fields. To achieve this, in so far as possible, without disturbing the thought flow in the story, the APA style commonly used to cite sources using extensive text reproduction in the social sciences was used in this work.

In process, every effort has been made to credit authors or experts who might have contributed first time postulations or have otherwise been the most widely accepted publisher of the ideas. Should this not have been achieved for an author please write to the editor of Minds-Eye Manuscripts at www. Minds-eye @bresnan.net and that will be corrected by posting the over-site on the internet at www.aminds-eye journey.net.

ABOUT THE AUTHORS

"Offspring" is a collaborative work by a Marine and a Professor! Lodema R. Anderson-Newsom (One of the first women assigned to combat U.S. Marines) and Dr. David M. Yourtee (Professor Emeritus UMKC and Fulbright Scholar) came together recognizing from their different experiences the critical need for us all to start looking with utmost seriousness into securing the distant future for the worlds' children.

Lodema contributed her perspective from the many tragedies she witnessed in the course of her military service. She and her fellow Marines clearly saw the need for peace and justice for all children. David brought his thoughts into the book after witnessing the terrible plight and cruelty he saw children suffer as he traveled on humanitarian research in developing countries.

Although this may seem to be an unusual author team, they found that heir different experiences and perspectives contributed strongly to the purpose of the book.

The authors offer the work with the vision that it may stimulate others to become **"Navigators for the Future"**!

This is a Minds-Eye Manuscript *Tm

www/aminds-eyejourney.net
Attending to the future
through knowledge of the past and present!

"Offspring" is sequel to a series of books in "The Future Navigator Trilogy". Books in that series are as follows.

1. "The Future Navigator" (ISBN: 9780692405888).
   This book lays down the foundation for the series and identifies the people and their challenges against the cataclysms of today who become the Navigators, otherwise known as "Vistaviens".
2. "On the Edge of Forever" (ISBN: 9781366621450).
   In this work the Future Navigators reveal just what is "Forever", showing that there is no justification for killing another because of a different philosophy about the governance of the here-after.
3. "The Omega Shield". (ISBN:9781389895647)
   This book treats the concerns that cruel, and in-human ways are increasing and changing the way people hold value to each-other (example, the global internet brain inconsiderately proselytizing children).

   A soft bond version "Eternity and the Omega Shield" (ISBN9781389925757) contains the text of both 2 and 3.

Minds-Eye Manuscripts, LLC was first established in 2000 with purpose to address present and future history. About the Minds-Eye Books created from the manuscripts:

"Engaging search for higher meaning in life…challenging rational thinking about the value and future of humans"
--*Online Review of Books and Current Affairs*--

"Vital read as we will become increasingly aware of our present journey toward survival or extinction."
--*Mind Quest*—

This Book was printed by Blurb Incorporated.

Copies can be purchased directly through their book store at www.blurb.com/bookstore.

Other books in the Future Navigator series can be obtained directly through the Blurb book store.

~~~~~~~~~~~~~~~~

Online interviews, questions, and/or concerns regarding this book will be entertained by writing to the e-mail Minds-Eye @ bresnan.net.

~~~~~~~~~~~~~~~~